Communicating Uncertainty

Media Coverage
of New and Controversial Science

LEA's COMMUNICATION SERIES
Jennings Bryant/Dolf Zillmann, General Editors

Selected titles in Journalism (Maxwell McCombs, Advisory Editor) include:

Black • Mixed News: The Public/Civic/Communitarian Journalism Debate

Friedman/Dunwoody/Rogers • Communicating Uncertainty: Media Coverage of New and Controversial Science

Garrison • Computer-Assisted Reporting, Second Edition

Hachten • The Troubles of Journalism: A Critical Look at What's Right and Wrong with the Press

McCombs/Shaw/Weaver • Communication and Democracy: Exploring the Intellectual Frontiers in Agenda-Setting Theory

Merritt • Public Journalism and Public Life: Why Telling the News is Not Enough, Second Edition

Wanta • The Public and the National Agenda: How People Learn About Important Issues

For a complete list of other titles in LEA's Communication Series, please contact Lawrence Erlbaum Associates, Publishers.

Communicating Uncertainty

Media Coverage
of New and Controversial Science

Edited by

Sharon M. Friedman
Lehigh University

Sharon Dunwoody
University of Wisconsin–Madison

Carol L. Rogers
University of Maryland

LEA

1999

LAWRENCE ERLBAUM ASSOCIATES, PUBLISHERS

Mahwah, New Jersey   London

Lawrence Erlbaum Associates, Inc., Publishers
10 Industrial Avenue
Mahwah, NJ 07430

Cover design by Kathryn Houghtaling Lacey

Library of Congress Cataloging-in-Publication Data

Communicating uncertainty : media coverage of new and controversial
science / Sharon M. Friedman, Sharon Dunwoody, and Carol L. Rogers, editors.
p. cm. — (LEA's communication series)
Includes bibliographical references and index.
ISBN 0-8058-2727-7 (cloth : alk. paper). — ISBN 0-8058-2728-5
(pbk. : alk. paper).
1. Science in mass media. 2. Science news. 3. Mass media—Audiences. 4. Discoveries in science. I. Friedman, Sharon M. II.
Dunwoody, Sharon. III. Rogers, Carol L. IV. Series.
P96.S33C66   1998
500—dc21   98-38311
                                                          CIP

Books published by Lawrence Erlbaum Associates are printed on acid-free
paper, and their bindings are chosen for strength and durability.

Printed in the United States of America
10 9 8 7 6 5 4 3 2

Contents

Preface

Perhaps the most common outcome of the scientific process is not facts, but uncertainty. Ambiguity about what is true and what is not is so ubiquitous that one could define scientific expertise not so much in terms of accumulation of knowledge but by the skill of recognizing and managing uncertainty. The acknowledgment and management of uncertainty is one hallmark of good science. But how do journalists fare when trying to convey the complexities, ambiguities, and controversies that are the visible manifestations of scientific uncertainty?

Examining scientific uncertainty and how it is constructed and interpreted is one of the goals of this volume. Exploring the actions and reactions that result when journalists report about scientific uncertainty is another goal. This volume concentrates on new and controversial science, types of science that often find their way into the public arena. Although we believe that all science is inherently uncertain, chapter authors focus on areas where public communication of science is an integral part of the action and where journalists are most active.

Another one of our goals is to look closely at three of the actors involved in the scientific communication process—scientist, journalist, and audience—and analyze how each actor responds to and copes with scientific uncertainty. To do so, we go beyond anecdotes and "war stories," however fruitful, to feature research by leading science communication scholars. We also seek to explore interactions among the three actors and ask communication scholars to focus on specific scientific issues whose uncertainties have received much attention in the public arena.

To add multiple voices to the conversation, yet another goal of this volume, we incorporate many different points of view in panel and roundtable discussions. Among the natural and physical scientists who participated in these discussions are a Nobel Laureate and the director of the National Science Foundation (NSF), both of whom are also past presidents of the American Association for the Advancement of Science (AAAS); a MacArthur Foundation grant-winning scientist and author in his own right; and the director of major environmental assessment efforts by the Environmental Protection Agency. Social scientists are represented by a specialist in science, ethics, and public policy, and by the former head of a social science division of the NSF, who is now provost/vice chancellor of a major university. Journalists include a Pulitzer Prize winner, past presidents of both the Council for the Advancement of Science Writing and the National Association of Science Writers, and award-winning science writers and editors from *The New York Times*, Dateline NBC, *Business Week*, *The Dallas Morning News*, and a freelance writer and book author who is a former environmental reporter for *The Boston Globe*.

THE VOLUME'S ORIGINS

Some people might wonder why we chose to highlight the specific subject of scientific uncertainty rather than the larger issue of scientist–journalist interactions. As some readers might recall, our earlier edited volume, *Scientists and Journalists: Reporting Science as News* (Friedman, Dunwoody, & Rogers, 1986), took a broad view by describing the connections between scientists and journalists that characterize the science communication process. Many people urged us to update that book, but instead, we chose to focus our attention on scientific uncertainty to bring more clarity to issues and interactions. However, we found that as we narrowed the topic, we enlarged it in another perspective by concentrating on highly public and controversial issues with great potential societal impact. This view, too, provided a rich base for analyzing scientist–journalist interactions.

Six of the chapters and the two panel discussions in Parts I and II of this volume are based on a day-long symposium on "Science, Uncertainty, and the Media" organized by the three co-editors for the 1996 annual meeting of the AAAS. Using feedback from the symposium, speakers reworked their presentations into the expanded and more fully developed chapters that appear in the book. Two chapters in Part I and all of the chapters in Part III were specifically developed to add further dimensions to this volume. The roundtable discussion at the end of Part III is based on a private meeting that took place at the 1996 AAAS meeting.

INTENDED AUDIENCES

This volume is designed for a variety of readers. The most obvious are scientists and science journalists. Although scientists are famous for denigrating media coverage of science, many years of experience by science communication researchers suggest that scientists are consumed with curiosity about public communication processes. Many scientists purchased *Scientists and Journalists*, and we still hear from researchers for whom the book was a catalyst for their thinking. This volume would also be directly relevant for journalists who write about scientific, environmental, health, medical, agricultural, or technological issues as well as for freelance writers and public information or public relations practitioners in these fields.

Academic scholars and graduate and undergraduate students in a number of fields should find the book useful both in and out of the classroom. In journalism and mass communication, these fields include science and environmental communication, health and medical communication, public journalism, and public re-

munication, health and medical communication, public journalism, and public relations. It should also prove interesting to those teaching and studying in the fields of science, technology and society, the sociology or philosophy of science, and other social sciences. Many of the chapter authors are among the premier science communication researchers, and therefore they reflect the state of the art of scholarship in their particular domains. Their chapters, with their citations, make the entire text relevant as a source of conceptual knowledge as well as a jumping off point for individuals seeking supplemental work.

Last, but not least, is a subset of the general public who would find this book appealing and important. Many of the people in this subset would have an interest in science and its representations in the mass media. Others would be more interested in the application of the information in this book to areas of scientific uncertainty that directly affect them in some way, such as environmental and health disputes. It is our hope that all of these individuals find this book useful and stimulating.

ACKNOWLEDGMENTS

The editors deeply appreciate the significant amounts of time and energy given to this endeavor by the authors of the chapters in this volume. We also thank the scientists and journalists who took time out of their busy schedules to participate in the panel and roundtable discussions. We could not have made our deadline without the wonderful editing assistance of Kathy Campbell, for which we are very grateful. Our appreciation also goes to the News and Information Office of the American Association for the Advancement of Science for providing meeting rooms on several occasions. Credit is due to Spinal Tap, Mr. Guffman, and the theater group in Blaine, Missouri, who kept us laughing while we worked into the night during our editing frenzies in Washington, Madison, and Bethlehem. Finally, our sincere thanks go to those family members, friends, colleagues, and students who encouraged us to follow up *Scientists and Journalists* with this new book.

REFERENCE

Friedman, S. M., Dunwoody, S., & Rogers, C. L. (1986). *Scientists and journalists: Reporting science as news.* New York: The Free Press.

—*Sharon M. Friedman*
—*Sharon Dunwoody*
—*Carol L. Rogers*

Introduction

One day, a local cement plant announced a plan to save money in a new way. Instead of purchasing its traditional fuel, it proposed to burn hazardous wastes and get paid for doing it by industries seeking to get rid of the wastes. People in the surrounding community protested, concerned about potential hazardous emissions from the incinerator—including small amounts of dioxin—falling on downwind areas, particularly a nearby school. Arguments ensued, experts debated, government regulators evaluated, and finally the cement plant was given the go ahead by state environmental regulators to burn many different types of hazardous wastes with certain restrictions. Far from being reassured by the state agency's action, community members were upset and unsettled. Uncertainty remained a dominant feature in the neighborhood—uncertainty about the plant's operator and its standards; uncertainty about safety predictions made by scientists; and uncertainty about the potential health risks to school children from the incinerator's emissions and residues.

This true story is not a rare instance, but rather an example of how scientific uncertainty affects all of our lives. Scientists are not sure about the degree of health risks facing people from long-term exposure to low levels of chemicals or radioactivity. They actively debate the existence of a threshold below which the human body's mechanisms can repair damage caused by low-level exposure over time. Even after many years of such debate, there is no consensus. Scientists also face uncertainties involving many other issues because they either lack knowledge or disagree over interpretations of the data. Name the issue—AIDS, climate change, genetic engineering, whether the universe is a closed or ever-expanding system, cloning, the impact of nature versus nurture on behavior, the basic nature of matter, pesticide effects—and you will find it filled with areas where scientists do not always know what to expect or predict.

Uncertainty is a feature of all our lives. We are uncertain about tomorrow's weather, about the outcome of a basketball game, and about the qualities of a particular political candidate or activity. However, most people seem to have become habituated to these types of uncertainties and rarely seem bothered by them.

Scientific uncertainty is another matter. When scientists advise people to avoid eating or drinking a particular substance to improve their health, some people listen. Others, however, angrily accuse scientists of changing their minds too often about such advice. Tell people that they might be at risk from an environmental hazard and they will probably become outraged because scientists cannot agree on the level of risk they face. People are definitely not habituated to scientific uncertainty!

In particular, in areas of science that are new or controversial, the uncertainty itself becomes a public focus. It is in emerging and contested fields of science that uncertainty is paramount and most visible to the public. The mass media play an active role in influencing our perception of uncertainty in these issues. They report the discoveries and advances, but they also highlight the disagreements in both how scientists should proceed and how best to manage what they do not yet know. Managing uncertainty involves enormous stakes. Public policies often have to be developed long before scientists have clear answers to important questions. For example, how should the United States establish climate change regulations when predictions over the degree and pace of the change vary widely among experts? Governmental decisions that have to be made based on incomplete or disputed data can have major impacts on a nation's economy and lifestyle.

Three important actors—the scientist, the journalist, and the public—are among many constituencies who must interpret and respond to scientific uncertainty. The role of scientific experts in the formulation of public and governmental opinion about new and controversial science is formidable. They have a stake in what they believe to be true, with value judgments they make intertwined with their knowledge of science. According to sociologist Brian Campbell (1985), "Uncertainty within science is a question for negotiation, decision and argument" (p. 429). Scientists seek factual accounts of the world around them, but in the process, they negotiate what the facts mean and how they should be interpreted with other scientists and government officials. Facts alone are rarely sufficient for policy formation because policy, by definition, is an application of knowledge.

In addition, data can be interpreted in multiple ways. For example, a 1988 draft report by the Environmental Protection Agency (EPA) contained a wide range of assessments of the dose of dioxin expected to cause the risk of one additional cancer in one million people.[1] Made by scientists in various U.S. and foreign regulatory agencies during the 1980s, the assessments ranged from .006 to more than 10 picograms per kilogram per day, a span of almost five orders of magnitude (EPA, 1988, p. 4). Yet, these assessments were all based on essentially the same study. In this example, the basic facts were the same, but the interpretation of the data by various scientists led to widely varying assessments.

Like scientists, journalists often confront scientific uncertainty. In many of the stories they write, they describe advances or controversies that are full of questions for which there are no easy answers. In fact, journalists are very active in uncertainty coverage because controversy and debate are important criteria for newsworthy stories. Not only do they write about what scientists know, but more frequently now than in the past, they also write about what scientists do not know. How they present and describe this uncertainty affects how readers, viewers, and

---

[1]The assessment comparison was originally related by Dr. Dorothy Patton of the EPA.

listeners interpret it. In addition to reflecting how scientists negotiate and express uncertainty, journalists also can foster or downplay perceptions of uncertainty by the way they construct stories. For example, by pitting one expert's or group's views against another's, journalists can heighten perceived uncertainty. A story that offers a confident point of view, in turn, may diminish such perceptions. Besides describing scientists' views, journalists also highlight those of laypersons and emphasize how uncertain issues have an impact on people's lives. Because of the mass media's pervasiveness, how they construct scientific uncertainty can often have significant effects.

Audiences also construct their understandings of scientific uncertainty. People who read or view what journalists present bring their own perceptions to controversial or emerging issues. Whether they are pro-science or anti-science, whether they favor more or less government regulation, whether they fear or applaud brave new technologies, their perceptions, attitudes, and interpersonal interactions color their interpretations of what scientists say and journalists report.

Therefore, these major actors in the science communication process interpret and respond to scientific uncertainty in their own ways. This is not to say that science is only a construction of the three actors and that scientific facts do not exist. Rather, it means that facts can be interpreted, negotiated, and built on in many ways, a process encouraged by highly uncertain science issues more frequently than not. The three actors start with facts and then construct their interpretations of the uncertainty related to these facts layer upon layer.

SOME IMPORTANT DEFINITIONS

This book explores the ways in which scientists, journalists, and the public cope with the uncertainties of what is "true" in science as well as how scientific uncertainty is constructed. To help guide our readers, here are operational definitions for some key terms used throughout this volume. In our minds, *scientific uncertainty* means uncertainty brought about by either a lack of scientific knowledge or disagreement over the knowledge that currently exists, although chapter authors occasionally employ a different definition.

New science represents more to us than just an overnight breakthrough that occurs perhaps unexpectedly and may occasion a scientific shout of "Eureka!" Although such exciting developments are important, they are not the only ones we consider new. Advances that occur more slowly and appear to be emergent—that is, developing over a period of time of some months or even a year or two—also come under this term.

Controversial science means areas of science in which experts disagree: where there are disputes and opposing points of view. Occasionally, controversy indicates a total lack of a scientific consensus, but it can also arise when minority views collide with those of the bulk of scientists.

The terms *science* and the *mass media* are used in this volume in their widest sense. *Science* not only encompasses the natural and physical sciences, but also the social and behavioral sciences as well as medicine, environmental sciences, technology, and engineering. *Science writing* includes coverage of the accumulation of knowledge in these fields, as well as the political, economic, and social aspects of science. A few authors refer to specific types of writers, such as environmental journalists, as well.

When we discuss the *mass media*, we include any medium that communicates to large numbers of individuals: newspapers, television, radio, magazines, books, and the ever-expanding Internet and World Wide Web are the prime sources.

A BRIEF OUTLINE

Part I examines participants in the scientific uncertainty arena and how scientists, journalists, and audiences react to, cope with, and manage uncertain issues. It also describes how scientists and journalists jockey for control over uncertain science. The panel discussion at the end of this section is a spirited discourse on how the three actors handle scientific uncertainty.

Part II explores instances of scientific uncertainty in the public arena, highlighting studies involving uncertainty and biotechnology, dioxin, human resources for science, and human behavior. The panel discussion that concludes this part reacts to several of these specific issues and adds other perspectives about handling uncertain science.

Part III concentrates on issues of audience and methods for more effective communication about scientific uncertainty. It focuses on the importance of understanding audiences and their needs, how to explain complex information to readers and viewers, and how to better understand and present statistical evidence through systematic thinking. The roundtable discussion at the end of this section is a wide-ranging review of journalistic practices and their impact on the treatment of scientific uncertainty.

In this volume, we try to tease apart constructions of scientific uncertainty to help readers understand how these constructions affect scientific and lay beliefs about science and technology as well as how government policies and regulations dealing with uncertain issues are influenced and formed. Within this framework, we also examine the variety of the interactions among the actors in the uncertainty drama. We hope this rich tapestry gives readers valuable insights into the intricacies of science communication at work.

REFERENCES

Campbell, B. L. (1985). Uncertainty as symbolic action in disputes among experts. *Social Studies of Science*, *15*, 429–453.

Environmental Protection Agency. (1988, June). *A cancer risk-specific dose estimate for 2,3,7,8 TCDD* (Draft).

Part I

Interpreting Uncertainty

Chapter 1

Scientists' Representations of Uncertainty

Stephen C. Zehr

Stephen C. Zehr is an associate professor of sociology at the University of Southern Indiana. His research focuses on how science is represented in public discussions of environmental problems; currently, he is examining the ways that policymakers use economic expertise in developing strategies to manage global climate change. His previous writings include research on acid rain and ozone depletion as well as on other aspects of global climate change controversies.

Because science involves producing knowledge about what was previously unknown, uncertainty is a normal and necessary characteristic of scientific work. Scientists regularly engage parts of the world unfamiliar to them. This is not unique to science; many other workers, such as physicians or mechanics, regularly inhabit an uncertain world as well. Thus, the fact that uncertainty among scientists is prevalent is less interesting and significant than the attempt to reveal how uncertainty is actively managed by scientists. This chapter focuses on different features of the management process. It demonstrates that scientific uncertainty is not simply something that scientists try to eliminate through their research. Scientists also actively construct and effectively use it in scientific articles and in public science contexts.[1]

This chapter is divided into three sections. The first reviews the ways that scientists handle uncertainty in the laboratory and in scientific discourse in professional journal articles. The second focuses on the construction and management of scientific uncertainty in public science settings, such as political hearings and the mass media, where, although uncertainty could potentially undermine the authority of science in these settings, it is often used instead to enhance the image of science. The third section reviews several cases of

---

[1]See Smithson (1989, 1993), and Stocking and Holstein (1993), for a discussion of the construction of scientific ignorance, of which uncertainty is a part.

scientific uncertainty in public science that illustrate the processes identified in the second section of this chapter. These cases include the Mackenzie Valley Pipeline Inquiry in the Canadian western Arctic, a television show about the Shroud of Turin, and U.S. Congressional hearings on acid rain.

UNCERTAINTY IN LABORATORY WORK AND SCIENTIFIC DISCOURSE

Laboratory Work

Like many other workers, scientists are beset daily with unsolved problems that demand resolution. These problems, the uncertainties they create, and the subsequent decisions that scientists must make involve diverse levels of activity (Star, 1985). For example, experimental materials may have acted in unexpected ways, a particular technique may have been incorrectly applied or interpreted, observations may have been made by less-than-trustworthy assistants or other scientists, organizational politics may be unclear, or future funding may be insecure.

Scientific work often involves moving among these activities to resolve uncertainties as they arise. If an experiment produces unexpected results, a scientist must decide whether it was caused by an improper technique, observational error, or flawed expectations. At the same time, repeating the experiment may demand more resources than are available, creating yet another level of uncertainty. Scientists then rearrange different elements of their world to make it more orderly and, they hope, to reduce uncertainty (Latour, 1987). Occasionally, the resolution of uncertainty at one level also removes uncertainty at another. For example, if more funding is obtained, part of it may be used to purchase more reliable equipment, which in turn reduces the uncertainty of a particular technique.

Scientific work does not just reduce uncertainty; it actively constructs it (Smithson 1989, 1993). This feature of science makes it unique among other work activities. Most nonscientific work involves removing uncertainties constructed elsewhere. Plumbers, for example, try to fix problems in other people's homes that typically were not of their own creation. Scientists, on the other hand, find problems in their own work by asking questions and probing for gaps in their own realm, thus identifying uncertainties that require their special skills and knowledge to address. Science is as much an uncertainty generator as it is a certainty producer.

When uncertainties are generated in their laboratories, scientists often transform them either into universal certainties or uncertainties. In the first sense, scientists are making scientific claims to universal truth. In the second sense, they are making claims about a universal gap in knowledge (Stocking & Holstein, 1993). This transformation from local, or laboratory-generated, claims to universal claims occurs in scientific discourse directed to other scientists, such as professional meetings or journal articles, or to a broader public. This chapter considers discourse directed to other scientists first.

Scientific Discourse

To construct certain claims to truth, scientists often remove contingencies from their statements (Gilbert & Mulkay, 1984; Latour & Woolgar, 1979). Such contingencies call attention to specific technical, social, or political conditions of the local context of a claim to truth. For example, the following hypothetical scientific statement is filled with contingencies: "When we ran that test last Friday, we obtained results that we think suggest a correlation between internal exposure to mannitol and heart irregularities in rats." The correlation between mannitol and heart irregularities appears to be contingent on which test was used, when that test was performed, how the results were evaluated, what kind of exposure was selected, and what type of animal was involved. These contingencies create uncertainty in the claim. What if a different test had been used? Were test conditions last Friday unique in some way? Were we wrong in our interpretations of the test results? Are the effects only present with internal exposure and with rats?

This type of statement, according to Gilbert and Mulkay (1984), is more typical of informal, local scientific contexts, such as discussions in the laboratory among colleagues. However, as this statement moves into more formal and more universal settings, it often loses some of these contingencies. Eventually, the statement may read: "Exposure to mannitol causes heart irregularities." This type of statement is more likely to appear at the end of peer-reviewed articles or scientific textbooks. The elimination of contingencies in the statement also leads to the perception of much more certainty about the connection between mannitol and heart irregularities. The connection no longer appears contingent on the conditions of the local context.

Gilbert and Mulkay (1984) suggested that these two versions reflect two repertoires used by scientists, called *contingent* and *empiricist*. A *contingent repertoire* leads the reader or listener to infer that the state of nature could be otherwise if certain contextual conditions (e.g., psychological makeup of researcher or funding) are varied. The first version of the scientific statement incorporates a contingent repertoire. An *empiricist repertoire*, in contrast, leads the reader to believe that scientists' actions and beliefs follow unproblematically and inescapably from the empirical characteristics of the natural world (pp. 55-58). The second version of the results of the rat experiment just discussed uses an empiricist repertoire; that is, it appears as a matter-of-fact statement about mannitol and heart irregularities. These two repertoires are important in scientific work because they help scientists transform local uncertainties into more certain knowledge in articles and textbooks.[2]

In their discourse, however, scientists do more than merely present certainties; they also carefully construct uncertainties in the state of knowledge (Smithson, 1993; Stocking & Holstein, 1993). These uncertainties play an important role in the communication of knowledge. For example, a typical peer-reviewed scientific article begins with a literature review that carefully maps out what is known about the subject. This part of the article depicts much certainty in the state of scientific knowledge.

Soon, however, the author begins to point out gaps in the body of knowledge. Questions are raised, limitations of previous research are identified, and conjectures are put forth. Areas of uncertainty and ignorance begin to emerge as the author, in effect, asks readers to agree that these areas require further investigation.

This knowledge gap—and its associated uncertainty—is important because it helps demonstrate the novelty and significance of the author's claims to truth. After constructing the knowledge gap, the author presents a method, data, and specific claims that appear to partially fill it in. Without the gap, the significance of these claims would not be readily apparent. In the final section of an article, the author typically constructs further knowledge gaps, often carefully tailored to allude to broad ramifications of the results (e.g., implications for policymaking) or to the author's future research contributions.

Other techniques are also used to construct uncertainty. These have been reviewed by Stocking & Holstein (1993). They noted that scientists may use caveats to acknowledge limitations in their knowledge claims. Contingencies may be added to statements, reversing the contingent-to-empiricist process previously described. Drawing on Myers (1990), they described how biologists use such rhetorical devices as *echoic speech* (placing knowledge claims in direct quotes), *ironic turns* (for example, relabeling an observation as a precon-

---

[2]Other tools are used to transform local uncertainties into universal certainties. See, for example, Latour (1987), Lynch (1985), and Pinch (1981).

ception), and *asserting negative evidence* (stating that no evidence has been gathered to support a claim). Each device is used to construct uncertainty about opponents' claims during a scientific controversy over definitive claims to truth.

The identification of these devices is significant in that it reveals how scientists can manage their uncertainty claims. In other words, uncertainty claims do not simply represent an uncontrollable feature of scientific work or, for that matter, some underlying reality or a state of objective knowledge. Rather, uncertainty is constructed in particular situations with certain intended effects (Shackley & Wynne, 1996).

In Myers' analysis, scientists may manage their own uncertainty by constructing uncertainty about opponents' claims and contrasting them to try to raise their own credibility. In other settings, uncertainty claims may serve other purposes. This approach to managing uncertainty does not mean that scientists are being disingenuous or biased. Rather, they are simply using uncertainty claims as a rhetorical tool to persuade others or simply to describe and organize some state of knowledge (Stocking & Holstein, 1993). This is a significant part of our next topic, public science.

SCIENTIFIC UNCERTAINTY IN PUBLIC SETTINGS

I use the term *public science* broadly to refer to contexts in which scientists make scientific claims before nonscientists. Major arenas for public science include the popular press, television shows, public hearings, government inquiries, public lectures, and science exhibits in museums. Uncertainty claims in public science can be viewed as the product of a joint venture among scientists and other spokespeople for science, such as journalists, museum curators, policy advisors, and politicians (Gieryn, 1996; Nelkin, 1995). Often, we cannot determine the sole proprietorship of an uncertainty claim. For example, in mass media articles on global climate change, writers often incorporate direct quotes from scientists about scientific uncertainty, making it appear that scientists themselves are the sole source of these claims (Zehr, 1996). However, because writers typically have much information and many quotes from which to choose, scientific uncertainty must be understood as jointly emerging from scientists who were interviewed and from writers themselves.[3]

---

[3]See Friedman, Dunwoody, and Rogers (1986), Hansen (1993), and Nelkin (1995) for further discussion of this issue.

The standard interpretation of public science assumed a distinct hierarchy and separation between real science and its public representation. In this view, real science was done in one context—the scientific laboratory away from the public—and occasionally popularized for public consumption (Hilgartner, 1990). *Popularization*, for many scientists, meant at best, simplification and at worst, pollution of scientific knowledge. As Hilgartner convincingly showed, this perspective on public science as either simplified or corrupted cannot be supported on theoretical grounds, even though it serves as a useful rhetoric for scientists to use in describing public science. Instead, it is important to understand that public science is simply another occasion for performing real scientific work (Hilgartner, 1990; Shinn & Whitley, 1985). Scientific knowledge is essentially being constructed in these public settings, just as it is in the scientific laboratory or on the pages of a peer-reviewed journal article (for an interesting example, see Gieryn & Figert, 1990).

There are, of course, differences between public science and laboratory science. First, public audiences tend to be more diverse than scientific audiences. Recent studies of public science suggest that, in practice, scientists and spokespeople have largely failed at understanding these audiences and effectively integrating scientific information into their lay knowledges (Lewenstein, 1995; Wynne, 1995).

Second, public science can reinforce the authority of science in society. Because the public has little contact with the scientific laboratory and professional journal articles, public science provides scientists with unique opportunities to defend and augment their authoritative position in society (Gieryn, Bevins, & Zehr, 1985; Turner, 1980).

Third, public science is mediated by individuals, such as journalists, politicians, or museum curators, who incorporate into one account or text multiple spokespeople for science. Unlike a professional journal article, which presents a single voice with a single version of knowledge, public science typically features multiple speakers with multiple versions of knowledge. This appearance of uncertainty may confuse the public, giving scientists an opportunity to manage that confusion for their own purposes. This is the topic to which we turn next.

Management of Uncertainty

When scientific uncertainty appears in public science, we might predict an abatement of the perceived authority of scientists as legitimate and definitive knowledge providers. In their popular image, scientists have special techniques and powers that enable them to produce objective knowledge and push back the realm of uncertainty. However, if scientists and their audiences share the same uncertainties, then why should scientists hold this special authority and, for example, have their work be deemed worthy of public funding?

Early sociological treatments of public science assumed such a reduction in authority. Hence, these studies focused on how scientists hide or downplay the uncertainties of the laboratory and knowledge production process, while presenting a more certain version of knowledge for public consumption (Mulkay & Gilbert, 1982; Nelkin, 1975; Pinch, 1981). Transformation of local uncertainties into universal certainties in articles and texts was also assumed to occur in public science as well. The construction of more certain versions for public consumption, according to these analyses, would help protect the public image of science.

More recently, however, it has become apparent that much scientific uncertainty is revealed in public science and that it can be carefully managed and used to achieve specific goals. Campbell (1985) was one of the first to recognize this in a case study of science related to a public controversy. Campbell noticed that experts on one side of an issue used claims about scientific uncertainty to support their position and that these claims were accepted as authoritative in themselves. For example, in Campbell's model, a scientist might claim that scientific definitions of a wetland area are too incomplete or uncertain to support a policy position that would lift restrictions on wetlands use. To stall construction on a nuclear reactor, an expert could deem studies of risks associated with it to be inconclusive. These uncertainty claims often appear objective and authoritative in public science because it appears that scientists are frankly and openly admitting incomplete knowledge. Campbell's findings about the management of scientific uncertainty have been confirmed by subsequent studies, which have also identified the key features of the process. Four of them are described in detail in the following sections.

Uncertainty in General. Because multiple spokespeople for science are used in many instances of public science, scientific uncertainty may appear to lie within science in general rather than in the claims of any one scientist.[4] An individual scientist may make knowledge claims that, on the surface, appear quite certain. However, when several such claims exist, divergent data, interpretations, or consequences may emerge, producing the appearance of scientific uncertainty. This form of scientific uncertainty may be caused more

---

[4]The concept of *science in general* comes from work that examines public understandings of science (Michael, 1992). Michael suggested that the public uses two discourses to understand science: The first, *science in general*, occurs when science is talked about as an abstract entity or principle; the second, *science in particular*, is a discourse directed toward specific phenomena or problems. Here, I expand the concept of science in general to include what scientists in general are saying about a broad science-related problem.

by the specific features of public science, which invite such divergent claims, than by uncertainty in the state of knowledge.

A couple of illustrations may be useful. First, public accounts may emphasize scientific controversy by including claims from scientific experts with a variety of theoretical perspectives and research interests. People who pull together these different claims may do so with the intention of operating within a norm of objectivity (Tuchman, 1972). Journalists, for example, may present opposing scientific opinions to maintain a fair and balanced description of an issue in their articles (Nelkin, 1995, pp. 84-88). Members of Congress and their staff may arrange hearings so that at least one expert offers a different opinion from their own views. A recent major museum exhibit, *Global Warming: Understanding the Forecast*,[5] included opposing scientific positions on global warming and climate change. This presentation, the exhibit designers suggested, illustrated the problem's complexity and provided a representative depiction of the science of climate change (Milner, 1992). In the scientific community, the implied uncertainty of these positions may be understood as a product of different assumptions, methodological approaches, or topic areas. However, in the more limited space of public science, this tacit knowledge may be left out, leading to an appearance of contradictory claims.

Second, science writers and other public science actors often look for unique, esoteric, and cutting-edge research projects to enhance the novelty of their articles (Hilgartner & Bosk, 1988). Novelty becomes increasingly important when an issue, such as global climate change, has been in the news for some time. One way to create novelty is to link new scientific research projects to a larger issue. Each new research project is described as ongoing and incomplete, but the implication is that it may, in the future, answer some important question. As this process continues, readers may interpret these ongoing and incomplete (but potentially fruitful) projects as important indicators of the degree of scientific uncertainty, even if there is actually broad agreement within the scientific community.

For example, many mass media accounts over the past 10 years have situated new and interesting scientific research projects such as studies of bore hole records, snow cover, glacier and ice sheet melting rates, and changes in ocean acoustics within the broad category of global warming (Zehr, 1996). Each new project is represented both as a possible detector of global warming and as very preliminary. The accounts of each new project make it appear to readers that

---

[5]This exhibit was a joint production of the Museum of Natural History in New York and the Environmental Defense Fund. The exhibit ran at the Museum of Natural History from May 15, 1992 to January 19, 1993 and subsequently traveled to several other museums in the United States.

scientists are much more uncertain than they actually are about whether global warming is occurring.

Salience of Uncertainty. Claims about scientific uncertainty also tend to be salient features of public science accounts (Stocking & Holstein, 1993). In the mass media, for example, uncertainty claims may appear in the headline or first paragraphs of an article—perhaps to encourage readers to form an inquisitive attitude toward subsequent information (Collins, 1987)—or in the form of caveats to previous, more certain claims (Stocking & Holstein, 1993). Uncertainty claims also often appear in direct quotes from scientists, which accent their significance (Zehr, 1996). In political debates about environmental problems such as global warming, scientific uncertainties are shared by both scientists and the policy community (Shackley & Wynne, 1996). In each instance, claims about scientific uncertainty are highly visible and salient features of the account.

Elimination of Uncertainty. Several case studies found that a timetable for resolution often accompanies scientific uncertainty claims. For example, policy statements about global climate change typically identify when and how key uncertainties will be reduced (Shackley & Wynne, 1996). Science television shows, such as *NOVA* often identify some point at which scientific uncertainties explored in the episode (e.g., the ability to predict the behavior of hurricanes more precisely) will be eliminated. According to Shackley and Wynne, this temporal framework helps to manage and domesticate scientific uncertainty so that it does not alter basic social relations and order between, for example, science and the public. Although there is scientific uncertainty now, Shackley and Wynne suggested, the public is offered a view of the future in which scientific certainty returns.

Transformation of Uncertainty. When scientific uncertainty appears in public science settings, it could reduce the perceived authority of science. However, representations of scientific indeterminacies and ignorance are likely to be even more damaging to science. *Indeterminacy* involves situations in which not all the parameters of a system and their interactions are fully known. *Ignorance* refers to situations in which it is not known what is not known (Shackley & Wynne, 1996). Both are less manageable by scientists and their spokespeople in public science arenas, and, hence, tend to be reconstructed or collapsed into the more manageable category of scientific uncertainty, in which the parameters around a system are sufficiently known to make a qualitative judgment (Shackley & Wynne, 1996; Smithson, 1993). For example, when official documents on global warming identify the estimated average temperature increase as falling within a range of 1.5°C to 4.5°C, they are placing parameters around an indeterminate forecast. Scientific uncertainty remains over precisely how much the Earth will warm up, but the deeper indeterminacies and ignorance are eliminated from public discussion.

Implications of Uncertainty

Many more such features of scientific uncertainty in public settings undoubtedly exist. What are some of the implications of uncertainty in these settings? What does scientific uncertainty accomplish, and why is it significant?

Some of these features have implications for those who speak for science. These were just briefly mentioned and will be quickly reviewed here. Uncertainty claims help scientists and spokespeople for science create an appearance of objectivity. By admitting some uncertainty, they are protected against charges of dogma or bias that might come with more definitive accounts. Uncertainty also adds an element of novelty to public accounts, thereby enhancing audience interest. Science shows, such as *NOVA*, commonly contrast the uncertainties of present research with a forecast of a more certain future to help manage public perceptions of science.

Uncertainty also affects particular social relations between scientists and different public sectors. One study of policy development on global climate change suggested that scientific uncertainty provides a useful boundary between the policymakers and the scientists who advise them (Shackley & Wynne, 1996). Uncertainty, these authors suggested, is used effectively by scientific advisors and policymakers in their separate communities, while also helping to socially order the boundary between them. To put it another way, members of each community lay claim to, effectively use, and flexibly interpret scientific uncertainty within their own communities; at the same time, scientific uncertainties become a common discursive object and facilitator of social order across these two communities.

For example, agreement on a timeframe for the resolution of scientific uncertainty tends to be useful both to scientists and policymakers. Scientists need not take a definitive position now, when they are skeptical of its accuracy, but they can still justify the authority of science by alluding to a more definitive future after the scientific research has been conducted. Policymakers can use current scientific uncertainties to justify inaction when a policy decision might be unfavorably received.[6] The future timeframe offers both groups a rational basis to delay decisions without appearing to be ineffective. In this way, the timeframe for elimination of scientific uncertainty serves as a shared "boundary-object" (Star & Griesemer, 1989) that socially orders the two communities.

CASE STUDIES OF UNCERTAINTY IN PUBLIC SCIENCE

Now that some general features of the construction of scientific uncertainty in public science have been considered, three cases in which claims about scientific uncertainty were important features of public science are discussed in more detail. Each case illustrates one or more of the features previously described.

Mackenzie Valley Pipeline Inquiry

The first case, analyzed by Campbell (1985), involves the Mackenzie Valley Pipeline Inquiry. This inquiry was ordered by the Canadian government in 1974 to study the social, economic, and environmental impact of pipelines to carry natural gas in the Canadian western Arctic. The head of the inquiry board interpreted the mandate broadly enough to enable not only consideration of the pipeline's immediate effects, but also the broader socioeconomic and political development of the northern part of Canada. The inquiry lasted for 3 years, generating extensive debate over the impact of pipelines on the biota of the western Arctic (Campbell, 1985). In this case, as in many others, different organizations enlisted scientists to provide expert testimony. These experts polarized into two camps: critics and defenders.

In his analysis, Campbell identified two areas of debate that emphasize scientific uncertainty. First, the experts debated the adequacy of knowledge about the impact of pipeline development. Industry proponents were required to demonstrate that their particular plans would have limited negative environmental effects. Their scientific experts—the defenders—cited scientific studies suggesting that negative effects would be minimal. Critics, on the other hand,

---

[6]Stocking and Holstein (1993) review several studies that discuss this point. They include Brown and Lyon (1992); Campbell (1985); Funtowitz and Ravetz (1990); and Miller (1992). Also see Proctor (1995).

did not need to muster an equal amount of evidence;[7] they simply claimed that the defenders' knowledge was inadequate because insufficient research had been conducted to demonstrate the environmental safety of the pipeline. They presented a different interpretation of the evidence that had been put forth by the defenders without necessarily claiming that the data were wrong.

The second area of debate developed after critics were successful in convincing inquiry board members that much scientific uncertainty still existed. This debate centered on the relative significance of scientific uncertainty (Campbell, 1985). The defenders argued that uncertainty was a normal feature of science and that it was not significant enough to stall a decision about the pipeline. In Campbell's terms, they argued that the uncertainty was sufficiently manageable for the pipeline to proceed. Critics, on the other hand, argued that the uncertainty was not manageable.

This case demonstrated, according to Campbell, that scientific uncertainty claims can have the same authoritative force as more certain knowledge claims. That is, claims about uncertain knowledge can be accepted as certified scientific knowledge and used effectively in political arenas. Once critics were successful in convincing inquiry board members that scientific uncertainty existed, Campbell pointed out, defenders authoritatively claimed that scientific uncertainties were sufficiently manageable for the major project to proceed.

Television Show on the Shroud of Turin

A second case consists of scientific uncertainty in a British television program on the Shroud of Turin. Titled "Shroud of Jesus: Fact or Fake," the show was first broadcast on November 3, 1982 and repeated on August 21, 1983 (Collins, 1987). The Shroud of Turin is a linen cloth held and carefully protected at a cathedral in Turin, Italy. In certain lighting conditions, markings on the cloth appear to be an image of a crucified man, possibly Jesus Christ. The show depicted scientific dating techniques used to determine whether the shroud could have covered Christ. The program began with a description of past scientific analyses of the shroud. In this section of the program, according to Collins, viewers saw a world of certainty. Scientists were shown at work reenacting tests and experiments that produce definitive results. It appeared that the scientists in the program were obtaining results at the same time as the

---

[7]See Nelkin (1975) for a more extensive discussion of how critics of a major project typically need not muster equal evidence to offset the proponents' expertise. They merely need to be good at pulling apart, or deconstructing, the proponents' position.

viewing audience. In one instance, a test was conducted that clearly depicted the presence of blood (Collins, 1987).

However, each of these tests provided only a small piece of certain information; the actual date of the shroud remained a mystery. After this opening sequence, viewers were brought into the present where several scientists made brief statements, each offering a different opinion on the authenticity of the shroud. What Collins calls a "window of uncertainty" was opened. Viewers were invited to make their own conjectures about the outcome of the debate. Finally, near the end of the show, viewers were presented with a glimpse of the future in which the next test—radiocarbon dating—will be decisive. This future was depicted as a world of scientific certainty (Collins, 1987).

In his analysis, Collins suggested that television generally depicts science as a producer of certainty. However, on occasions where a scientific controversy is heated or when a case involves fringe or pseudoscience (such as the shroud), the program may depict this brief window of uncertainty. This gives the public a brief glance, albeit limited, at science in action. Although Collins did not mention it explicitly, this window of uncertainty helps dramatize the scientific process. Viewers may genuinely feel the same curiosity as the scientists depicted in the program. However, once this window of uncertainty is constructed, it must subsequently be closed to reconfirm the certainty-producing world of science.

This case again illustrates the construction and careful management of scientific uncertainty in public science. These uncertainty claims on television may not be limited to controversies and fringe science, as Collins suggested. *NOVA* viewers, for example, can attest to the prevalence of uncertainty claims on these shows. The *NOVA* show "Hurricane!" (1989), for example, provides rather dramatic footage of Hurricane Gilbert and depicts meteorologists at work attempting to predict its U.S. landfall. Throughout the show, the audience is reminded of the limitations and uncertainties of predicting hurricanes and weather in general. However, near the end of the show, an expert scientist suggested that in the future, there is a good chance that science will accurately predict the landfall of hurricanes.

Acid Rain

A third case involves scientific uncertainty in political debates over acid rain policy (Zehr, 1994a, 1994b). This case illustrates how scientific uncertainty can emerge from science in general. *Acid rain*, or the more inclusive term *acid deposition*, refers to the chemical interaction of sulfur dioxide or nitrogen oxide with water to produce acidic compounds. These compounds eventually precipitate out of the atmosphere, often hundreds of miles from the source of the pollutants.

A controversy over acid rain emerged in the late 1970s and early 1980s. Debates about the exact connection between industrial emissions in the Midwest and acid rain in the northeastern United States and Canada—and how much damage it caused—focused extensively on scientific uncertainty and its implications for policy. Opponents of stricter pollution control legislation used scientific uncertainties to imply that more research was needed. Proponents of the legislation suggested that enough scientific knowledge was available for policymakers to take immediate action. In this sense, the acid rain case looks very similar to the Canadian pipeline case described earlier.

By pushing the analysis further, however, we begin to recognize that uncertainty is a much more common feature of public science than it might appear to be on the surface, and it could be intrinsic to public science itself. Scientific uncertainty is something that we should expect to find. The acid rain case shows how easily an appearance of uncertainty emerges in public science because it incorporates many scientific voices. Any one of these voices may suggest much certainty. However, the many voices taken together often evoke uncertainty, whether intentional or not.

During the 1980s, approximately 80 congressional hearings were held on acid rain, allowing many scientific experts to testify. These experts individually tended to be quite definitive about the state of scientific knowledge in their field. However, scientific uncertainty crept in because of differences in how specific data, concepts, and methods were interpreted and described.[8]

For example, in congressional testimony, the concept of acid rain was flexibly constricted or expanded in scale depending on the interpretive goal of the expert (Zehr, 1994b). In one hearing, acid rain was interpreted in four ways: as rain that is acidic, as acidic deposition, as a problem related to airborne pollutants, and as a problem in the Adirondacks and Canadian Shield (Hearing before the Committee on Environment and Public Works, U.S. Senate, May 25, 1982). Each interpretation and account alone appeared clear and concise to the audience, but across these accounts some uncertainty inevitably emerged. To what, specifically, did acid rain refer? Was it simply a process that occurs in nature? Or did it refer to a specific problem in a particular part of the country?

---

[8]This is referred to in the sociology of science literature as *interpretive flexibility* (Pinch & Bijker, 1987). The basic idea is that nature underdetermines scientific representations of it. Thus, there is the possibility for much flexibility in how nature is interpreted and described. Interpretive flexibility is especially visible in scientific controversies and less visible in areas where there is more agreement among scientists.

In another hearing, acid rain was described by scientists as a relative condition. However, the basis of comparison was flexibly altered. Several scientists compared it to some baseline of normal rain, whereas others compared it to the amount of acidity added to the ecosystem through different processes. One consequence was the appearance of scientific uncertainty. Most scientists who testified agreed that pH values of rain at an average of 4.1 had been detected in the Adirondacks. Since the pH scale is logarithmic, and hence confusing to some, they also attempted to interpret these observations.

Some scientists interpreted the 4.1 average as abnormal by comparing it to normal rain, for which they used the figure pH 5.6. They pointed out that acidic rain was anywhere from 10 to 50 times more acidic than normal rain—certainly a major difference. Other scientists called into question the 5.6 figure by observing that at some remote parts of the world, rain had been found to be as low as pH 4.7 to pH 5.0. These scientists did not object to data about acid rain levels in the Northeast; rather, they compared them to a different standard. With this comparison, acid rain levels could be interpreted as less abnormal. Another scientist calculated that the amount of actual acidity that the rain would add to the soil would be trivial compared to acidity produced by forests in the Northeast through their acidic humus layers. This scientist argued that naturally created acidity would be a thousand times greater annually than acidity added through acid rain (Zehr, 1994b).

At this hearing, scientists offered flexible interpretations of average acid rain levels in the Northeast. Even though the scientists used the same data, they altered the basis of comparison in their descriptions, which resulted in an appearance of scientific uncertainty. Political actors were left to judge for themselves which interpretation was correct. They tended to make these judgments based on which interpretation was most consistent with their political views, thus further extending the controversy.

This hearing illustrates that scientific uncertainty can emerge within science in general in public science settings. Any context that allows for or encourages multiple voices for science also encourages the construction of scientific uncertainty. This has often been frustrating to political decision makers (the acid rain case is a good example) as well as to other public groups. To the extent that we understand scientific uncertainty as a normal and expected occurrence, this frustration may be reduced or be replaced by nonscientifically based or hybrid knowledges that combine scientific and lay knowledge. (For further discussion, along with examples, see Irwin & Wynne, 1996).

CONCLUSION

I began this chapter by describing how uncertainty must be interpreted as a normal and necessary part of scientific research. Scientists' day-to-day laboratory practices involve managing this uncertainty and, at least occasionally, transforming it into more universal certainty in the form of certified scientific knowledge. Scientists' discursive practices are very important in this transformation process. In the arena of public science, early studies demonstrated how scientists and other science workers tend to gloss over the contingencies and other uncertainties of laboratory life as they reconstruct knowledge for public dissemination. However, more recent studies suggest that scientific uncertainty is a salient feature of public science. This uncertainty does not necessarily decrease the authority of science. Rather, uncertainty can be effectively managed by spokespeople for science to achieve their specific goals.

We should expect uncertainty to remain salient in public science, given the expanding number and scope of issues that elicit scientific uncertainty. For example, the key environmental problems of the 1960s and 1970s were largely local, while the environmental issues of today have not only increased in number, but also are national and international in scale. As the scope of these problems increased, so has the amount of scientific uncertainty. Many of these issues and problems also entail nonscientific questions of morality, politics, and economics that add to their complexity and to uncertainty. Clearly, for example, the ethics of genetic engineering and the global equity measures to slow global warming fall outside of the scientific purview.

Given the uncertainties inherent in these important issues, scientists and nonscientists need to be aware of the processes associated with their construction and management. Scientists can do a better job of openly representing the uncertainties that are part of their work. They can also be more aware of how their more certain knowledge claims can be easily transformed into an appearance of uncertainty in public science settings. Nonscientists can become more aware of how scientific uncertainties are constructed and how they can become authoritative claims in themselves. If nonscientists fail to become aware of the management of scientific uncertainty, they open themselves to manipulation by scientists and other groups and organizations that use science for their own benefit. This lack of awareness tips the balance of power further in the direction of those best able to represent and interpret these uncertainties—a potentially dangerous arrangement for issues, such as genetic engineering and global warming, that touch the lives of many people. Widespread awareness of how scientific uncertainties are managed, however, helps demystify science and increases the amount of influence that the public can exercise over decisions that affect their lives.

ACKNOWLEDGMENTS

Thanks go to the editors of this volume, Ronda Priest, and Holly Stocking for helpful comments on earlier drafts of this chapter.

REFERENCES

Brown, M. S. & K. A. Lyon. (1992). Holes in the ozone layer: A global environmental controversy. In D. Nelkin (Ed.), *Controversy: Politics of technical decisions* (3rd ed.) (pp. 59–79). Newbury Park, CA: Sage.

Campbell, B. L. (1985). Uncertainty as symbolic action in disputes among experts. *Social Studies of Science, 15*, 429–453.

Collins, H. M. (1987). Certainty and the public understanding of science: Science on television. *Social Studies of Science, 17*, 689–713.

Friedman, S. M., Dunwoody, S., & Rogers, C. L. (1986). *Scientists and journalists: Reporting science as news.* New York: The Free Press.

Funtowicz, S. O. & J. R. Ravetz. (1990). *Uncertainty and quality in science for policy.* Theory and Decision Library, Series A 15. Dordrecht: Kluwer.

Gieryn, T. F. (1996). Policing STS: A boundary-work souvenir from the Smithsonian exhibition on "Science in American Life." *Science, Technology, & Human Values, 21*, 100–115.

Gieryn, T. F., Bevins, G. M., & Zehr, S. C. (1985). Professionalization of American scientists: Public science in the creation/evolution trials. *American Sociological Review, 50*, 392–409.

Gieryn, T. F., & Figert, A. E. (1990). Ingredients for a theory of science in society: O-rings, ice water, C-clamp, Richard Feynman, and the press. In S. E. Cozzens & T. F. Gieryn (Eds.), *Theories of science in society* (pp. 67–97). Bloomington, IN: Indiana University Press.

Gilbert, G. N., & Mulkay, M. (1984). *Opening Pandora's box: A sociological analysis of scientists' discourse.* Cambridge, UK: Cambridge University Press.

Hansen, A. (Ed.). (1993). *The mass media and environmental issues.* Leicester, England: Leicester University Press.

Hilgartner, S. (1990). The dominant view of popularization: Conceptual problems, political uses. *Social Studies of Science, 20*, 519–539.

Hilgartner, S., & Bosk, C. L. (1988). The rise and fall of social problems: A public arenas model. *American Journal of Sociology, 94*, 53–78.

Hurricane! (1989, November 7). Written, produced, and directed by Larry Engel and Thomas Lucas. *NOVA.* Boston: WGBH/Public Broadcasting Service.

Irwin, A., & Wynne, B. (1996). *Misunderstanding science? The public reconstruction of science and technology.* Cambridge, UK: Cambridge University Press.

Latour, B. (1987). *Science in action: How to follow scientists and engineers through society.* Cambridge, MA: Harvard University Press.

Latour, B., & Woolgar, S. (1979). *Laboratory life: The social construction of scientific facts.* Beverly Hills, CA: Sage.

Lewenstein, B. V. (1995). Science and the media. In S. Jasanoff, G. E. Markle, J. C. Petersen, & T. Pinch (Eds.), *Handbook of science and technology studies* (pp. 343–360). Thousand Oaks, CA: Sage.

Lynch, M. (1985). *Art and artifact in laboratory science: A study of shop work and shop talk in a research laboratory.* London: Routledge & Kegan Paul.

Michael, M. (1992). Lay discourses of science: Science-in-general, science-in-particular, and self. *Science, Technology, & Human Values, 17,* 313–333.

Miller, K. (1992). Smoking up a storm: Public relations and advertising in the construction of the cigarette problem 1953–1954. *Journalism Monographs, 136* (December).

Milner, R. (1992). Earth's hot topic. *Natural History, 101* (5), 65–66.

Mulkay, M., & Gilbert, G. N. (1982). Accounting for error. *Sociology, 16,* 165–183.

Myers, G. (1990). *Writing biology: Texts in the social construction of scientific knowledge.* Madison: University of Wisconsin Press.

Nelkin, D. (1975). The political impact of technical expertise. *Social Studies of Science, 5,* 35–54.

Nelkin, D. (1995). *Selling science: How the press covers science and technology* (Rev. ed.). New York: Freeman.

Pinch, T. (1981). The sun-set: The presentation of certainty in scientific life. *Social Studies of Science, 11*(1), 131–158.

Pinch, T. J., & Bijker, W. E. (1987). The social construction of facts and artifacts: Or how the sociology of science and the sociology of technology might benefit each other. In W. E. Bijker, T. P. Hughes, & T. J. Pinch (Eds.), *The social construction of technological systems* (pp. 17–50). Cambridge, MA: MIT Press.

Proctor, R. N. (1995). *Cancer wars: How politics shapes what we know and don't know about cancer.* New York: Basic Books.

Shackley, S., & Wynne, B. (1996). Representing uncertainty in global climate change science and policy: Boundary-ordering devices and authority. *Science, Technology & Human Values, 21,* 275–302.

Shinn, T., & Whitley, R. (Eds.) (1985). Expository science: Forms and functions of popularization. *Sociology of the sciences yearbook.* Boston: Reidel.

Smithson, M. (1989). *Ignorance and uncertainty: Emerging paradigms.* New York: Springer-Verlag.

Smithson, M. (1993). Ignorance and science: Dilemmas, perspectives, and prospects. *Knowledge: Creation, Diffusion, Utilization, 15,* 133–156.

Star, S. L. (1985). Scientific work and uncertainty. *Social Studies of Science, 15,* 391–427.

Star, S. L., & Griesemer, J. (1989). Institutional ecology, "translations" and boundary objects: Amateurs and professionals in Berkeley's Museum of Vertebrate Zoology, 1907–1939. *Social Studies of Science, 19,* 387–420.

Stocking, S. H., & Holstein, L. W. (1993). Constructing and reconstructing scientific ignorance: Ignorance claims in science and journalism. *Knowledge: Creation, Diffusion, Utilization, 15,* 186–210.

Tuchman, G. (1972). Objectivity as strategic ritual. *American Journal of Sociology, 77,* 660–679.

Turner, F. M. (1980). Public science in Britain, 1880–1919. *Isis, 71,* 589–608.

Wynne, B. (1995). Public understanding of science. In S. Jasanoff, G. E. Markle, J. C. Petersen, & T. Pinch (Eds.), *Handbook of science and technology studies* (pp. 361–388). Thousand Oaks, CA: Sage.

Zehr, S. C. (1994a). The centrality of scientists and the translation of interests in the U.S. acid rain controversy. *Canadian Review of Sociology and Anthropology, 31,* 325–353.

Zehr, S. C. (1994b). Flexible interpretations of "acid rain" and the construction of scientific uncertainty in political settings. *Politics and the Life Sciences, 13,* 205–216.

Zehr, S. C. (1996, August). *Public representations of uncertainty about global warming and climate change.* Paper presented at the Annual Meeting of the American Sociological Association, New York.

Chapter 2

How Journalists Deal
With Scientific Uncertainty

S. Holly Stocking

*S. Holly Stocking has worked for **The Los Angeles Times,** The Associated Press and the **Minneapolis Tribune.** She earned her PhD at Indiana University, where she now teaches courses in science writing and literary journalism. She has written extensively on media coverage of scientific knowledge, ignorance, and uncertainty and is the coauthor of three science-based books, including **How Do Journalists Think? A Proposal for the Study of Cognitive Bias in Newsmaking.***

Breast implants. Gulf War syndrome. Global warming. Acid rain. Every day, journalists are bombarded with news releases and press packets from scientists, scientific journals, scientific societies, and from industry, special interest groups, environmental groups, and consumer groups, all of whom have an interest in shaping public interpretations of science. Some of the materials that land on journalists' desks downplay the uncertainties of knowledge claims bearing on public choices; others do not. Some interpret findings as unqualified breakthroughs; others interpret the same findings as self-serving hype. Some claim near consensus, if not certainty, with respect to what scientists think they know; others counter by stressing the controversial nature of such claims.

How do journalists deal with this barrage of scientific claims and counterclaims? If you listen to many critics, the answer is about as well as Southerners deal with blizzards—which is to say, with a lot of slipping and sliding, and sometimes by falling flat on their derrieres! On the one hand, journalists are frequently accused of making scientific claims appear more solid and certain than they are; on the other hand, there are times when journalists are lambasted for making science appear more uncertain and baffling than it, in fact, may be.

So who is right? Indeed, is any of the criticism justified?

WHAT RESEARCHERS AND SCHOLARS SAY

Those who study science news have addressed such charges, although the data they have gathered are severely limited. The majority of this small, disparate group of studies are analyses of media content intended to address other research problems. Some are case studies, and most investigate mainstream American news media, particularly the elite print press.[1]

The majority of these studies, too, come from a tradition of research that assumes that journalists' accounts of science are biased and distorted and that scientists' accounts of science, in contrast, are objective and accurate, assumptions that a growing number of scholars have called into question in recent years. However, the existing research does shed some much needed light on the critics' claims.

Journalists Make Science More Certain Than It Is

Among the findings considered most robust, especially by those working in the tradition that assumes media, not science, are where problems lie in the public communication of science, are those suggesting that journalists present science as more solid and certain than it, in fact, is. Multiple studies, for example, support the view that journalistic accounts of science tend to contain fewer caveats than scientific accounts. Other studies suggest that science news contains less in the way of other kinds of information that might temper the extravagances of individual research claims, including information about related research and about the process by which findings were developed. Studies also suggest that journalistic accounts of science convey considerable, and many would argue unwarranted, certainty with respect to the potential outcomes of ongoing research efforts.

Loss of Caveats

The particular work suggesting that science news contains fewer caveats than the scientific research it describes comes from several streams of research and scholarship.

Social scientists Carol Weiss and Eleanor Singer (1988), in their careful, quantitative treatment of mainstream media coverage of the social sciences,

---

[1]Television has not been studied much because of the difficulties of doing such research. Studies tend to exclude books, small local media, wire service news, business media, advocacy media, and emerging media on the information highway.

found that journalists tend to transform provisional findings into certain findings. Likewise, discourse analyst Jeanne Fahnestock (1986), in fine-grained comparisons of articles about scientific findings appearing in *Science* magazine with accounts of the same topics in popular science and news magazines, found that the popularized versions exaggerated the scientific claims, playing down the qualifiers and caveats present in the original.[2] For example, one study's carefully hedged observation in the scientific literature about the relation between gender and mathematical ability became a definite conclusion in the popular literature. In *Science* magazine, the authors of the study (Benbow & Stanley, 1980) wrote, "*We favor the hypothesis that* sex differences in achievement in and attitude toward mathematics result from superior male mathematical ability, which *may* in turn be related to greater male mathematical ability in spatial tasks" (cited in Fahnestock, 1986, p. 287). In *Newsweek*, this statement became, "The authors' conclusion: 'Sex differences in achievement in and attitude toward mathematics result from superior male mathematical ability.'" (cited in Fahnestock, 1986, p. 287). Fahnestock found that other popular media, ranging from *The New York Times* to *Reader's Digest*, shared this tendency to increase the certainty of Benbow and Stanley's findings.

Quantitative content analyses of media coverage of the risks associated with natural and man-made hazards have also documented a tendency to minimize uncertainties (see, e.g., Singer & Endreny, 1993), as have qualitative studies of television documentaries (Collins, 1987; Hornig, 1990).

Moreover, the findings of social science studies assessing the accuracy of media accounts of science are consistent with the conclusions of these content studies. That is, scientists who complain about the accuracy of media coverage have complained the most about omissions in journalists' accounts, especially the omission of caveats and other qualifications (see, e.g., Singer & Endreny, 1993; Tankard & Ryan, 1974).

Single-Source Stories

In addition to documenting a relative poverty of caveats, investigators have found a tendency among a significant number of journalists to limit themselves to single sources in reporting science stories. In their study of media coverage of the social sciences, for example, Weiss and Singer (1988) found that a vast majority of journalists who wrote about scientists' findings appeared to accept the scientists' word on faith, seeking out other scientists for their reactions only in a minority of cases.

---

[2]The popularized versions also stressed the *uniqueness* of the findings.

Even in cases where controversy would seem to demand multiple sources, a sizeable proportion of journalists may use very few. In a study of the Alar controversy, for instance, Friedman, Villamil, Suriano, and Egolf (1996) found more than one half of the journalists covering the dispute over whether this growth-inhibiting chemical used by apple growers was harmful quoted just one to two sources.[3] If we assume that scientists sometimes suggest uncertainty in the findings by offering a different interpretation of the data, the study's conclusions, or its implications, the fact that journalists quote a limited number of sources may itself minimize the amount of scientific uncertainty reported in their stories.

Lack of Context

Some journalistic accounts of science have also neglected historical context, failing to indicate, for example, whether a new study departs from or extends prior research. Indeed, Tankard and Ryan (1974) cited "continuity of research with earlier work ignored" (p. 221), as one of the top problems in science reporting; more recently, Pellechia (1997) found that fewer than 60% of the science articles that she examined during three decades mentioned either prior research or future studies.

As a case in point, Weiss and Singer (1988) noted that, during their study:

> *Time* ran a story about an NIMH [National Institute of Mental Health] report on the link between children's viewing of television violence and subsequent aggressive behavior. A few months later *Time* ran another story on the (positive) effects of television viewing on children. No mention was made of the NIMH report (p. 133).

Although they did not explicitly say so, the concern of the authors seemed to be that without such mention (and with what were likely few caveats associated with the findings), readers who did not see the NIMH story might interpret the new, more positive report—and particularly the recommendations based on the new findings—as more definitive than it was, and so draw unwarranted conclusions about the value of television for their children.

Summing up their concerns for the lack of context in media accounts, Weiss and Singer (1988) quoted a social scientist in their study who commented, "My study was just out there, sitting there. It didn't have any tie-in to the whole body of research [on the subject]" (p. 133).

---

[3]Specifically, the authors reported that about 20% of the articles about Alar quoted 3 sources, 20% quoted 4 to 7 sources, and 5% quoted between 8 and 13 sources (p. 11). This suggests that 55% quoted only 1 to 2 sources. Indeed, the authors reported that one third of the articles quoted only 1 source (p. 11).

Product Over Process

Not only do journalists tend to present science with relatively few caveats, few sources, and little historical context, according to studies, but they also appear more interested in the carefully crafted results (or products) that scientists produce than in the messy, interpretative, and often very social processes by which they are produced.[4]

Sociologist Dorothy Nelkin (1995) made this point in her account of contemporary media coverage of science, as did communications scholar Marcel LaFollette (1990) in her historical look at American magazine coverage of science. Weiss and Singer (1988) also found very few discussions of the methods of science in the stories about social science they examined. Singer and Endreny (1993), in their study of the risks associated with complex technologies, natural disasters, diseases, and other hazards, found similar patterns, as did Pellechia (1997) in her study of science coverage in three U.S. newspapers over three decades.

Product-oriented news, each author suggested in her own way, works to solidify and mystify scientists' claims. In doing so, it might be argued, it often works to obscure scientific uncertainties.

A Triumphant Quest

Some scholars who formally monitor media content have concluded that when the process of science is actually reported, it tends to be presented as a quest whose future outcome is assured: Scientists will find the answer; they will find the key that unlocks the mysteries of influenza, cancer, and genetic disease.

LaFollette (1990) and Nelkin (1995), based on their extensive observations of the news media, each made this point. Science, each suggested, is often presented in the media as a triumphant quest for certainty. Put another way, *uncertainty* is presented in the media as reducible and resolvable at a time when a growing number of critics (see, e.g., Smithson, 1989) argue that much uncertainty, by simple virtue of the complexity of social, biological, and physical systems, may be irreducible, and indeed may not be resolvable at all.

---

[4]Put in social constructionist terms (discussed later in this chapter), they are more interested in the carefully crafted constructions of science than in the much less deliberate, and perhaps more revealing, acts of constructing science.

Journalists Make Science
Appear Uncertain and Baffling

Although the bulk of the existing work on science news suggests that journalists make scientific claims appear more solid and certain than they are in traditional scientific forums, a few studies suggest that journalists on occasion make scientific claims appear more uncertain and baffling than most scientists with the relevant expertise believe them to be.

Unexplained Flip-Flops

Indeed, the very certainty of individual accounts of science, when followed in rapid succession by equally certain but contradictory accounts, may be expected to exaggerate uncertainty on occasion, as when today's apparently certain study on the nutritional value of butter appears to contradict yesterday's study on its nutritional dangers.

This amplification of uncertainty may be particularly acute when such inconsistencies are presented without explanation. As a case in point, Weiss and Singer (1988) described the media coverage of the Global 2000 symposium at the 1983 meeting of the American Association for the Advancement of Science. The symposium was organized by futurist Herman Kahn and economist Julian Simon to rebut previously reported, more pessimistic conclusions about world trends in population, resources, and the environment. The resulting journalistic accounts tended to say only that these analyses were more optimistic than previous doom-and-gloom reports. Indeed, only 3 of the 13 reporters who filed stories on this session tried to explain the reasons for the discrepancy (Weiss & Singer, 1988, pp. 133–134). The resulting coverage, it could be argued, left the impression that the science on these matters was more in flux than might have been the case if the particulars of the differing conclusions had been clarified and the reasons for them explained.

Equal Weight to Majority and Fringe Scientists

In general, journalists tend to give more attention to information offered by sources who are visible in a culture (often *officials*) than they do to information offered by sources who are less visible; this is no less true in science than it is in other domains. In particular, journalists tend to give more attention to the work of scientists who are highly visible in the scientific community than they do to the efforts of scientists who are in the minority or on the fringes (Hansen, 1994; Shepherd, 1979; Stocking, 1985).[5]

However, sometimes, particularly in science addressing contentious public issues, journalists have been found to pit scientist against scientist, with little or no discussion of the reason for disagreements, and often without mention of the relative degree of scientific acceptance of the differing views. The resulting accounts of science give equal, but unequally deserving, weight to "dueling experts," thus making the science appear more controversial and more uncertain than the bulk of scientists believe it to be (Dearing, 1995).

For example, in the case of the scientific link between tobacco and lung cancer, scientists whose work supports the interests of the tobacco industry, although they were not given much credence among nonindustry scientists, were for a long time given equal time in the American press (Miller, 1992). More recently, in the global climate change debate, fringe scientists, many of them funded by industry with huge stakes in the outcome of the controversy, have been given almost equal weight with majority scientists (Wilkins, 1993). Indeed, it has been suggested that socially significant and economically contentious issues, such as global climate change, may be especially prone to this kind of coverage (Schneider, 1996).

In addition, on occasion journalists have devoted entire stories to the work of fringe or minority scientists. For example, some years ago *The New York Times* devoted an entire story in the science section to the minority position in the science of species loss. Although noting the minority status of the views presented, the attention given to the story implied that science in this arena was far more "iffy" than the majority of scientists in the field at the time assessed it to be (Stocking, 1992) .

Equal Weight to Scientists and Nonscientists

Sometimes, too, journalists have been found to give equal weight to scientists and nonscientists. Journalists have been found to give equal weight,

---

[5]Shepherd (1979) found that scientists who were less visible in the scientific literature on marijuana, as measured by citation counts, were given more weight in mass media accounts than scientists who were more visible in the scientific literature in the field. However, a point that Shepherd himself and others interpreting this study appear to have missed is that the work of highly cited scientists received more attention in the press than the work of less highly cited scientists; this is because many of the journalists' sources, who were administrators themselves, cited the work of the scientists who were most active in the field. Stocking (1985), likewise, found that the more a study was cited in the scientific literature, the more likely it was to show up in press accounts. To my knowledge, these are the most rigorous studies comparing visibility in the scientific literature with visibility in the popular press.

for example, to the testimony of nonscientists who believe themselves to be victims of hazardous substances, and to the evidence of scientists who are unable to find the suspected link (see, e.g., Greenberg, Sandman, Sachsman, & Salomone, 1989). Media coverage of scientific issues that have gone to court may be especially susceptible to such media balancing acts. The case of media coverage of a trial about creationism is a case in point (Taylor & Condit, 1988), along with the more recent case of silicone breast implants, which pitted women with diffuse symptoms against scientists who could find no link between the women's symptoms and their implants (Angell, 1996). Such situations worry scientists who believe that nonscientists lack the knowledge and skills to be granted such authority.

Accounting for Different Patterns of Media Coverage

If the data directly addressing patterns of coverage of scientific uncertainty are slim, they are even slimmer concerning the factors that create these patterns. However, extrapolating from existing social science research, mostly about media coverage of nonscience domains, we can make some guesses as to the factors involved.

In particular, it is not unreasonable to speculate that characteristics of individual journalists, such as their knowledge levels and concerns for the values of scientists, have some influence on how scientific uncertainty is covered. At the same time, decades of social science research on media coverage of nonscience domains suggest that such individual characteristics are likely to have far less influence than other factors, including various media routines and organizational constraints under which journalists work. With the exception of the occasional studies noted below, such speculations should be considered as hypotheses that, with a little work, could be tested.

Individual-Level Factors

Ignorance, Education, and Experience.   Journalists' lack of scientific knowledge or training is one of the most commonly cited reasons for reporting patterns that media critics define as problematic. Just why this is so is not clear. Perhaps it is because human beings tend to blame individuals over systems, or perhaps because, among all the likely problems, it appears to be the most fixable. Whatever the reason, the evidence to date does little to support the view that ignorant journalists are the culprits.

Although it is true that American journalists have little training in the natural sciences (Weaver & Wilhoit, 1996), it is far from clear that this translates into different ways of handling scientific uncertainties. In their study of media coverage of the social sciences, which attended only indirectly to media treatment of scientific uncertainty, Weiss and Singer (1988) did not find any relationship between formal training in the social sciences and the ability of journalists to develop stories that their sources judged as competent (that is, accurate, complete, and offering appropriate emphasis). They did find a relationship, although it was not strong, between the journalists' abilities to develop competent stories and their years of work experience (pp. 82-83).

Certainly it makes sense to think that knowledge, whether acquired from training or experience, matters in the treatment of scientific uncertainty. Indeed, those of us who are educators in science communication take this as an unquestioned assumption; so do scientists who organize workshops that address issues of uncertainty.

For example, if journalists understand that single studies do not make knowledge, they may be more eager to include caveats about the findings of a new study, perhaps even to seek them out if the scientists with whom they are talking fail to mention them. If reporters understand that correlation does not equal causation, they will know, when they see a study reporting a correlation between ear infections and pacifiers that they should not jump to the conclusion that pacifier use causes ear infections; it may simply be the case that children who get ear infections find some relief in using pacifiers. To report that pacifier use is linked to ear infections without mentioning this possibility, as was the case in an article that ran in *The Washington Post* (Squires, 1996), is to obscure the inherent uncertainties in a correlational study of this sort.[6]

Journalists' Concern for Scientists' Values and Allegiance to Their Own Profession's Values and Standards.

In one study, journalists who expressed concern for social scientists' criteria for stories (i.e., factual accuracy, appropriateness of emphasis, and completeness of information) were more likely than journalists who did not express such concerns to satisfy them in the eyes of the scientists evaluating their work (Weiss & Singer, 1988, pp. 76–77). Given this, we might expect journalists who are sensitive to scientists' apparent concerns for the loss of caveats in media accounts to take pains to include such caveats.

---

[6]A more recent study, reported in 1998 (Van), found a correlation between heart disease and a lack of flossing. The study, done by dental researchers, is subject to a variety of interpretations, only some of which appear to have been covered by journalists.

Certainly, with the growing professionalization of journalism and of science and environmental reporting, in particular, professional societies in journalism have endorsed or organized a number of initiatives designed to offer guidelines to journalists in their coverage of complex scientific issues. These initiatives usually take the form of workshops and publications and often involve input from scientists, scientific societies, or communications scholars allied with scientific societies. The resulting dialogue inevitably involves issues of scientific uncertainty and often stresses the need for caveats in journalists' stories. It seems reasonable to assume that individual journalists will be influenced by emerging professional standards with respect to managing scientific uncertainty to the extent that they make use of these initiatives and to the extent that they ally themselves with their professional societies and with the definitions of responsibility that such groups endorse.

Indeed, Lisa Holstein and I found anecdotal evidence to that effect in the work we did on the construction of ignorance in scientists' and journalists' accounts (Stocking & Holstein, 1993). Veteran science writer Victor Cohn's *News and Numbers* (1989) and *Reporting on Risk* (1990), which both discuss journalists' handling of uncertainty, were mentioned frequently in our talks with journalists as guidelines they use in their reporting.

Media Routines and Organizational Demands

Decades of communications research and scholarship in mass communications suggest that an individual journalist's knowledge or concerns may matter less than we might think, and certainly may matter less than other factors, in how a particular story is reported or written. As any working journalist will tell you, individual reporters may know or want something to be so, but they may not be able to use their knowledge or concerns to write the kind of stories that might satisfy critics simply because their behavior is constrained by the routines and other organizational demands of the business.

Media Routines.   If media accounts tend to solidify uncertain science, for example, the reason may be attributed more to media routines than to ignorance or a lack of appropriate concerns or standards on the part of individual journalists.

The routine demands for information that fits journalists' notions of news may be especially influential in solidifying uncertain findings. The routine demands for novelty and significance, in particular, may be expected to shape news involving scientific uncertainty. As Fahnestock (1986) pointed out, "There is simply no way to address the public with the significance of findings that are so carefully hedged [that] their reality seems questionable" (p. 283). Journalists, who need stories that will be regarded as significant by their editors and peers, will be led to ignore all but those hedges that have the most obvious implications for their audiences. The result is a story that may appear more certain to the public than it does to scientists who read the scientific literature and have a more fully rounded picture of the research and its context.

Other patterns of media coverage of scientific uncertainty that critics have deemed problematic also may be traced to media routines. The case in which news media played up the uncertainties in the science of species loss, for example, appears to have come about when a highly knowledgeable freelance science writer went searching for a story that defied conventional scientific wisdom about the loss; he did this knowing that contrarian stories are novel and therefore newsworthy (Stocking, 1992).[7]

Media routines also seem to contribute to the pattern in which scientists, regardless of the weight of evidence on their side, are presented as equally deserving experts. American mainstream journalists, in particular, are expected to routinely seek opinions from all sides, with an eye toward balancing one view against the others in their account.[8] Sociologist Gay Tuchman (1972) has called this balancing routine the ritual of journalistic objectivity.

Sources who understand this ritual, and other media routines, often manipulate them to their own ends (see, e.g., Dunwoody & Griffin, 1993; Nelkin, 1995; Stallings, 1990). Such was the case when a handful of dissenting scientists in the late 1990s clamored to be given equal time against the consensual views of an international panel of 2,500 scientists studying global climate change (Gelbspan, 1997b).[9]

Organizational Demands.   Accounts of scientific uncertainty tend to vary from one medium to another. This is due, at least in part, to differing organizational demands, such as the need to tailor messages for specific

---

[7]His story, originally published in *Science,* was picked up by mainstream media, including *The New York Times.*

[8]Dunwoody and Peters (1992) suggested that American journalists may be more prone to the balancing routine than German journalists who appear to think they have relatively more freedom to make validity judgments on their own.

[9]Gelbspans' book *The Heat is On* (1997a) provided a sobering look at how a group of dissenting scientists, funded by the fossil fuel industry and various conservative groups, worked to raise doubts about the majority scientific views of global climate change and influence the global climate change debate. News media, which traditionally strive for fairness on controversial matters, often unwittingly became allies of these scientists in sowing the seeds of doubt among policymakers and the public alike.

audiences. Although individual journalists have somewhat hazy images of their audiences (Hansen, 1994), writers, editors, and producers collectively attempt to shape their accounts to accommodate their audiences' knowledge level and interests. Thus, a story for media catering to a business audience may be expected to highlight different aspects of the climate change story, including interpretations of scientific uncertainty, than a story for the environmental advocacy press or even for the mainstream media (Jacobi, 1991, pp. 33–37).[10]

Pressure from advertisers also might be expected to affect coverage of uncertainty in science. In their review of studies on the relationship between media content and tobacco advertising, Weis and Burke (1986) found a history of media vulnerability to tobacco industry threats to pull their advertisements. Hayes and Reisner (1991) found farm magazines similarly vulnerable to advertiser threats. For example, a magazine that depends on advertising from an insecticide manufacturer may attend more to the uncertainties of a claimed scientific link between insecticides and cancer than a magazine that does not accept such advertising.

Ownership patterns, too, may affect coverage of uncertainty. In one of the few studies of advertiser influence on media accounts of science, researchers found differences in the way the stories about smoking and cancer were reported in the *Weekly Reader*, a grade school newsweekly owned by a unit of the largest shareholder in a tobacco company, and the *Scholastic News*, its independently owned competitor. *Weekly Reader* stories were more likely than *Scholastic News* stories to give tobacco industry sources the same weight as nonindustry scientists (Balbach & Glanz, 1995). As a result, the *Weekly Reader* was more likely than *Scholastic News* to create the impression of uncertainty about claimed links between smoking and cancer.

In recent years, the traditional wall between the business and editorial sides of the media has been breached in many outlets, with editors assuming ever more responsibility for the bottom line of the business and publishers keeping close watch on editorial content. To the extent that this is so, concerns about capturing audiences and not alienating advertisers or owners (stockholders in the case of publicly owned companies) may come to take precedence over traditional editorial concerns, with the result that uncertainty claims that undermine business interests may be expected to be given less coverage and prominence than uncertainty claims that support such interests.

---

[10]See Jacobi's text (1991) on magazine writing for examples of variations in the interpretations of scientific uncertainty as a function of audience.

RESEARCH NEEDS

It is easy to forget that the bulk of these assertions, although they definitely make sense, are but speculations with respect to journalists' accounts of uncertainties in science. We are swimming in uncertainty and downright ignorance when it comes to the questions at hand—how journalists deal with uncertainty (the patterns of content) and what factors account for the observed patterns (the patterns of influence). For those who want to grapple with these matters, there are many challenges ahead.

Conceptual Challenges

Uncertainty

Concurrent with formulating the foregoing speculations as testable hypotheses, we need to decide what we mean by *scientific uncertainty*. Journalists who cover science, medicine, the environment, and other issues involving science are exposed to a variety of oral and written expressions that often are subsumed under the term. These include, but are not limited to, the following:

- Words and phrases (e.g., "*suggests*" or "*may*").
- Caveats specifying limits to the knowledge at hand (e.g., "sampling or chance could account for the observed variation").
- Simple assertions (or claims) that knowledge is preliminary or uncertain ("these data are too preliminary to suggest that Americans make changes in their diet").

We need to examine systematically the content of both scientific and public discourse to see how various actors characterize scientific uncertainty and how (and if) they perceive and act on such characterizations.[11]

---

[11]Krimsky (see chap. 10, this volume) has noted the need to sort out various types of uncertainty related to evidence, such as insufficient data, contradictory data, different interpretations of data, uncertainty about causality, predictive uncertainty about models or extrapolations, and uncertainty about the quality of information. According to Krimsky, "The idea that scientists may disagree or that there is uncertainty does not provide sufficient information for an informed reader." (personal communication on February 19, 1996)

Ignorance

Ignorance, in the sense of absence of scientific knowledge, is another concept in need of scholars' attention.[12] Sometimes, *ignorance* is expressed in explicit statements, as in "We simply don't know," "Scientists have not conducted any studies on that," "It's a problem that baffles scientists," or "It appears to be a problem that's insoluble." Sometimes, such explicit statements are not visible but might be if journalists went looking for them.

The central questions are these: How is the absence of scientific knowledge expressed in scientific and public discourse, and how do journalists deal with such expressions? In my view, when we focus on uncertainty in books such as this one, we risk obscuring the fact that there is a great deal in the world that science does not address at all. Many chemicals in use on our planet have never been tested. Many medical treatments, including many kinds of surgeries, have not gone through clinical trials. Some pollutants have become so pervasive that it has become impossible to find the kind of control groups that make good science. And, when it comes to the implications of what we think we know, the language of uncertainty often obscures the outright absence of knowledge, or even of research, in the face of systems that are becoming ever more complex.

Certainty

Finally, what constitutes certainty, particularly to a journalist? Is it when there is no obvious disagreement among scientists? Is it when the disagree-

---

[12]Smithson (1989) proposed a complex taxonomy of ignorance, which subsumes both uncertainty and absence of knowledge (p. 9). Specifically, *ignorance* in his taxonomy consists of two major subcategories: *error* and *irrelevance*. Under *error* is distortion and incompleteness; under *irrelevance* is untopicality, taboo, and undecidability. Under *distortion*, furthermore, lies confusion and inaccuracy; and under incompleteness lies uncertainty and absence.

Ignorance in this particular chapter appears to be what Smithson called absence of knowledge. In that sense, I am making a much more restricted use of the term ignorance than Smithson did. In contrast, my use of uncertainty in this chapter is broader than Smithson's, an attempt to stay close to the ways that I anticipated the majority of other contributors to a volume on "uncertainty" would use the term. Serious scholars should note that in other published works (Stocking & Holstein, 1993), and Stocking (1998), I use the term *ignorance,* as Smithson did, to describe not only uncertainty and ignorance as discussed here, but also many other ways of non-knowing. Ignorance, rather than uncertainty, is the preferred organizing term for those wishing to develop a sociology of scientific ignorance (SSI) to complement the existing sociology of scientific knowledge (SSK). For a discussion of the pressures on scholars to use the term "uncertainty" over "ignorance," see Stocking (1998); for mention of the tendency of scientists to use "uncertainty" to deflect attention from ignorance in the sense of the absence of knowledge, see Zehr in this volume.

The obvious differences in the way various scholars use the terms ignorance and uncertainty, and in the ways of same scholars may use these terms in various contexts, only emphasize the need for careful observation and interpretation with respect to this subject.

ments in science are simply not very visible? Or, is it when scientists make claims without issuing caveats? And faced with apparent certainty, what do journalists do? To what extent, and under what circumstances, will journalists—on their own—question apparent certainty or seek out the views of a dissenting minority (as the freelance reporter did in the case of the science of species loss presented earlier)?

Theoretical Challenges

The bulk of the foregoing research relevant to media coverage of scientific ignorance and uncertainty comes from a traditional theoretical position known as *objectivism*. As such, it tends to operate on assumptions that scientific ignorance and uncertainty, like scientific knowledge, are givens in nature, unproblematic, and, except in the case of bad science, uncontaminated by social factors. Scientists routinely uncover these givens; journalists, whose protections from social contamination lack the rigor of scientists', routinely distort them. So commonplace are such assumptions that it can be difficult, particularly for scientists, to imagine any other way of looking at the matter. However, there are other ways.

Scholars working in a more recent framework—a *social constructionist framework*—do not assume that ignorance and uncertainty are natural givens. Indeed, scholars working in this framework have adopted the view, prevalent in the sociology of scientific knowledge, that scientists' claims are just that—claims that are subject to social interpretation and negotiation. Like their counterparts, scholars working in the emerging sociology of scientific ignorance assume that scientists' claims that something is not known are either inherently social or at least partially subject to social processes (Proctor, 1995; Smithson, 1989; Stocking & Holstein, 1993; Stocking, 1998). Scientists, for example, have to work to convince others that types of ignorance—knowledge gaps and particular caveats, for example—"exist." In doing so, they must make use of rhetorical strategies, professional and political allies, and other social and material resources.[13]

In some of these social constructionist accounts of scientific ignorance and uncertainty, scientists are portrayed not as uniformly offering more caveats than

---

[13]Indeed, J. R. Ravetz has raised the possibility that ignorance may be even more prone than knowledge to social construction because, in his view, ignorance claims often lack both "the positive, articulate argumentation behind knowledge claims" and "their standing as self-sufficient objects of discourse" (personal communication, on July 11, 1993).

journalists but as flexibly interpreting their claims depending on the social context, much as journalists do who work for various media (Stocking & Holstein, 1993). Zehr (1994; chap. 1, this volume), for example, showed how scientists made scientific claims about acid rain appear more certain in some contexts and less certain in others. It thus seems that scientists tell—or *sell*, to use Nelkin's (1995) term—different versions of scientific uncertainty to differ- ent people, depending on their audience and what they hope to achieve. Indeed, scientists sometimes offer fewer caveats than journalists do. Hilgartner (1990), for example, cited one instance in which *People* magazine offered more information about the uncertainty of an estimate of the role played by diet in the development of cancer than did accounts in more scientific forums. Arguing that the boundaries between "science" and "popular science" are not easily drawn, he suggested that scientists flexibly interpret what is appropriate sim- plification and what is distortion, tending to judge their own simplifications as appropriate and those of nonscientists as distorted. According to Hilgartner, such interpretations serve scientists well, working as a "powerful tool for sustaining the social hierarchy of expertise" (p. 519).

Hilgartner's analysis can be interpreted as problematizing the very notion of media "problems," leading us to ask whose interests are served when particular patterns of media coverage of ignorance or uncertainty are defined as *problem- atic* in the first place. Whose interests are served, for example, by defining as a problem the equal weighting in media accounts of nonscientists' testimonials and scientific evidence? Does it serve the interests of the recipients of silicone breast implants or the interests of the survivors of the Gulf War? Or does it serve the interests of those particular scientists whose research has failed to support links between physical ailments and exposure to silicone implants or chemicals in the Gulf?

Asked this way, the answers appear to suggest themselves. Many of the patterns of media coverage of ignorance and uncertainty that have been iden- tified as problematic have been so labeled by scientists who have much to lose if others' observations are accorded weight comparable to their own in the popular press.[14]

---

[14]This is not meant to suggest that scientists are exclusively self-interested in their definitions of problems. Nor is it to suggest that media are without problems in covering scientific ignorance and uncertainty. It is meant only to call attention to the facts that definitions of problems vary and that variations can be linked to interests. As noted in Stocking and Holstein (1993), in another context: "Such interests may be political or economic, but they need not be. They can be selfish, but they need not be. A scientist's interests may be in advancing or protecting the public good." (p. 190).

From this perspective, efforts designed to understand the patterns of media coverage of scientific ignorance and uncertainty and the reasons for such patterns (efforts such as this book and the scientific session that led to parts of this book) can themselves become the object of investigation by scholars who take a social constructionist approach to science.[15]

CONCLUSION

Claims about the absence or uncertainty of knowledge are becoming increasingly visible in discussions of public controversies involving science. Given the data to date, it is tempting to make the categorical statement, as many scientists do, that journalists distort science by eliminating important caveats and making findings appear more certain than they actually are. However, as our own work suggests, journalists occasionally make scientific knowledge appear far less certain than scientists believe it to be; sometimes, much to the consternation of scientists, journalists also point out downright ignorance.

The question, of course, is how do media describe (or construct) scientific uncertainty and ignorance? What accounts for differences that might be observed? As argued in this chapter, our answers to these questions are themselves very limited. Considerable work is needed before we can describe with any confidence how journalists deal with (or construct) uncertainty and ignorance in science, let alone explain why they do as they do, and what, if anything, ought to be done, and can be done, about identified problems.

REFERENCES

Angell, M. (1996). *Science on trial: The class of medical evidence and the law in the breast implant case.* New York: Norton.

Balbach, E. D., & Glanz, S. (1995). Tobacco information in two grade school newsweeklies: A content analysis. *American Journal of Public Health, 85* (12), 1650–1653.

Benbow, C. P., & Stanley, J. C. (1980). Mathematical ability: Is sex a factor? *Science, 210,* 1262–1264.

Cohn, V. (1989). *News & numbers: A guide to reporting statistical claims and controversies in health and related fields.* Ames, IA: Iowa State University Press.

---

[15]The fact that social constructionist scholars have been invited to write chapters for this volume is itself worthy of comment by social constructionists motivated to examine a collection such as this one.

Cohn, V. (1990). *Reporting on risk: Getting it right in an age of risk.* Washington, DC: Media Institute.

Collins, H. M. (1987). Certainty and the public understanding of science: Science on television. *Social Studies of Science, 17* (4), 689–713.

Dearing, J. W. (1995). Newspaper coverage of maverick science: Creating controversy through balancing. *Public Understanding of Science, 4,* 341–361.

Dunwoody, S., & Griffin, R. J. (1993). Journalistic strategies for reporting long-term environmental issues: A case study of three Superfund sites. In A. Hansen (Ed.)., *The mass media and environmental issues* (pp. 22–50). Leicester, England: Leicester University Press.

Dunwoody, S., & Peters, H. P. (1992). Mass media coverage of technology and environmental risks: A survey of research in the U.S. and Germany. *Public Understanding of Science, 1,* 199–230.

Fahnestock, J. (1986). Accommodating science: The rhetorical life of scientific facts. *Written Communication, 3,* 275–296.

Friedman, S. M., Villamil, K., Suriano, R. A., & Egolf, B. P. (1996). Alar and apples: Newspapers, risk and media responsibility. *Public Understanding of Science, 5,* 1–20.

Gelbspan, R. (1997a). *The heat is on: The high stakes battle over Earth's threatened climate.* Reading, MA: Addison-Wesley.

Gelbspan, R. (1997b, May 15). Hot air, cold truth: Why do we pay attention to greenhouse skeptics? *The Washington Post,* p. C1.

Greenberg. M. R., Sandman, P. M., Sachsman, D. B., & Salomone, K. L. (1989). Network television news coverage of environmental risks. *Environment, 31* (2), 16–20, 40–43.

Hansen, A. (1994). Journalistic practices and science reporting in the British press. *Public Understanding of Science, 3,* 111–134.

Hayes, R. G., & Reisner, A. E. (1991). Farm journalists and advertiser influence: Pressures on ethical standards. *Journalism Quarterly, 68* (1/2), 172–178.

Hilgartner, S. (1990). The dominant view of popularization: Conceptual problems, political uses. *Social Studies of Science, 20,* 519–539.

Hornig, S. (1990). Television's *NOVA* and the construction of scientific truth. *Critical Studies in Mass Communication, 7* (1), 11–23.

Jacobi, P. (1991). *The magazine article: How to think it, plan it, write it.* Cincinnati: Writer's Digest Books.

LaFollette, M. C. (1990). *Making science our own: Public images of science, 1910–1955.* Chicago: University of Chicago Press.

Miller, K. (1992). Smoking up a storm: Public relations and advertising in the construction of the cigarette problem 1953–1954. *Journalism Monographs, 136.*

Nelkin, D. (1995). *Selling science: How the press covers science and technology* (Rev. ed.). New York: Freeman.

Pellechia, M. G. (1997). Trends in science coverage: A content analysis of three U.S. newspapers. *Public Understanding of Science, 6,* 49–68.

Proctor, R. N. (1995). *Cancer wars: How politics shapes what we know and don't know about cancer.* New York: Basic Books.

Schneider, S. H. (1996, August). *Characterizing and communicating scientific uncertainty.* Remarks made at summer science session: Aspen Center for Global Climate Change, Aspen, CO.

Shepherd, R. G. (1979). Science news of controversy: The case of marijuana. *Journalism Monographs, 62.*

Singer, E., & Endreny, P. M. (1993). *Reporting on risk.* New York: Russell Sage Foundation.

Smithson, M. (1989). *Ignorance and uncertainty: Emerging paradigms.* New York: Springer-Verlag.

Squires, S. (1996, November 28). Pacifiers linked to ear infections. *The Washington Post*, p. Z05.

Stallings, R. A. (1990). Media discourse and the social construction of risk. *Social Problems, 37* (1), 80–95.

Stocking, S. H. (1985). Effect of public relations efforts on media visibility of organizations. *Journalism Quarterly, 62* (2), 358–366, 450.

Stocking, S. H. (1992, February). *When scientists' agendas hit the newsroom: Media coverage of the science of endangered species.* Paper presented at the annual meeting of the American Association for the Advancement of Science, Chicago.

Stocking, S. H., & Holstein, L. W. (1993). Constructing and reconstructing scientific ignorance: Ignorance claims in science and journalism. *Knowledge: Creation, Diffusion, Utilization, 15* (2), 186–210.

Stocking, S. H. (1998). On drawing attention to ignorance. *Science Communication, 20 (1),* 165–178.

Tankard, J. W., & Ryan, M. (1974). News source perceptions of accuracy of science coverage. *Journalism Quarterly, 51* (2), 219–225, 334.

Taylor, C. A., & Condit, C. M. (1988). Objectivity and elites: A creation science trial. *Critical studies in Mass Communication, 5,* 293–312.

Tuchman, G. (1972). Objectivity as a strategic ritual: An examination of newsmen's notions of objectivity. *American Journal of Sociology, 77,* 660–680.

Van, Jon (1998, February 17). Oral germs can damage heart, study finds. *Chicago Tribune*, p. N6.

Weaver, D. H., & Wilhoit, G. C. (1996). *The American journalist in the 1990s: U.S. news people at the end of an era.* Mahwah, NJ: Lawrence Erlbaum Associates.

Weis, W. L., & Burke, C. (1986). Media content and tobacco advertising: An unhealthy addiction. *Journal of Communication, 36* (4), 59–69.

Weiss, C. H., & Singer, E. (1988). *Reporting of social science in the national media.* New York: Russell Sage Foundation.

Wilkins, L. (1993). Between facts and values: Print media coverage of the greenhouse effect, 1987–1990. *Public Understanding of Science, 2,* 71–84.

Zehr, S. C. (1994). Flexible interpretations of "acid rain" and the construction of scientific uncertainty in political settings. *Politics and the Life Sciences, 13* (2), 205–216.

Chapter 3

Public Responses to Uncertainty

Edna Einsiedel
Bruce Thorne

Edna Einsiedel is currently collaborating with colleagues in Europe, the United States, and Japan to examine the intersection between public perceptions, media coverage, and public policy on biotechnology. She is a professor of communication studies in the Graduate Program in Communications at the University of Calgary. Her research interests also include the social construction of technology and the public understanding of science.

Bruce Thorne teaches mass communication theory in the Bachelor of Public Relations program at Mount Saint Vincent University in Halifax, Nova Scotia, Canada. He holds a master's degree from the University of Calgary and has concentrated his research in the social construction of biotechnology. His most recent work examines the interrelationship between popular understandings of nature and biotechnology.

A quick perusal of news coverage of science issues shows that uncertainty is a common element. Consider some of the more recent issues in the news: Is Mad Cow disease transmissible to humans and, if so, how does transmission occur? Is genetically engineered food safe? What do we know about the amounts and distribution of toxic chemicals being used and released into the environment, and what are their potential impacts? Which foods cause cancer or help impede its development?

Many times increased science knowledge is associated with greater uncertainty, as is illustrated by the following excerpt from an article in *The New York Times* on the discovery of a gene responsible for some forms of breast cancer:

> Just two years ago, a team of scientists won a fevered race to find an elusive gene that causes breast cancer in women who inherit it. And researchers hoped, with bated breath, that it might be the answer to breast cancer.

> But science is rarely so neat and simple, and the gene, known as BRCA1, for breast cancer 1, has turned out to be an enigma. . . .

> Women who inherit a changed, or mutated, form of the gene have as much as a 90 percent chance of developing breast cancer and as much as a 60 percent chance

of developing ovarian cancer. Beyond that rudimentary understanding, however, ignorance reigns. (Kolata, 1996, p. B1)

At a time when science and technology underlie most of the major public issues of the day, and when many of these issues are laced with varying degrees of uncertainty, the understanding of uncertainty—what it is, how it is framed by actors in a social system, what people do with it—becomes an increasingly critical endeavor.

In this chapter, we examine uncertainty from the public's point of view by addressing three issues: What are the different forms public uncertainty can take and what factors influence them? What is the significance of these various forms when we consider how the public deals with science and scientific knowledge? In addition, how do the media and other contributors to the information environment interact with the public to construct different versions of knowledge and uncertainty?

CATALOGING PUBLIC UNCERTAINTY

Dimensions of Uncertainty

We begin with the proposition that *uncertainty* is a social construction, one that is negotiated among actors in a social system that includes various publics. Seen in this light, uncertainty is manifested by individuals in a number of different ways, for different reasons, and with varying outcomes. Consider the following dimensions of uncertainty:

1. I don't know anything about X; I will leave it to experts to tell me what I need to know.
2. I don't know about X; that's okay because it isn't that important or relevant to me.
3. I don't know much about X, and I don't want to know any more.
4. I don't know much about X and I want (or need) to know more, so I intend to learn more about it.
5. I don't know about X; no one else knows much (or anything definitive) about X, and there's not much we can do about it.
6. I don't know about X, but my friends and family know quite a bit about it; I'd better find out more about it, or I might be left out.
7. I don't know about X and I don't have the skills to find out; therefore, I can't really learn more about it until I acquire these skills.
8. I don't know about X, and I can't get the information so I can't really learn more about it until the information becomes more accessible.

FIG. 3.1. Dimensions of uncertainty.

1. I don't know anything bout X; I will leave it to experts to tell me what I need to know. One of the characteristics of the Information age has been an explosion of information, prompting people to turn to experts for assistance. Trust has been identified as a crucial element in the public acquisition of science information from expert sources (Wynne, 1995). In studying radiation workers in a nuclear reprocessing plant, Wynne, McKechnie, and Michael (1990) also found that ignorance was maintained as part of the division of labor. Because there were experts within the company and in regulatory bodies whose job it was to be familiar with the science and because it would be time-consuming to achieve such familiarity themselves, these workers saw their ignorance as entirely justified in terms of trust and cost-effectiveness.

2. I don't know about X; that's okay because it isn't that important or relevant to me. Importance or relevance is always relative, of course; people often selectively pursue or attend to information or accept a state of uncertainty for reasons of mental economy, interest, or utility. Years ago, Afghanistanism became part of the newsroom lexicon to describe stories or events that were so far away, geographically or psychologically, that editors assumed their readers would neither know much about the place nor be interested. (Russian and American involvement in Afghanistan during the 1980s, of course, may have increased public interest and rendered the term temporarily inaccurate).

3. I don't know much about X, and I don't want to know any more. This active resistance to knowledge may occur for a variety of reasons. Michael (1992) observed, for example, that people avoided information about radiation because they thought such information was embedded in motivations to sell nuclear power. On other occasions, knowledge might be considered a painful burden. Consider, for example, this brief personal anecdote in *The New York Times*:

> I went to the National Institutes of Health in Bethesda, Maryland, to learn about a genetic disorder that I may have inherited from my father's side of the family. In the end, I would find out just enough to know that I didn't want to know more. Knowing I had a gene predisposing me to an incurable condition, I decided, would only hobble rather than help my existence. (Siebert, 1996, p. A13)

4. I don't know much about X and I want (or need) to know more, so I intend to learn more about it. In this dimension of uncertainty, the need for more

information is often prompted when people learn that they are exposed to a previously unrecognized risk. For example, a newly diagnosed disease or a recently discovered neighborhood pollution problem can prompt a successful search for new information. A number of case studies have documented the development of expertise among lay publics (see, e.g., Brown, 1992; Epstein, 1995), challenging notions about knowledgemaking and the public as passive audience, about science as a closed or autonomous arena, and about who has cultural authority and currency in science and medicine. This acquisition of expertise and its effective use in political and medical domains has been well documented, for example, among AIDS activists (Epstein, 1995).

5. I don't know about X; no one else knows much (or anything definitive) about X, and there's not much we can do about it. It might be appropriate to call this the age of uncertainty, given the explosion of research efforts in many science-related areas (such as health and the environment), the public interest in better health or environmental measures, the media interest in covering research findings, and the limits of studies themselves, (particularly epidemiological or ecological findings. (See, e.g., Taubes, 1995).

A number of health and environmental risks have received widespread media attention in the last 10 years, leaving the public at various times beset with anxiety, reduced to indifference, or simply waiting until more definitive evidence turns up. Often, the public is given little credit for tolerating uncertainty, despite findings that certain publics are perfectly capable of judging whether findings detailed in newspaper science stories are incomplete or require further validation (Hornig, 1993).

6. I don't know about X, but my friends and family know quite a bit about it; I'd better find out more about it, or I might be left out. Knowing what others think can sometimes influence a person's opinions. Studies of the spiral of silence phenomenon (Noelle-Neumann, 1993) suggest that societies may threaten deviant individuals with isolation and that this fear of isolation is felt by members of society who consequently try to assess the social climate of opinion. The result is that people express opinions when they think they are in the majority and withhold them when they think they are in the minority.

7. I don't know about X and I don't have the skills to find out; therefore, I can't really learn more about it until I acquire these skills. The most obvious examples of this dimension of uncertainty are found in the relation between basic language skills and information acquisition: The former is the stepping-stone to the latter. Literacy, in this sense, expands to include learning the technical language of a particular branch of science or medicine, a skill that facilitates information access and enables communication. In describing the

success of AIDS activists in influencing biomedical research, for instance, Epstein (1995) maintained that the activists' familiarity with the language of biomedicine enabled them to influence the institutions of biomedicine:

Once they could converse comfortably about viral assays and reverse transcription and cytokine regulation and epitope mapping, activists increasingly discovered that researchers felt compelled, by their own norms of discourse and behavior, to consider activist arguments on their merits. (p. 419).

8. *I don't know about X, and I can't get the information so I can't really learn more about it until the information becomes more accessible.* Even if people have the skills they need, there may be structural reasons why some information is not available to them. These barriers may exist to protect the privacy of others (e.g., individual tax records), to protect corporate interests (e.g., trade secrets), or to protect the state (e.g., national security). Bauer and Joffe (1996) also cited *taboos* as cultural barriers that preserve traditions or social order; what they call *a protected right to preserve ignorance* facilitates interpersonal interactions, maintains social coherence, and enhances economic order.

Other Factors

The eight dimensions of uncertainty just described are not mutually exclusive. For example, knowledge may be actively rejected because of its content and because of the social values it represents. For instance, a parent may insist that his or her child not be exposed to sex education programs in school not only because of their content (the parent might feel that knowledge encourages promiscuity), but also because his or her reference group norms demand such rejection. This illustration indicates that two categories of factors, *individual* and *social-structural*, impinge on and shape perceptions of uncertainty and subsequent coping strategies.

Individual factors include such elements as personal skill levels, social activity (e.g., I need to keep up with my friends), and general and specific motivations (e.g., I need to keep informed in order to function well in this society or as a citizen; I need to find out more about a specific subject because the information will help me address a problem; I prefer not to know about something because it may cause me distress).

Social-structural factors, on the other hand, relate to issues of externally controlled access to information. The issue of universal access to information technologies, for example, revolves in large part around structural and policy factors. To be more specific, if people who cannot afford personal computers are interested in learning about and accessing the Internet, they will not be able to act on their interest unless computers are readily available in public places.

Social-structural factors, such as laws, also may determine what information people can obtain. It is usually these structural factors that are invoked when issues about equity and power are raised with regard to information availability and accessibility.

It is not unusual to find situations in which the use or nonuse of information is the product of the interplay among individual and social-structural factors. For instance, the issue of testing for *sickle-cell anemia*—a hereditary red blood cell disorder—became quite controversial in African-American communities during the 1970s (Gary, 1974). Because this health problem affected a large proportion of African Americans, a number of states mandated testing for the sickle-cell trait. In explaining why there was considerable resistance to the tests among African Americans, Gary outlined a number of reasons that illustrate the mix of factors operating at that time:

- The absence of a cure for the disease, making it difficult if not impossible to eliminate the problem.
- The inadequacy or absence of counseling available to those identified with the trait.
- The social stigma attached to testing and especially to a positive outcome, not to mention the potential for subsequent discrimination against those seeking jobs and insurance.
- The disagreement about what further information ought to be provided once the trait was identified (e.g., should those with the trait be counseled against having children or should the information be limited to what was known about the disease?).
- The disagreement in the medical literature about outcomes of the disease, such as longevity of patients.

What does this example, as well as our discussion of the eight dimensions of public uncertainty discussed earlier, tell us about publics and science? It affirms that uncertainty can be a state of mind occasioned by our information environment or social relations. It also can be negotiated in the sense that we actively resist information or make a conscious decision to relegate expertise to institutional or other sources. Uncertainty is also a resource to be used for negotiating social identities. The acquisition (or rejection) of knowledge may be part of how a person constructs an identity of good citizen, smart consumer, or resistant worker. In other words, uncertainty can be a resource used by individuals in much the same way that it is also often used by scientists or journalists (Stocking & Holstein, 1993).

Why do we need to differentiate among these dimensions of uncertainty? This question clearly has research as well as policy implications, issues to which we turn next.

UNCERTAINTY AND ITS IMPLICATIONS FOR COMMUNICATION

For information producers, such as researchers, scientists, and public relations professionals, learning how to communicate with public audiences more effectively has always been important. The solutions to problems created by a lack of skills versus a lack of interest, or by lack of individual motivation versus information inaccessibility, are going to be different. For example, in examining why breast cancer screening participation rates are lower among particular groups of women, researchers may find the answers in a variety of factors. The reasons some women choose uncertainty about their personal health may be structural (the inaccessibility of information or of screening clinics), cultural (differing conceptions of health), or personal (I don't want to find out; I find the examination experience extremely uncomfortable).

We need a clearer picture of how people navigate through the various dimensions of uncertainty to help us recognize not only how audiences receive and cope with new information, but also when audiences can be knowledge producers themselves. It is the portrait of these audiences drawn by previous research that we turn to next.

The Construction of Science Publics

Two portraits of the public and its understanding of science have recently emerged. The two apparently conflicting theoretical approaches are called the *scientific literacy model* and the *interactive science model* (Layton, Jenkins, Macgill, & Davey, 1993).

Scientific Literacy.   The *scientific literacy model* is represented by a stream of studies, most notably the long-standing work of political scientist Jon Miller (1987) in the United States, Edward Hirsch's work on cultural literacy (1988), and our own in Canada (Einsiedel, 1990, 1994). These studies suggest that knowledge of particular basic scientific ideas and concepts is required for people to function well in a variety of cultural contexts. Scientific knowledge within this framework is generally portrayed as fixed and certain.

For example, a set of basic ideas and concepts can include knowing that hot air rises, that the oxygen we breathe comes from plants, or that the Earth revolves around the sun and not vice versa. It also can include knowledge of applied sciences such as health or environmental studies, for example, understanding the connection between smoking and lung cancer or that burning fossil fuels is connected to the appearance of a hole in the ozone layer, which in turn reduces our protection against harmful solar radiation.

Rationales for raising public awareness and understanding of science in this cognitive sense have ranged from the importance of such literacy to a civic and democratic culture to its importance for personal efficacy to its value as preparation for the world of work. Such rationales suggest that to be scientifically literate is a societal good, with the consequent implication that lack of such skills represents a deficiency. Hence, the scientific literacy model has also been labeled the *cognitive deficit model* (Layton et al., 1993).

Interactive Science.   In comparison, the *interactive science model* takes as a given the uncertainties embedded in the scientific enterprise and the idea that science cannot be separated from its social and institutional connections. In terms of how publics are conceptualized, this perspective argues that publics can be quite knowledgeable about science, particularly when their occupations or personal interests require certain levels of understanding. As Wynne (1991) maintained, ordinary social life is marked by contingency and uncertainty as the norm, and adaptation to uncontrolled factors is routine. Similarly, science is often an uncertain enterprise, with many of its findings open to conflicting interpretations and providing considerable grounds for disagreement among so-called experts.

Building a Continuum

The scientific literacy model has been criticized, and those criticisms are not without merit. Operational definitions of science knowledge may differ among researchers, making it difficult to build a consensus about what such knowledge is. The need for audiences to be literate may be arguable, as is the issue of what they ought to be literate about. It is simplistic to look at audiences as homogeneous, or at least stratified according to how attentive they are to science. Attentiveness varies with time, place, and issue, and science is a subject whose contours change for different publics at different times.

Having said this, we think there may be some good arguments against getting rid of the scientific literacy model entirely. These two models of scientific understanding can be seen as the ends of a continuum: The scientific literacy model is at one end depicting a well-bounded and fixed set of ideas and activities, and the interactive model is at the other end, marking an enterprise characterized by constant uncertainty. For example, although there is generally a lot of agreement about the connections between cigarette smoking and lung cancer or between sun exposure and skin cancer, there is considerably less agreement about the links between alcohol consumption and breast cancer. This difference in the degrees of agreement about what things are known and what are not known is something proponents of both the scientific literacy or interactive science model are likely to accept.

The public also has different degrees of knowledge and uncertainty, as discussed earlier. Although this may be acceptable in some instances, in other instances, disparities in knowledge become an important social problem. In some situations, the need for public education is acute, making it imperative to provide information to the public (and yes, on occasion, using a top– down approach). For example, the mortality rates attributed to smoking—not to mention the costs to the public health system—have made public education programs not just desirable but necessary. Such voluntary measures have had to be complemented in some countries with structural disincentives such as higher tobacco taxes, restrictions on advertising, or restrictions on smoking in public spaces.

Numerous examples also exist in the environmental arena. For instance, environmentalists have worked to get the public to understand the notion of endangered species and to encourage actions such as the boycott of ivory-based products to try to stop the slaughter of elephants. Environmentalists have also promoted an understanding of the complex notion of biodiversity and have pursued active roles in shaping the public's understanding of other issues.

Many of the examples or case studies used to support the interactive science model concern situations in which members of the public are directly involved with a particular issue. Wynne (1991), for example, studied farmers dealing with radiation in their immediate environment and talked to workers in a nuclear plant. Other researchers have looked at families coping with a form of Downs' syndrome and the elderly dealing with a domestic energy question (Layton et al., 1993). In these instances, there is no question that scientific knowledge intersects with other stocks of public knowledge, that knowledge seeking depends on motivation, social networks, and so forth.

On the other hand, what do we do in cases where personal involvement in an issue is minimal or nonexistent, when there is a widespread lack of public knowledge about it, and when such ignorance is judged detrimental to some acknowledged social good? The scientific literacy model has, in fact, demonstrated considerable utility when we look at specific areas of application, particularly at health or environmental issues where public experience may be lacking. How does a concept make it into the public consciousness unless it has visible issue entrepreneurs—sources who actively promote particular points of view—championing its cause?

For example, when the AIDS virus was first identified, health educators found a great deal of public uncertainty about what caused the disease and who was susceptible to it. Given that the consequences of public ignorance about AIDS would have been devastating for society as a whole, a critical first step was to identify the level and nature of public knowledge and uncertainty.

We argue that integrating the scientific literacy and the interactive science frameworks can result in a more fertile approach to understanding publics and their approaches to scientific uncertainty. We need to know what different publics know. We also need a fuller understanding of the contextual uses of scientific knowledge by the public and how the public negotiates through the thickets of uncertainty and the information environment.

Mass Media

To understand the context within which various publics navigate through uncertainties in this information environment, we need to discuss the role and nature of information sources that contribute to it. A significant source of information for the public, of course, is the mass media. Quite often, people's knowledge of science and technology issues is influenced by mass media content. This is not to say that the media determine how people think about an issue in a linear fashion (see, e.g., Dunwoody & Neuwirth, 1991), but simply that, over time, the media can be an important—if not the only—source of information for various publics on many issues. Factors that may influence public understanding of scientific uncertainty include the media's role in the social representation process, their agenda-setting function, and their reliance on particular sources of information.

Social Representations.   All forms of news, entertainment, and media commentary play a role in the process of social representation because they convey new ideas, present particular images, and employ particular concepts and vocabularies (Moscovici, 1984). Media content routinely interprets scientific information to make it interesting, relevant, and comprehensible for audiences. People may draw on these messages as they set out to understand science and scientific uncertainty in ways that make sense within their personal frames of reference.

Social representations emerge when people reconcile their existing knowledge (however limited or indirect) with information from any number of outside sources, including the mass media. For example, most people's social representations of cancer combine information from personal experience (perhaps from observing the disease firsthand) with information and imagery accumulated from outside sources. These outside sources can include media accounts, health education materials, discussions with friends, and popular culture. In this way, any social representation of the term *cancer* embodies many kinds of information, some of which may be derived from the mass media.

Agenda Setting. In addition to interpreting scientific information on behalf of the public, the mass media also play an important role in determining which science-related stories (and, by extension, which scientific information) are the focus of public attention at any given time. With regard to scientific uncertainty, when and how the media play this agenda-setting role is significant. For example, the considerable lag between the time the first clinical concerns about AIDS were raised in the early 1980s and the time the disease received broad public awareness in the mid-1980s has been attributed to lack of media coverage (Rogers & Chang, 1991).

Source Use. How the media cover science-related stories is similarly critical. Reporters' reliance on particular sets of sources over others may provide audiences with a partial picture of an issue. This can be a function of reporters' trust in and familiarity with certain sources to the exclusion of others and of the ability of particular sources to attract and focus the attention of the press. For example, Nelkin (1995) described how journalists' love affair with space coverage and their long-standing, congenial relationship with NASA led to a dearth of attention to questions about space shuttle safety prior to the Challenger disaster.

Other Factors. The media may be uncomfortable reporting on scientific uncertainty because they assume the audience may be uneasy about ambiguity or indifferent to it. This concern about pleasing audiences, a component of so-called market-driven journalism, may lead reporters and editors to avoid such stories altogether or to suggest some sort of closure or resolution to stories containing elements of scientific uncertainty.

Despite the media's power to present the public with large amounts of seemingly up-to-date and valid information, the public's use of this information is not linear. Media information must be seen as part of a tangled web within a larger information environment through which individuals negotiate, sometimes actively seeking or screening out information, sometimes passively absorbing new information, sometimes actively participating in the construction of knowledge, and, at other times, accepting that certain thickets of uncertainty will always be part of the information landscape.

Politics and Big Business

It is important to note that this information environment hosts a wide range of political, moral, and commercial influences that are not strictly scientific in nature. This media-centered information environment is often a focus of the marketing and public relations activities of various institutions wishing to promote particular certainties about science-related issues. The biotechnology industry, for example, has promoted ideas about biotechnology products that often downplay or ignore attendant risks and highlight so-called benefits (Thorne, 1996). Priest (1995) observed that industry and government sources of information on biotechnology, all of whom have interests in promoting it, tend to dominate news coverage of biotechnology issues. Not surprisingly, these information frames tend to downplay uncertainties in areas such as ethics, morality, or risks in favor of information that touts economic or health benefits.

Considering the power of business and scientific institutions to influence the nature of media coverage and the increasing commercialization of science, public uncertainties are rarely focused on the state of the science but are centered more on uncertainties about whom to trust. For example, the tobacco companies' long-standing claims about the nonaddictive nature of tobacco and the U.S. government's denials of the health impacts of Agent Orange have strained public trust. The increasing climate of mistrust is one that hardly serves the scientific establishment, the industries concerned, government regulators, or even the public itself.

In response, Nelkin (1996) argued that social studies of science and technology must pay more attention to the economic and political contexts of science. Such attention must also explore "the powerful pressures—from special interests seeking scientific legitimation or competitive industries seeking market opportunities—that drive the direction of science and technology and shape their social impact"(p. 35).

In an increasingly technocratic world, the media must also explore more fully the political and commercial contexts that underlie various scientific and technological certainties. It has been suggested that science and technology stories are often political stories (in the broadest sense of the term), but are not always treated as such by journalists and editors. A greater emphasis on the political and commercial nature of scientific information may contribute to a more open and democratic future for scientific practice, and it may help avoid the swings between public resignation and hostility that characterize many issues of scientific uncertainty.

Researchers and others who communicate with the public should regard the various expressions of uncertainty with a healthy respect. They offer opportunities not only to engage in dialogue, to educate, and to negotiate a collective understanding, but also to understand how knowledge and uncertainties are negotiated.

CONCLUSION

We argued that in looking at conceptualizations of publics and science, the notion of public knowledge or uncertainty needs to be problematized. As part of the process, we identified eight dimensions of uncertainty and discussed how uncertainty is socially negotiated using various sources of information within the contexts of social relations and cultural frameworks.

While recognizing that audiences actively negotiate their way through information environments, we also pointed out the limitations imposed on the public's information environment by social-political, cultural, or structural impediments, often reflected in the dominance of particular voices over others. A special threat also may be posed by the media's nonrecognition of the political and economic contexts for the practice of science, resulting in public uncertainties being translated into disbelief and potential long-term damage to public trust in expertise or institutions associated with science.

Some solutions might lie in greater research and media attention to science as a political, commercial, and social institution or story. Exploring the dimensions and interactions of publics and uncertainties goes a long way toward helping our understanding of their multifaceted character and their place in the social world of science.

REFERENCES

Bauer, M., & Joffe, H. (1996). Meanings of self-attributed ignorance: An introduction to the Symposium. *Social Science Information, 35* (1), 5–13.

Brown, P. (1992). Popular epidemiology and toxic waste contamination: Lay and professional ways of knowing. *Journal of Health and Social Behavior, 33,* 267–281.

Dunwoody, S., & Neuwirth, K. (1991). Coming to terms with the impact of communication on scientific and technological risk judgments. In L. Wilkins & P. Paterson (Eds.), *Risky business: Communicating issues of science, risk, and public policy* (pp. 11–30). New York: Greenwood.

Einsiedel, E. F. (1990). *Scientific literacy: A survey of adult Canadians.* Report to the Social Sciences and Humanities Research Council, University of Calgary, Calgary, Alberta, Canada.

Einsiedel, E. F. (1994). Mental maps of science: Knowledge and attitudes among Canadian adults. *International Journal of Public Opinion Research, 6* (1), 35–44.

Epstein, S. (1995). The construction of lay expertise: AIDS activism and the forging of credibility in the reform of clinical trials. *Science, Technology, & Human Values, 20* (4), 408–437.

Gary, L. E. (1974). The sickle cell controversy. *Social Work, 19* (3), 263–272.

Hirsch, E. (1988). *Cultural literacy.* New York: Vintage.

Hornig, S. (1993). Reading risk: Public response to print media accounts of technological risk. *Public Understanding of Science, 2* (2), 95–109.

Kolata, G. (1996, February 2). More questions about breast cancer gene. *The New York Times,* p. B1.

Layton, D., Jenkins, E., Macgill, S., & Davey, A. (1993). *Inarticulate science.* East Yorkshire, England: Studies in Education Ltd.

Michael, M. (1992). Lay discourse of science: Science-in-general, science-in-particular, and self. *Science, Technology, & Human Values, 17* (3), 313–333.

Miller, J. (1987). *Scientific literacy in the United States: Communicating science to the public.* New York: Wiley.

Moscovici, S. (1984). The phenomenon of social representations. In R. Farr & S. Moscovici (Eds.), *Social representations* (pp. 85–100). New York: Cambridge University Press.

Nelkin, D. (1995). *Selling science: How the press covers science and technology* (Rev. ed.). New York: Freeman

Nelkin, D. (1996). The evolution of science studies. In S. Aronowitz, B. Martinson, & M. Menser (Eds.), *Technoscience and cyberculture* (pp. 31–36). New York: Routledge & Kegan Paul.

Noelle-Neumann, E. (1993). *The spiral of silence: Public opinion—our social skin.* Chicago: University of Chicago Press.

Priest, S. (1995). Information equity, public understanding of science, and the biotechnology debate. *Journal of Communication, 45* (1), 39–54.

Rogers, E., & Chang, S. (1991). Media coverage of technology issues: Ethiopian drought of 1984, AIDS, Challenger, and Chernobyl. In L. Wilkins & P. Paterson (Eds.), *Risky business: Communicating issues of science, risk, and public policy* (pp. 75–96). New York: Greenwood.

Siebert, C. (1996, January 5). At the mercy of our genes. *The New York Times,* p. A13.

Solomon, J. (1993). Reception and rejection of science knowledge: Choice, style, and home culture. *Public Understanding of Science, 2* (2), 111–122.

Stocking, S. H., & Holstein, L. W. (1993). Constructing and reconstructing scientific ignorance: Ignorance claims in science and journalism. *Knowledge, 15* (2), 186–210.

Taubes, G. (1995, July 14). Epidemiology faces its limits. *Science, 269,* 164–169.

Thorne, B. (1996). *Faust or famine? The rational construction of biotechnology.* Unpublished master's thesis, University of Calgary, Calgary, Alberta, Canada.

Wynne, B. (1991). Knowledges in context. *Science, Technology, & Human Values, 16* (1), 111–121.

Wynne, B. (1995). Public understanding of science. In S. Jasanoff, G. Markle, J. Peterson, & T. Pinch (Eds.), *Handbook of science and technology studies* (pp. 361–388). Thousand Oaks, CA: Sage.

Wynne, B., McKechnie, R., & Michael, M. (1990). *Frameworks for understanding public interpretations of science and technology.* Lancaster, UK: Lancaster University, Centre for Science Studies and Science Policy.

4

Scientists, Journalists, and the Meaning of Uncertainty

Sharon Dunwoody

Sharon Dunwoody is a former science reporter who now teaches science writing and conducts research on various dimensions of media coverage of science. She is Evjue-Bascom Professor and director of the School of Journalism and Mass Communication at the University of Wisconsin-Madison. In addition to coediting **Scientists and Journalists: Reporting Science as News** *with Sharon M. Friedman and Carol L. Rogers in 1986, she wrote* **Reconstructing Science For Public Consumption,** *published by Deakin Press in Australia in 1993.*

INTRODUCTION

The making of a mass media science story is a complex endeavor, indeed. Any single tale in a newspaper, on a TV news program, or on a website is the product of a complicated dance between scientists and journalists, both trying to cast the story in ways that make sense to them.

Complicating matters further is that meaning is only partly under the control of these storymakers. At the receiving end of the production line waits an audience capable of making sense of the intended message in sometimes unexpected ways. Equipped with a formidable array of interpretive frameworks, readers and viewers are likely to construct story meanings that fit their own perceptions as easily as they don a favorite sweater.

Sources, journalists, and audiences may all approach a science topic or issue with different notions of what is true and what is not. Although some kind of objective scientific truth may take hold in the long run, whose version of reality survives in the short run reflects, to a great degree, the distribution of power among the information producers as well as the interpretive finesse of the audience. This interpretive jostling has implications for the communication of scientific uncertainty. In this chapter, I concentrate on the first two of these three information producers: journalists and scientists.

The struggle for interpretive control between journalists and scientists is an unequal one. Although journalists typically keep many of the narrative decisions in their court, the scientific culture often succeeds spectacularly at determining the meaning of the science covered. Yet, that control over meaning can erode in two circumstances: when the science itself is new and when it is controversial.

Journalists are drawn to both those conditions. Emergent and controversial science stories constitute a big chunk of what we call *science news*, and they offer journalists the chance to play a greater role in constructing the popular version of scientific reality than they would have otherwise. Both conditions are awash in high levels of scientific uncertainty.

My Interpretation of Reality or Yours?

The typical mass media science story is not a fabrication, so it is important that none of us takes the notion of news as a constructed reality to its extreme. When NASA scientists announce that they may have found evidence for ancient microbial life in a Martian meteorite (McKay et al., 1996), there is every reason to believe that researchers have found something suggestive in a bit of ancient rock from elsewhere in the solar system.

But what to make of the tiny globs of carbonate in the rock, which harbor organic molecules and mineral compounds, is something else. Deciphering the origins of these substances is extremely difficult. The scientists responsible for the discovery are encouraged by the evidence for biological activity; although they acknowledge the difficulty of empirically eliminating competing explanations, they feel they have rendered the uncertainties manageable enough to allow a conclusion to emerge. Other scientists are unconvinced, arguing that the scientific uncertainties are simply too great to allow one interpretation to sink others; the carbonate could just as easily have come from inorganic processes, they contend, or be more down-to-Earth contamination from the Antarctic ice that entombed the rock for so long.

Journalists, in turn, shout "What a story!" and make room on their front pages or at the top of their news hour for the startling discovery. Some of those stories will celebrate the finding, downplaying uncertainty. Other stories will emphasize early differences of opinion among scientists, highlighting uncertainty.

Both scientists and journalists, thus, can influence the construction of scientific uncertainty in media accounts. Understanding the ebb and flow of that influence is crucial, for, in a global culture that relies heavily on storytelling as an arbiter of what is important and what is not, the mass media reign as our principal storytellers on the cusp of the 21st century.

The Main Points of This Chapter

To make the story I wish to tell in this chapter more manageable, I develop four main arguments:

1. The scientific culture has experienced a long and successful history of control over what constitutes popular science.
2. When a new piece of scientific knowledge enters the social arena, however, the uncertainties associated with the finding make it more difficult for science to speak with one voice. Journalists, thus, can play a larger role in making sense of the information by determining whose voices are heard.
3. Controversial science is an arena in which various scientific factions may actually use uncertainty as a rhetorical tool. In such a setting, journalists are invited to play a major role in constructing reality not only by the dueling scientists themselves, but also by journalistic practice, which recognizes the attractiveness of controversy as news and has cobbled together a variety of strategies to enhance its perception by the audience.
4. Scientists and journalists seem to be in the throes of developing a "shared culture," within which the meaning of science information is negotiated for public consumption. What does such negotiation mean for the communication of scientific uncertainty?

Although this chapter concentrates on the interpretive efforts of journalists and scientific sources, it is important that the reader not lose sight of the formidable ability of the audience to reconfigure information. Several chapters in this volume speak to such ability (for example, see the chapters by Einsiedel, Priest, and Rogers), so I do not dwell on it here. Yet, information producers routinely overestimate their influence on readers or viewers by confusing "need to know" with "readiness to accept *my* version of reality." Audiences may indeed need to know, but all too often it is on their own terms.

SCIENCE RULES!

As society becomes more complex, our reliance on experts increases. For much of the 20th century, science has served as a major source of expertise. Von Schomberg (1993) characterized our reliance on science as "functional," arguing that science has gained the status of authority by demonstrating sustained competence at evaluating evidence. Toumey (1996) noted that we have so thoroughly bought into the problem-solving abilities of science that "an *appearance* of scientific authority can be easily conjured from cheap symbols and ersatz images like . . . the solemn sounds of Greek or Latin terminology, visual images of shiny laboratory paraphernalia, or graphs and charts that pop up on the monitors of humming computers" (p. 6). In a world of increasing skepticism, we still trust science more than almost any other way of knowing. As Bill Nye the Science Guy puts it in the opening credits of his popular TV science program, "Science rules!"

We certainly trust science's authority more than we trust the authority of journalism. Although we readily admit our belief in science's ability to uncover truth, we are much less enamored with the evidentiary skill of journalistic practice. We rarely question the veracity of a report in *The New England Journal of Medicine*. Yet, journalistic claims of objectivity and reporters' attempts to balance disparate views as a surrogate for determining who is right often meet with rank skepticism on the part of audiences. The status differential between scientist and journalist is great, indeed.

This difference can have a profound impact on who controls the meaning of a story. Although journalists assert that they are the ultimate arbiters of story content, the authority of science is so pervasive that most scholarly studies of media coverage of science easily detect the fingerprint of science in the construction of meaning. The following are three patterns that illustrate this point.

The first pattern is that the scientific culture is an extremely effective purveyor of story ideas. One of the most important story judgments made by a journalist is the initial one: What is this story about? This decision will drive the reporter's choice of sources and the questions posed to those sources, as well as the organizational scaffolding of the story itself. The entire interpretive framework for a story, thus, may derive from that initial step (for a fuller discussion of this process, see Stocking & Gross, 1989).

Although it is clearly the journalist who makes the topic choice, studies of those choices suggest that sources have ample opportunity to define the universe of possibilities from which stories are plucked. Like all sources, scientists (or, more typically, the organizations that employ them) make overt attempts to influence story choice via press releases, video news releases, press conferences, tip sheets, and a variety of personal contacts. Additionally, the process of peer review, essential to the maintenance of science, creates a bevy of journals to which journalists routinely have access (Kiernan, 1997).

These efforts to influence choice are often successful, for two reasons. First, researchers find that, although journalists may only use a fraction of the information that comes across their desks, they tend to make their selections from that available pool rather than digging up stories on their own (Dunwoody & Shields, 1986; Weaver & Elliott, 1985; Whitney & Becker, 1982). Put another way, sources routinely define the boundaries within which story choices are made.

Second, when the pool of information available to a science reporter contains material perceived to come directly from scientists themselves (i.e., articles written by scientists for peer-reviewed journals as opposed to press releases about research written by public information personnel), science journalists opt disproportionately for those materials (Jones & Meadows, 1978). In one study of daily information selection patterns of science writers, for example, journalists tossed 85% of the press releases they received, but kept 85% of the science journals, phone contacts, and other materials that seemed to come directly from the scientists (Dunwoody & Kalter, 1991). This journalistic preference for information from high-status sources—information ostensibly untouched by "biased" individuals such as public relations folks—is powerful indeed and gives scientists a great deal of control over representations of uncertainty.

The second pattern is that once a science topic becomes news, mainstream science's notion of what matters continues to drive the interpretive framework of stories, sometimes for months or years. Scientists often grumble that mavericks can overwhelm media coverage of science issues, and they occasionally find support for that position when a savvy extremist dominates an issue (see the following section on coverage of emergent and controversial science). However, the more typical pattern revealed in the research literature is that journalists will readily follow the interpretive lead of respected sources.

Sociologist Mark Fishman (1980, 1982) illuminated the generic pattern in a study of media coverage of city and county government in a small West Coast community. Fishman himself worked as an apprentice journalist for a weekly newspaper in the area and observed fellow reporters from other newspapers. What he found was that journalists unquestioningly bought into the reality structured for them by sources. For example, organizations responsible for finding and punishing wrongdoing in society—police, courts, etc.—have divvied that process into a series of events: investigation, arrest, arraignment, trial.

Fishman found that journalists assimilated those interpretive structures by defining news as happening only at those moments. Other parts of the process remained invisible.

A similar pattern emerged in a study of media coverage of a major scientific meeting (Dunwoody, 1979). Science writers came to the meeting to cover it, and they adopted the science organization's interpretation of what was important, faithfully deriving their stories from meeting sessions or press conferences. Although the reporters complained about the dearth of news made available to them, only a very few could abandon the meeting structure itself and redefine their mission as one of seeking to interview particular scientists or to write about particular topics.

Even when an issue is controversial, there is a good chance that the scientific culture will be able to maintain some interpretive control. Perhaps the best-studied science issue from the perspective of control was the national brouhaha over attempts to fiddle with plant and animal DNA in the 1970s. This precursor to today's sophisticated biotechnology research was just getting under way, and scientists across the country who wished to take the first tentative steps at recombining DNA ran into resistance from their local university communities, who feared that the efforts could unleash aberrant life forms.

Scholars who studied media coverage of this issue found that mainstream scientists played a much greater role in setting the media agenda than did community leaders or scientific outliers (Pfund & Hofstadter, 1981). As a result, coverage emphasized recombinant DNA as a scientific or technical challenge, not as a philosophical or political one (Altimore, 1982). Goodell (1986) argued that scientists were even successful, in the mid-1970s, at moving journalistic accounts away from the issue that started the controversy—safety—toward a focus on the developing biotechnology industry.

Finally, the third pattern revealing the underlying authority of science is that science reporters are reluctant to criticize science. Although journalistic work is predominantly reactive, the occupation saves its highest honors for investigative reporting, a form in which reporters labor to bring major problems to public attention. Such reporting often requires a large resource commitment from both reporters and their media organization, but the potential payoff is great. A good investigative project can be a major contender for the journalistic version of the Nobel Prize: the Pulitzer. Additionally such work comes closer than any other journalistic activity to fulfilling the "watchdog" role of the American mass media, a role that urges the media to maintain independence from sources of political power and to champion the interests of the populace (Donohue, Tichenor, & Olien, 1995).

Protess et al. (1991), in a study of investigative reporting in the United States, characterize investigative reporting as "the journalism of outrage":

> More than a newsgathering process, the journalism of outrage is a form of storytelling that probes the boundaries of America's civic conscience. Published allegations of wrongdoing—political corruption, government inefficiency, corporate abuses—help define public morality in the United States. Journalistic exposés that trigger outrage from the public or policy makers affirm society's standards of misconduct. (p. 5)

The independence of journalists so crucial to investigative reporting, however, can bring reporters into direct conflict with sources. So one measure of source power is the extent to which a source can deflect such independent behavior and, thus, minimize "the journalism of outrage."

Although no one has systematically studied the extent of investigative reporting in science, anecdotal accounts unanimously describe it as scarce indeed. John Crewdson, a senior writer (not, he is quick to note, a science writer) for the *Chicago Tribune*, is a Pulitzer Prize-winning investigative reporter who has become known for his critical reporting about science. For example, he has disputed scientist Robert Gallo's claim to have discovered the AIDS virus (Crewdson, 1989) and uncovered fraud in a major breast cancer study (Crewdson, 1994). Crewdson (1993) attributed the dearth of critical reporting about science in part to science writers' belief that science is good and good for us:

> When Professor Schmidtlapp says he's discovered something big, the science writers, their collective belief reaffirmed (and their own stature enhanced), don't draw their guns and make him put his cards on the table. They don't flyspeck his raw data, don't check his funding sources, don't scrutinize his previous articles for mistakes. They don't interview his enemies or call his lab technicians at home for an off-the-record assessment of the great man's work. They like science, they probably admire Schmidtlapp and they're excited by the prospect that he's right. (p. 12)

Just as important, being critical is anathema to journalists who must maintain a good relationship with their sources. According to Crewdson (1993):

> For regular [not science] reporters, the best stories are the ones that politicians and bureaucrats don't want them to have. But if Schmidtlapp thinks he's found a cure for cancer he's hardly going to keep quiet about it. The only question is which reporter will get the first crack. The best stories a science reporter can get are the ones somebody wants to put out. To get there first he needs continuing access to the most important scientists. (p. 12)

This need for continuing access runs afoul of a long-standing imbalance: Journalists traditionally have needed the information that scientists can provide more than scientists have needed the public visibility that journalists can provide (Dunwoody, 1986, 1993; Nelkin, 1995). The less needy tend to dominate such a lopsided exchange, and that has allowed scientists to set many of the important ground rules for interaction. Even today, some scientists will not hesitate to cut off a journalist who displeases them. I argue in the last section of this chapter that the balance of power has begun to shift in recent years as scientists have come to value public visibility, but like all high-status sources, scientists continue to insist that the only way to see science is through their eyes.

WHEN THE SCIENCE IS NEW OR CONTROVERSIAL

Science's interpretive control over its popularized self can founder in two settings: when new findings are reported and when a particular piece of science becomes controversial. In both cases, science writ large is either unable (in the former) or unwilling (in the latter) to speak with one voice. Journalists, thus, have an opportunity to play a greater role in selecting both whose voices and how many voices will appear in a story. Both those judgments can have a profound effect on the communication of uncertainty.

Emergent Science

Scientists get ahead by being first. They are eager to spot something new in data worthy of a priority claim. Overwhelmingly, they make those claims in the pages of peer-reviewed journals, although they are occasionally tempted to enlist the mass media in that effort as well.

Reporters are also eager to learn about new findings, for such information coincides with the emphasis of their business on the new and the novel. This news emphasis is so strong, in fact, that journalists will use journal publication or meetings to give otherwise timeless science information a timely edge: "In today's issue of *Science* magazine" or "at yesterday's meeting of the American Astronomical Society" can make science information palatable not only to an editor but also to readers or listeners.

The scientist making a priority claim would, not surprisingly, like to control the interpretive ground and infuse press accounts with her version of reality. However, the novelty of a priority claim signals the presence of uncertainty, and that emphasis on uncertainty may drive journalists to seek more voices in their stories.

I emphasize the word *may* because even in the presence of a novel claim, journalists may default to one voice: that of the individual claim maker. Science writers have long been accused of writing too many one-source stories and, although the normative balance has shifted to an emphasis on querying a variety of sources for any given account (Blum, 1997), recent studies of source use in science and medical stories still find a heavy representation of single sources. For example, in one study of medical coverage in five daily newspapers in The Netherlands in 1991, researchers found that only 38% of the stories with identified sources contained more than one of them (van Trigt, de Jong-van den Berg, Haaijer-Ruskamp, Willems, & Tromp, 1994).

Still, for a growing number of science reporters, a priority claim is likely to trigger a search for credible sources who can react to the claim itself. A recent study of coverage of research in *The New York Times,* the *Chicago Tribune* and *The Washington Post,* for instance, found that, although the inclusion of additional voices speaking in support of a study remained at about the same level for more than 20 years (1966–1990), the inclusion of other voices critical of the research in question increased steadily over time (Pellechia, 1997).

The search for contrasting voices probably reaches its peak when a priority claim triggers uncertainty in the journalists themselves by violating their personal expectations. Here are two examples:

• Some years ago, science writers covering a large science meeting heard a sociologist offer empirical results on behalf of a genetic predisposition to criminal behavior. The claim clearly conflicted with the reporters' understanding of such predispositions, and that conflict sent the journalists to the telephones to seek reactions of other sociologists around the country.

• When two chemists announced in a press conference at the University of Utah in 1989 that they had achieved room-temperature nuclear fusion, many science journalists reacted with skepticism. *Los Angeles Times* science and medicine editor Joel Greenberg (1997), for example, explained afterward:

It seemed like a textbook case of a story to avoid. The claim . . . seemed fantastic. The research paper had yet to be published in a refereed journal. And no one at Princeton or anywhere else fusion research had been pursued for many years had come close to such a result. Most science writers knew this was a sensational story that almost certainly would prove to be not true, at least not to the point of the university's claims. (p. 100)

But those science writers also knew that the story would be front-page news for their competitors, so hundreds flew to Salt Lake City to cover it. The two *Los Angeles Times* reporters who took notes at the press conference, said Greenberg, signaled their skepticism by including in their story a bevy of sources who urged that the report of successful "cold fusion" be viewed with extreme caution.

Another reason that increasing numbers of science writers are incorporating more voices in their stories about the latest discovery is that they have been burned by science's own quality control mechanisms. Work deemed "good" by science can sometimes fall apart, leaving both scientists and journalists with egg on their faces.

For example, a peer-reviewed paper in the June 7, 1996, issue of *Science* magazine reported that, although chemicals in the environment that act like natural estrogens may be less potent individually, when combined, their potency—and potential ability to disrupt reproductive function—increased dramatically (Arnold et al., 1996). Published at a time of increased public concern with estrogen mimics, the report garnered a lot of press. One year later, however, the research team published a letter of retraction in *Science*, noting that they had been unable to replicate their earlier work (McLachlan, 1997). Although many journalists ignored or simply did not see the retraction, others found themselves in the uncomfortable position of trying to explain the turnaround to readers (Lewis, 1997).

The presence of multiple voices in a media story about emergent science allows audience members to glimpse the lack of consensus that often accompanies any brand-new discovery. Yet, it may be difficult for readers to make judgments about what that lack of consensus represents. Are the scientific uncertainties so great that reasonable people cannot come to resolution? Is the finding so novel that other scientists simply have no useful expertise to bring to the table to help put the discovery in context? Additional voices would be functional in the former instance, but might be dysfunctional in the latter.

Additionally, as increasing access to information via the World Wide Web and other outlets allows individuals to range beyond their hometown media, readers will be able to assemble meaning on a grander scale by cobbling together stories about the same topic from a variety of places. It seems almost inevitable that such triangulation will make uncertainty a common take-home message.

For example, a study of the impact of weight on risk of dying, published in *The New England Journal of Medicine* on January 1, 1998, produced this lead in an Associated Press story in one of my hometown daily newspapers:

Is keeping down your weight a New Year's resolution? Here's some incentive from the world of medicine:

One of the biggest studies ever to look at the effects of weight on longevity concludes that thinner is definitely better at almost all ages, including well into middle age and beyond. (Haney, 1998)

Now contrast that lead with the one in the same day's *The New York Times:*

The largest study ever conducted of the health risks of obesity has found that it increases the likelihood of premature death but not as much as many medical experts had expected.

The research, being published today in *The New England Journal of Medicine,* analyzed the fates of 324,135 white adults who were followed for 12 years. The study found that the excess risk of dying associated with being fat was relatively modest and declined as people aged. By age 65, the increased risk was slight, and by age 74 it had disappeared. (Kolata, 1998)

A close reading of the two stories demonstrates that they, in fact, report the same findings, but the sources asked to comment in each give the data distinctly different interpretations: Scientists in the former *really* think weight matters, whereas those highlighted in the latter are much more circumspect. A reader of one of them might see, in that story, agreement on the meaning of the study's findings. Yet, taken together, the stories seem to trumpet a lack of consensus. Any reader of the pair (and many Web surfers would have access to far more than two versions) would be forgiven for concluding that scientific uncertainty is high.

Controversial Science

When science becomes controversial, science writ large splinters into points of view, often dueling ones. The kind of normative power wielded by "science as authority" can splinter too. This gives journalists the opportunity to play a major role in constructing popular understanding of the science in question. As in the arena of emergent science, a journalist's power lies in the ability to select voices. Yet, although exercising such freedom when the science is new is only grudgingly respected by the scientific culture, when it comes to controversies, journalists may actually be encouraged to play such a role by both science and the reporters' own occupation. Reporters are no longer inadvertent partners in the construction of science meaning. Instead, they become crucial players whose role is sanctioned by all concerned.

What Is in It for Science?   Coverage of controversial science may per-
form an important service for scientists with a stake in the issue at hand. Just
as newspaper and TV news accounts inform the public of the latest developments in an ongoing dispute, so do they inform scientists embroiled in the issue.

Remember that scientific controversies split science into factions, each of
which vies for control of what the science means. These competing subgroups
are often too polarized to communicate effectively with one another. So they
need other means of keeping tabs on each other and on public perceptions of
the issue.

The mass media often help meet this need. Scholars who study the role of
media in our larger society suggest that news not only alerts various segments
of the public to issues, but also functions to inform those embroiled in the issues
themselves. As public opinion scholar Vincent Price (1992) noted:

> News about other political actors offers elites an arena for learning about,
> understanding, and reacting to one another. Political elites use the media not only
> to communicate with their supporters and opponents in the attentive public but
> to talk among themselves as well. Statements they issue ostensibly to the general
> public (press conferences and appeals to the public through the media) are often
> intended as messages to other elites. (p. 81)

Scientists rely more than they like to admit on the mass media for information about science. A controversy raises the stakes even further for those
scientists on the front lines of the debate and renders them dependent on the
mass media to keep abreast of what others are doing and saying.

For example, the early stages of the cold fusion controversy in 1989 found
researchers looking to news media accounts to learn not only about the claims
made by the scientists in Utah, but also about how to build the cold fusion
apparatus itself. Lewenstein noted that some journalists served even more
explicit roles as go-betweens, querying the scientists and administrators in Utah
and then passing their information on to scientists elsewhere (Lewenstein,
1992a).

What Is in It for Journalism?   Editors also encourage journalists to recognize and highlight controversy. Long experience in the journalistic trenches
has made it clear that audiences pay attention to controversy. Even better,
researchers have established that conflict can serve as a powerful catalyst for
learning. Tichenor, Donohue, and Olien (1980) found that newspaper coverage
of a number of environmental controversies produced greater amounts of
interpersonal discussion of those issues among readers, which in turn led to

greater levels of knowledge. They concluded, "It is general level of conflict, in which newspapers play a reciprocal role, that appears basic to stimulating citizens to learn about an issue" (p. 147).

Yet, journalistic strategies for collecting and presenting controversial information may truncate readers' abilities to glean a reasonable picture of what is going on. In the process, these strategies almost certainly muddy reader perceptions of scientific uncertainty.

The big problem for journalism is that it has neither the time nor the expertise to determine if a source is telling the truth. When sources offer conflicting truth claims, reporters pull out of their toolboxes two strategies to counteract their inability to establish validity. One strategy is objectivity: If you cannot tell if someone is telling the truth, you can at least make sure that you accurately capture the message and attribute it. This focus on the journalist as a passive transmitter allows the occupation to make accuracy the most important characteristic of a story and often to bypass issues of validity altogether.

The other strategy is balance: If you cannot distinguish the true statements from the untrue ones, then the best strategy is to present an array of viewpoints. Readers and viewers will have access to all perspectives, according to this norm, making the truth available to them, albeit often mired in a variety of options.

The objectivity norm urges journalists to leave their own analytical skills at home and to concentrate, instead, on conveying what they see and hear. When a scientific controversy erupts, this may mean that a reporter will feel responsible for conveying a point of view, no matter how scientifically aberrant it may be.

Smith (1996) found this pattern in a study of media coverage of a predicted earthquake in Missouri in 1990. When a self-trained New Mexico climatologist named Iben Browning predicted that there was a 50–50 chance that a severe earthquake would shake the lower Midwest on or about December 3, 1990, the mass media leaped to cover the announcement. Smith's analysis of the first 6 months of coverage in large daily newspapers and on network news programs found journalists uncritically transmitting the prediction, for the most part. When scientists at the U.S. Geological Survey released a report debunking the prediction in mid-October 1990, journalists covered that uncritically, too. Smith concluded that the reporters covering the controversy were "more like stenographers than a vigorous fourth estate that watches over public institutions" (p. 215).

Similarly, a journalist from a Milwaukee newspaper sent to cover rumors of a haunted house in the small town of Horicon in the middle of Wisconsin wrote a series of stories that treated the reported supernatural events seriously, even covering the investigation of a parapsychologist who claimed to have found extrasensory hot spots in the house. The reporter explained that if people were truly alarmed by the rumors, then his newspaper had a responsibility to report even the reactions of psychics accurately and without judgment (Brunsman, 1988).

The balance norm also requires that a journalist suspend her analytical judgment, this time to give equal space to competing points of view regardless of their likelihood of being correct. In most cases, differing perspectives are reduced to two competing points of view, and the journalist then works to represent them accurately in any given story. Although the journalist's take-home message in a balanced account is that truth resides somewhere in the story, the reader may get a very different message: All points of view represented in the story are legitimate—sometimes equally legitimate—ones.

For example, religious fundamentalists in the 1970s and 1980s succeeded in getting legislation passed in several states mandating that Biblical explanations of creation be discussed in biology classes along with scientific ones. Scientists took these creation scientists to court, where judges nearly unanimously concluded that creationist explanations were not scientific and, thus, did not belong in the science classroom. The mass media covered these trials, of course. One study of such coverage found that the journalistic effort to give equal space to both sides of the issue "produced a journalistic leveling which rhetorically transformed competing discourses into equivalent ones" (Taylor & Condit, 1988, p. 293). The result, said the authors, was that "creation science appeared as the equal competing theory to evolution that creationists claimed it to be" (p. 306).

Efforts to balance stories may confer legitimacy on individuals as well as on rhetorical claims. Dearing (1995) examined media coverage of three scientific controversies in which scientific outliers—mavericks, if you will—got a great deal of visibility despite the fact that most scientists and journalists suspected they were wrong. He studied coverage of Browning's New Madrid earthquake prediction in 1990, biologist Peter Duesberg's claim that the HIV virus cannot be the cause of AIDS, and the cold fusion claims of chemists B. Stanley Pons and Martin Fleischmann in 1989. Dearing found that media accounts were generally more supportive than critical of the unorthodox scientific theories presented by the outliers, although relevant experts quoted in the stories (for balance) were themselves critical of the mavericks. In a survey of journalists who wrote the stories, Dearing learned that most did not consider the mavericks or their theories to be credible. Yet, he noted, in spite of their skepticism, these reporters represented the claims of these outliers in ways that gave those claims legitimacy.

These journalistic practices can make comprehension of scientific uncertainty difficult for audiences in two ways. First, in controversies, particularly, scientists and other experts will use uncertainty as a rhetorical tool. For example, scientists may interpret their own work as being reasonably well-grounded but may highlight the uncertainties in the work of others with whom they disagree (Pinch, 1981). They may depict the inherent uncertainties in the science as either manageable or unmanageable, depending on their position in the controversy. For example, in a debate in Canada over the ecological effects of building a natural gas pipeline, Campbell (1985) found that scientists' positions in the controversy were good predictors of their judgment of the adequacy of the available scientific evidence. As he put it, "Critics [of the pipeline construction] tend to claim uncertainty while defenders tend to claim adequate knowledge" (p. 439).

If journalists are normatively limited to reporting rather than interpreting, then audiences are left to sift through the dueling representations of uncertainty themselves.

Second, evidence grows that media coverage of controversial science can send the message to readers and viewers that the science is uncertain without ever mentioning the word *uncertainty* in stories. All that may be necessary to deliver that perception is to include competing views in a story without providing any sense of how the evidence lines up. That is, the message of the traditional balanced account may be "Well, who knows what's true?" even when a story reports on a controversy in which both science and society have agreed that truth lies more firmly on one side than on the other (for example, the extent of human contributions to global warming, the cause of AIDS, or the presence of ghosts in Horicon, Wisconsin).

IS THERE A SHARED CULTURE IN OUR FUTURE?

Not too long ago, scientists and journalists held each other at arms' length. Relationships between the two groups foundered regularly on rocky shores, and both groups dwelled on the problem in written commentary, in conferences, and at writing workshops (see, for example, Friedman, Dunwoody, & Rogers, 1986; Goldstein, 1986; Goodfield, 1981; Haslam & Bryman, 1994; Lewenstein, 1992b; Stocking & Dunwoody, 1982).

Although some scientists and journalists will see the picture as virtually unchanged today, I think that something of a revolution in the basic relationship is under way. Specifically, scientists are increasingly recognizing the value of public visibility. And as that perception of value rises, scientists are entering into more equitable relationships with journalists.

Scientists have always suspected that visibility has its good repercussions along with its bad. They have long perceived a link between such visibility and their ability to secure funding (Dunwoody & Scott, 1982). Yet, two other perceptions are, I think, more recent:

1. Scientists have increasingly come to realize that mass media serve as societal signals to what is important. This signaling is so effective, in fact, that coverage in the mass media can legitimize a scientist's work not only in the eyes of the public, but also in the eyes of other scientists. One illuminating study (Phillips, Kanter, Bednarczyk, & Tastad, 1991) compared the perceived value to scientists of a set of research reports published in *The New England Journal of Medicine* (NEJM) and subsequently covered by *The New York Times* with a similar set of *NEJM* reports that did not find their way into *The New York Times*. Those that received attention from the newspaper were cited in the scientific literature much more often than those that did not, suggesting that even scientists in the discipline interpreted media coverage as an "importance" signal.

2. As scientists and private commerce forge partnerships, scientists are increasingly interested in the marketing power of public visibility. Advertising aside, there is much mileage to be made if objective journalists write about a development that might soon be on the market. Both journalists and science journal editors have become increasingly attentive to scientists' potential conflicts of interest as a result.

Today, scientists not only care more about their public image, but they are also becoming increasingly sophisticated at packaging themselves for public consumption (Nelkin, 1994, 1995). However, because so much of science's visibility is mediated by journalists, this growing sophistication must get played out within that scientist-journalist nexus. The result, I would argue, is the slow but steady evolution of a shared culture.

The concept of a shared culture was developed by mass communication scholars Jay Blumler and Michael Gurevitch who, in a provocative essay in 1981, proposed that a situation of mutual dependence between sources and journalists encourages the growth of a working relationship in which both sides share an understanding of the rules of the game. That understanding evolves, they argued, to enable both sides to accomplish their respective goals and to do so in ways that minimize uncertainty. In such a culture, for example, participants share an understanding of what is fair. They may develop joint definitions of what is accurate. And they come to hold the same values for what's news.

Journalists and sources are not required to assimilate; indeed, individuals in both camps will opt out of the culture for a variety of reasons. Yet, according to Blumler and Gurevitch, "a shared culture is continually reestablished, even in the face of disagreement, because it is indispensable to undergird the relationship" (p. 482).

The most visible shared culture in American journalism is that between journalists and politicians. If anything, scientists and journalists have historically been notorious for their lack of shared understandings.

However, all that is changing. Journalists have always needed the information that scientists can provide, but the growing dependence of scientists on the visibility that journalists can provide is serving as a catalyst for vigorous scientific efforts to understand how journalists work and to participate in the construction of popular images of science. For example, a concern with the misunderstandings between scientists and journalists led NASA scientist Rick Chappell and journalist Jim Hartz to a year-long study of the relationship. Funded by The Freedom Forum's First Amendment Center, the study culminated in a report aimed at helping scientists and journalists to bridge "the widening gap between them" (Hartz & Chappell, 1997, p. xiii).

A shared culture has both advantages and disadvantages. On the plus side, it can indeed make work more efficient, as neither source nor reporter needs to worry about the other misinterpreting the rules of the information-gathering process itself. A science writer calling a scientist for comment about an embargoed journal report, for example, will raise no red flags in the mind of a researcher who understands the embargo process and is confident that the reporter does too. They will concentrate on getting the information right rather than worrying about logistics.

Yet, a shared culture is a negotiated world in which both actors contribute to the rules of the game. Although relationships between journalists and scientists are becoming more equitable, it is the scientists who maintain the lion's share of the power. It is entirely possible that a true shared culture for scientists and journalists would be one dominated more by scientists' rules than by those of the journalist.

I see that a bit already as I look out over the world of science journalism. Here are a few potential markers:

• Science journal embargoes, which restrict the publication of new research information to days selected by the journals themselves, have long been a feature of the science reporting landscape. Journalists now take the embargo for granted and, in fact, castigate fellow reporters who "break" an embargo by publishing a story early. Blumler and Gurevitch (1981) noted that one characteristic of a shared culture is that, when an individual violates one of the culture's rules, both journalists and sources turn on that person.

• Science is successfully making the argument that the only good science journalist is the science-trained science journalist. To date, studies of whether formal science training enables a writer to do a better job of covering science than a writer with, say, an English, political science, or journalism background have been inconsistent at best and have shown no performance differences (see, for example, Smith, 1996; Wilson, 1996). Despite the absence of good empirical evidence that background matters, however, newer training programs for science journalists increasingly privilege applicants with science degrees (Dunwoody, Crane, & Brown, 1996).

• Science is having renewed success in convincing journalists that accuracy is a characteristic of science information that can only be evaluated by science itself (for a more general example of this trend, see Shepard, 1996). Although this argument seems plausible on its face, it ignores a literature that suggests that judgments about accuracy are far more subjective than most of us realize (Dunwoody, 1982; Dunwoody, 1997; Tichenor, Olien, Harrison, & Donohue, 1970). If accuracy is indeed partly in the eyes of the beholder, then journalistic acquiescence in requests by scientists to allow them to routinely check reporters' stories for accuracy will have the long-term effect of ensuring that media science accounts represent science's version of reality.

What does all this mean for communication of scientific uncertainty in the mass media? The evolution of a shared culture means, I suspect, that scientists will maintain the upper hand in determining the characteristics of scientific uncertainty and will play an increasing role in deciding when and how those elements appear in mass media accounts.

This will be helpful to journalists when the issue is really one of limited scientific understanding. Scientists have long argued (legitimately, I think) that journalistic accounts too often eschew information about the uncertainty of the science in circumstances when available knowledge really does limit our understanding of what the science means. When uncertainty stems from what we do not know, it makes sense for media stories to help audiences understand those limitations through such strategies as explaining the limits of a study's methodology or describing the qualified nature of the findings. A shared culture in which scientists emphasize communication of such uncertainty would be a good thing.

Yet, journalists must take care to avoid letting a shared culture submerge their ability to see scientists' use of uncertainty as a rhetorical or political tool.

That tool will come into widespread use in scientific controversies, and, although journalistic coverage of such controversies will be welcomed by competing scientific camps, reporters' revelations of the strategic employment of uncertainty will not. Journalists will do their audiences a great service by helping them to see and understand those uses, but their ability to do so will rest on the evolution of a shared culture in which both scientists and journalists have a substantive hand in constructing the rules.

REFERENCES

Altimore, M. (1982). The social construction of a scientific controversy: Comments on press coverage of the recombinant DNA debate. *Science, Technology, & Human Values, 7,* 24–31.

Arnold, S. F., Klotz, D. M., Collins, B. M., Vonier, P. M., Guillette, L. J., Jr., & McLachlan, J. A. (1996). Synergistic activation of estrogen receptor with combinations of environmental chemicals. *Science, 272,* 1489–1492.

Blum, D. (1997). Investigative science journalism. In D. Blum & M. Knudson (Eds.), *A field guide for science writers* (pp. 86–93). New York: Oxford University Press.

Blumler, J. G., & Gurevitch, M. (1981). Politicians and the press: An essay on role relationships. In D. D. Nimmo & K. R. Sanders (Eds.), *Handbook of political communication* (pp. 467–493). Beverly Hills, CA: Sage.

Brunsman, B. J. (1988). Ghost story. *The Quill, 76,* 25–30.

Campbell, B. L. (1985). Uncertainty as symbolic action in disputes among experts. *Social Studies of Science, 15,* 429–453.

Crewdson, J. (1989, November 19). The great AIDS quest. *Chicago Tribune,* Section 5.

Crewdson, J. (1993) Perky cheerleaders. *Nieman Reports, 47,* 11–16.

Crewdson, J. (1994, March 13). Fraud in breast cancer study. *Chicago Tribune.*

Dearing, J. W. (1995). Newspaper coverage of maverick science: Creating controversy through balancing. *Public Understanding of Science, 4,* 341–361.

Donohue, G. A., Tichenor, P. J., & Olien, C. N. (1995). A guard dog perspective on the role of media. *Journal of Communication, 45*(2), 115–132.

Dunwoody, S. (1979). News-gathering behaviors of specialty reporters: A two-level comparison of mass media decision making. *Newspaper Research Journal, 1,* 29–39.

Dunwoody, S. (1982). A question of accuracy. *IEEE Transactions on Professional Communication, PC–25,* 196–199.

Dunwoody, S. (1986). The scientist as source. In S. M. Friedman, S. Dunwoody, & C. L. Rogers (Eds.), *Scientists and journalists: Reporting science as news* (pp. 3–16). New York: The Free Press.

Dunwoody, S. (1993). *Reconstructing science for public consumption.* Geelong, Australia: Deakin University.

Dunwoody, S. (1997) *What is accuracy in science news reporting?* Unpublished manuscript, University of Wisconsin-Madison.

Dunwoody, S., Crane, E., & Brown, B. (1996) *Directory of science communication courses and programs in the United States.* Madison, WI: University of Wisconsin.

Dunwoody, S., & Kalter, J. (1991). *Daily information choices among mass media science reporters.* Unpublished manuscript, University of Wisconsin-Madison.

Dunwoody, S., & Scott, B. (1982). Scientists as mass media sources. *Journalism Quarterly, 59,* 52–59.

Dunwoody, S., & Shields, S. (1986). Accounting for patterns of selection of topics in statehouse reporting. *Journalism Quarterly, 63,* 488–496.

Fishman, M. (1980). *Manufacturing the news.* Austin, TX: University of Texas Press.

Fishman, M. (1982). News and nonevents: Making the visible invisible. In J. S. Ettema & D. C. Whitney (Eds.), *Individuals in mass media organizations: Creativity and constraint* (pp. 219–240). Thousand Oaks, CA: Sage.

Friedman, S. M., Dunwoody, S., & Rogers, C. L. (Eds.). (1986). *Scientists and journalists: Reporting science as news.* New York: The Free Press.

Goldstein, J. H. (Ed.). (1986). *Reporting science: The case of aggression.* Hillsdale, NJ: Lawrence Erlbaum Associates.

Goodell, R. (1986). How to kill a controversy: The case of recombinant DNA. In S. M. Friedman, S. Dunwoody, & C. L. Rogers (Eds.), *Scientists and journalists: Reporting science as news* (pp. 170–181). New York: The Free Press.

Goodfield, J. (1981). *Reflections on science and the media.* Washington, DC: American Association for the Advancement of Science.

Greenberg, J. (1997). Using sources. In D. Blum & M. Knudson (Eds.), *A field guide for science writers* (pp. 94–101). New York: Oxford University Press.

Haney, D. Q. (1998, January 1). Thin people live longer, study says. *Wisconsin State Journal,* pp. 1A, 3A.

Hartz, J., & Chappell, R. (1997). *Worlds apart.* Nashville, TN: First Amendment Center.

Haslam, C., & Bryman, A. (Eds.). (1994). *Social scientists meet the media.* London: Routledge & Kegan Paul.

Jones, G., & Meadows, J. (1978). Sources and selection of scientific material for newspaper and radio programmes. *Journal of Research Communication Studies, 1,* 69–82.

Kiernan, V. (1997). Ingelfinger, embargoes, and other controls on the dissemination of science news. *Science Communication, 18,* 297–319.

Kolata, G. (1998, January 1). Obesity's link to early death is found less than thought. *The New York Times,* pp. 1, A14.

Lewenstein, B. (1992a). Cold fusion and hot history. *Osiris, 7,* 181–209.

Lewenstein, B. (Ed.). (1992b). *When science meets the public.* Washington, DC: American Association for the Advancement of Science.

Lewis, H. (1997). The false alarm and its coverage changed a policy. *ScienceWriters, 45*(3), 1–2.

McKay, D. S., Gibson, E. K., Jr., Thomas-Keprta, K. L., Vali, H., Romanek, C. S., Clemett, S. J., Chillier, X. D. F., Maechling, C. R., & Zare, R. N. (1996). Search for past life on Mars: Possible relic biogenic activity in Martian meteorite ALH84001. *Science, 273,* 924–930.

McLachlan, J. A. (1997). Synergistic effect of environmental estrogens: Report withdrawn. *Science, 277,* 463.

Nelkin, D. (1994). Promotional metaphors and their popular appeal. *Public Understanding of Science, 3,* 25–31.

Nelkin, D. (1995). *Selling science: How the press covers science and technology* (Rev. ed.). New York: Freeman.

Pellechia, M. G. (1997). Trends in science coverage: A content analysis of three US newspapers. *Public Understanding of Science, 6*, 49–68.

Pfund, N., & Hofstadter, L. (1981). Biomedical innovation and the press. *Journal of Communication, 31*(2), 138–154.

Phillips, D. P., Kanter, E. J., Bednarczyk, B., & Tastad, P. (1991). The importance of the lay press in the transmission of medical knowledge to the scientific community. *New England Journal of Medicine, 325*, 1180–1183.

Pinch, T. (1981). The sun–set: The presentation of certainty in scientific life. *Social Studies of Science, 11*(1), 131–158.

Price, V. (1992). *Public opinion.* Newbury Park, CA: Sage.

Protess, D. L., Cook, F. L., Doppelt, J. C., Ettema, J. S., Gordon, M. T., Leff, D. R., & Miller, P. (1991). *The journalism of outrage.* New York: Guilford.

Shepard, A. C. (1996, March). Show and print. *American Journalism Review,* 40–45.

Smith, C. (1996). Reporters, news sources, and scientific intervention: The New Madrid earthquake prediction. *Public Understanding of Science, 5*, 205–216.

Stocking. S. H., & Dunwoody, S. (1982). Social science in the mass media: Images and evidence. In J. E. Sieber (Ed.), *The ethics of social research* (pp. 151–169). New York: Springer–Verlag.

Stocking, S. H., & Gross, P. H. (1989). *How do journalists think?* Bloomington, IN: ERIC Clearinghouse on Reading and Communication Skills.

Taylor, C. A., & Condit, C. M. (1988). Objectivity and elites: A creation science trial. *Critical Studies in Mass Communication, 5*, 293–312.

Tichenor, P. J., Donohue, G. A., & Olien, C. N. (1980). *Community conflict & the press.* Newbury Park, CA: Sage.

Tichenor, P. J., Olien, C. N., Harrison, A., & Donohue, G. (1970). Mass communication systems and communication accuracy in science news reporting. *Journalism Quarterly, 47*, 673–683.

Toumey, C. P. (1996). *Conjuring science.* New Brunswick, NJ: Rutgers University Press.

van Trigt, A. M., de Jong–van den Berg, L. T. W., Haaijer–Ruskamp, F. M., Willems, J., & Tromp, T. F. J. (1994). Medical journalists and expert sources on medicines. *Public Understanding of Science, 3*, 309–321.

von Schomberg, R. (1993). Controversies and political decision making. In R. von Schomberg (Ed.), *Science, politics and morality* (pp. 7–26). Dordrecht, The Netherlands: Kluwer.

Weaver, D., & Elliott, S. N. (1985). Who sets the agenda for the media? A study of local agenda–building. *Journalism Quarterly, 62*, 87–94.

Whitney, D. C., & Becker, L. B. (1982). "Keeping the gates" for gatekeepers: The effects of wire news. *Journalism Quarterly, 59*, 60–65.

Wilson, K. M. (1996). *Drought, debate and uncertainty: Reporter misconceptions about climate change.* Unpublished manuscript, University of Kansas.

Chapter 5

Interpreting Uncertainty:
A Panel Discussion

Philip M. Boffey
Joann Ellison Rodgers
Stephen H. Schneider

Philip M. Boffey is a Pulitzer Prize-winning journalist who is now deputy editorial page editor of The New York Times. He has written about science for more than 30 years and is the author of The Brain Bank of America, an investigation of the National Academy of Sciences. He has served as president of the National Association of Science Writers and is a director of the Council for the Advancement of Science Writing.

Joann Ellison Rodgers specializes in medical journalism and has written five books and numerous articles in addition to lecturing on science and the mass media at The Johns Hopkins School of Hygiene and Public Health. She is deputy director for public affairs and director of media relations at The Johns Hopkins Medical Institutions and past president of the Council for the Advancement of Science Writing and the National Association of Science Writers.

Stephen H. Schneider teaches at Stanford University and was a senior scientist at the National Center for Atmospheric Research in Boulder, Colorado. He was honored in 1992 with a MacArthur Fellowship for not only his research on global climate change but also for his integrated approach to communicating that information to a variety of audiences. Founder and editor of the interdisciplinary journal Climatic Change, he has published widely and is a frequent commentator on global climate issues.

Question: Is uncertainty a more manageable problem for science writers than for other journalists?

Philip Boffey: Uncertainty is a smaller problem for science writers than for many other kinds of journalists. Let me give some examples of what I mean and some reasons why I think it is a smaller problem. It is not one we should ignore, but we should see it in perspective. With the coverage of foreign affairs, for example, our editorial board has had to struggle at times to determine what is going on in China and what various power struggles there mean for military and economic affairs in the region. This is because China is a very closed society and there are enormous cultural differences between China and the United States. North Korea is even more closed. Even with a number of observers, reporters, and stringers in these countries, we have little idea of what is happening and we are trying to fashion editorial policies in almost total ignorance.

Coverage of economics is another area where there is great uncertainty. A well-known and respected economist, Paul Krugman, talks about two major problems our country faces today: slowing productivity growth and poverty that we cannot seem to eradicate. But the economics profession does not have a clue about what should be done. Krugman describes the profession as being similar to the medical profession at the turn of the century. Economists know a few things that they should not do at the margins, some things that will make matters worse, like bloodletting. Meanwhile, they are trying desperately to find out what has happened to the economy in the last 20 years and are uncertain about what to suggest for the future.

With social issues, there is the same uncertainty. What brought New York City's crime rate down in 1996? Is it that the drug gangs are not shooting each other up anymore or that the bad guys are in jail? Is it because the New York cops put more officers on the street or is it because the cops have a computer system that analyzes where crimes are breaking out and lets them plan better crime prevention? Who knows, but we have a big drop in crime and great uncertainty as to what brought it about.

With science writing, the subjects are better defined. One of the reasons why uncertainty is less of a problem for a science journalist is because the scientific material we cover is mostly issued and argued publicly. This is not North Korea or China. While it is true that journalists cannot view a scientist's lab notes or sit on a peer review committee, the final product is out there in public. There can be a vigorous public debate about it and reporters and others can see what is happening.

The uncertainty in science also is easier to identify because of the scientific tradition of replicating or refuting studies and findings. It is a professional obligation for researchers to discuss the uncertainty of their findings. And finally, many types of science do not deal with the messiest parts of the human equation where there is choice and response that cannot be predicted.

Joann Rodgers: Science writers may have an easier time in dealing with uncertainty issues in the conventional sense if they just seek comments from a number of sources—the he said/she said approach. However, there is the more difficult aspect of trying to understand influences on scientists and studies that are not so visible and not very accessible. When I was a reporter outside of an institution looking in, I had no idea of what went on inside. It is very difficult until you work in an institutional culture to understand some of the barriers to getting science-based information to the public. It also is difficult to understand how science is manipulated, and I do not mean that necessarily negatively, but how the uncertainty around it is manipulated by the dynamics of an institution and the people who have power there. I think these factors make scientific uncertainty a hard issue to cover.

Stephen Schneider: In my experience, science journalists do a better job of handling uncertainty than most other reporters because, as beat reporters, they get to know both people and the subject over time. This makes it somewhat easier for them not to be fooled by the quick press releases and fast-breaking stories that claim too much. But there is a fundamental problem in journalism that works against having knowledgeable reporters on a beat. Some top editors, including Ben Bradlee, the former editor of *The Washington Post,* have said that once a reporter gets to know nearly everybody on a particular beat, he or she is now too biased and should be transferred to some other beat. To me, that sounds like someone who does not understand the scientific process will then be assigned to cover the science beat. It will be difficult for this new-to-science reporter to know the good from bad players and he or she will probably give disproportionate attention to those with much to claim, but little credible to say. The reporter will not handle uncertainty well because she or he possibly will not know the difference between objective and subjective probabilities [see the following]. Unlike these editors, I believe reporters can be both knowledgeable and unbiased if they are conscious of the bias problem. When reporters do not know people or concepts from the field they are covering, many things are hidden. Then they are more likely to be fooled into producing an unbalanced or inaccurate story.

Question: What factors influence how scientists discuss uncertainty and does this change with the audience?

Joann Rodgers: When we talk about strategies to deal with communicating uncertainty in the process of science, I think reporters and many others make an assumption that the people most intimately involved in generating science buy into the ideal view of how science operates—with peer review, publication, critique, replication, and validation. But, I want to argue that there are often conflicting and hidden agendas inside scientific institutions and universities that work against this ideal view. These include commercial factors, licensing agreements, personality conflicts, multidisciplinary turf battles, and market-place forces that are manipulated and factored into all the decisions built around how we communicate about science and all the uncertainties that go with it.

While most people generally believe that corporations often smooth over uncertainties involved in their research, they do not believe this of universities and other scientific institutions. However, universities are not just generators, users, and conduits of information. They also are major players in manipulating uncertainty and how it operates. Corporate, commercial, and technology trans-fer issues are beginning to outstrip the capacity of science-generating institu-tions to communicate about or even deal with uncertainty.

The press does not know about this. I rarely get a reporter on the other end of my telephone, even a science journalist, who knows that conflicts of interest exist much of the time. There are investigative reporters who do. They are, however, few and far between, and they do not pay much attention to science. The way scientists express uncertainty certainly depends on whether they are talking to their corporate board, their dean, the press, their peers, or a journal editor. They may tell very different stories and whisper in many ears.

Stephen Schneider: Scientists deal with different types of uncertainty and respond to them differently, and we must keep that in mind. One form involves objective probability. Take the case of a coin or die: We do not know which face will turn up when it is tossed, but we have objective probabilities as to what it will likely be. Here and in other similar areas where we have considerable knowledge of outcomes, we have an objective probability for a given outcome.

However, there is a second kind of probability that involves judgments: subjective probability. This occurs when scientists deal with complex systems, as I do in studying a climate-environmental system or with those who study health systems. In these complex systems, where there are many interconnected subcomponents, scientists often are uncertain about the extent and magnitude of these interconnections. As a result, they have to make judgments about these interconnections and, consequently, underlying assumptions are subjective. This leads to subjective rather than objective probabilities about how these systems behave, despite the myth that there can be objective probability when dealing with complex systems.

Because of the many judgments that have to be made, evaluating or assessing the state of science is important. Science and science assessment are not the same thing. *Science* strives to explain how natural or social systems work. The motivations vary, but the simple curiosity-driven search for explaining nature is the archetype. *Science assessment*, on the other hand, is the evaluation of the likelihood of various possibilities needed by decisionmakers—personal, corporate, or governmental—to address real world problems. Truth is not the objective—only best guesses of the state-of-the-art science. When one is in the policy arena, one is dealing with science assessment and this factor influences how scientists behave. Science assessment is a social process, but it is usually done with a large degree of openness. In explaining judgments made in a study, it would be very difficult at an assessment meeting for a scientist to consciously stand up in front of his or her colleagues and knowingly distort what he or she believes to be the subjective probabilities of any specific event. This does not mean that scientists lack biases, but to allow these biases to knowingly alter one's judgment about the likelihood of an outcome is a good ticket to a reputation problem. However, fighting biases in one's subjective judgment does not mean there is no controversy. Scientists may still advocate policy positions, but they then have to acknowledge other points of view in their presentations or they do not look very good to their colleagues.

One problem in some assessments is that scientists often do not separate what they know to be likely from what is only possible—and this leads to much confusion. Journalists cannot be expected to do this separation for themselves. The frequent lack in media accounts of differentiation of what is reasonably well-known from what is speculative leads many laypeople to believe that scientists do not know very much. This simply may not be true. There often are aspects of knowledge that are known—for which there is established experimental, empirical, and other evidence. Also, there are aspects in which scientists have considerable confidence, but still moderate degrees of uncertainty remain. And there are aspects that are completely speculative. These different degrees of uncertainty get jumbled up in both assessments and media coverage, and when this happens, a false impression is conveyed that nothing solid is known.

It takes some depth of understanding of scientific issues to be able to sort out what is known well from what is highly speculative and that sorting is necessary when both scientists and journalists discuss science assessment and uncertainty among themselves and with the public. I do not think the science assessment process is well-understood outside of the scientific community and, in fact, many scientists do not communicate degrees of uncertainty very well at all.

Even good science journalists do not convey much information about science assessment. *NOVA*, the weekly science program on the Public Broadcasting System, for example, highlights science at its exciting edges and often misses the deliberative, argumentative process out of which scientific truth, even if it is tentative, is likely to emerge. Because of television production values, even this kind of show must focus on exciting, visual science. But where scientists determine their truths is not just out in the field—that is where the information underlying the assessment comes from, of course—but in the community process of getting together with colleagues for discussions. Science assessment occurs in academic offices and hotel lobbies and often appears dull on camera. It is not the stuff of television or other media coverage.

Question: Do the tactics that journalists and scientists use to convey uncertainties get the message across to the audience?

Joann Rodgers: Even when reporters do what scientists and I think is an excellent job of qualifying the results of a study, the reality is that if the study relates to a prevalent human disease, readers and viewers interpret the stories through a filter of their own. The next day the phones ring off the hook from people who have read the story or heard about it on television or radio and these people are demanding the cure. Or, they are angry and fearful about reports that a drug or treatment has side effects. This happens despite carefully crafted language, carefully spelled out qualification, even a broad statement that says that treatment is 10 years away and much more experimentation is needed. People do hear what they need to hear and read what they want to read. They think that perhaps the institution and the investigator are not telling them everything and they want to check it out despite what the scientist or journalist has said.

Philip Boffey: In some ways, reporters can go too far. If they are going to write a story, they probably think the subject is somewhat important. So they will try to show that here is something that may affect people's health or their understanding of the universe, and only acknowledge dutifully that there are some uncertainties involved. But they are writing to convey, "Wow! Look here is a new surge in some new direction." They are not going to say that this study, which came out yesterday, may or may not mean anything. So while they need caveats in the story, those are more like "weasel" words stuck in somewhere in the flow of the article where they are hardly noticed. The only people who pay attention to them are the writer, or the editor who made the reporter put them in, or the scientist who says that he or she did not say the finding was definite, or the lawyer who wants to protect the media organization from litigation. What I am saying here is true for all journalism, not just science writing. Reporters are always faced with deciding on the truest interpretation they can put on what they are describing, and on how to achieve balance and tentativeness when that is needed.

Joann Rodgers: Scientists act as qualifiers. Often in our institution, for example, a scientist will want to bury the lead of a news release in the fifth paragraph or the third page. They do this, I believe, so people will not think they are going too far in what they say about their work. Of course, this tactic does not work because journalists are smart enough to figure out where the lead is in the story, and so is the public. The public assumes that all of the qualifiers are background noise after a while and they interpret the research from their own needs and perspectives.

Stephen Schneider: Scientists have a serious problem in communicating about science that I call the *double ethical bind*. On the one hand, your scientific ethics require the truth—the whole truth—which means lots of caveats that cannot be included in a two-page article, let alone a short sound bite for broadcast. On the other hand, you also want laypeople to know about and understand your research, particularly if you are working in a controversial area such as climate change. To work with the media effectively, particularly television, requires dramatic stuff and catchy phrases. What I advocate to handle this tricky situation is to use metaphors that convey the newness, the potential seriousness, and the uncertainty of what scientists are presenting. One involving the climate that I use all the time is that the climate is like dice and what humans may be doing is slowly loading them. This metaphor means that although weather is going to bounce around, there is an increasing probability that underlying climatic change also will emerge as the dice are loaded.

Scientists who do public outreach have an obligation to prepare a series of products of varying lengths about their research to provide to their colleagues, the media, and the public. For example, I have produced, in addition to my repertoire of sound bites, longer explanations for use in the more in-depth media, as well as written articles in *Scientific American* and books that are readable by laypeople. And, of course, I also have written scientific papers for my peers. For the small fraction of people who really care about what I think in depth, they can find the necessary caveats spelled out in the longer works.

But for the majority of people, simple phrases and metaphors that convey both urgency and uncertainty get the main idea across. While an individual journalist often does not write in all of these various lengths about some specific scientific subject, the collective of journalistic work done by the profession produces a similar variety of materials so that a layperson has many choices in seeking more scientific depth on a subject. People who get their information by reading only a general magazine or a business-oriented newspaper or by viewing the evening television news get very limited information about the environmental debate. They have to go to multiple sources that provide many viewpoints and greater depth to be well-informed.

Question: Differences and disagreements about what is professed as true in science frequently are linked to scientists' values. Are those values a part of what needs to show up in stories so that readers and viewers can become aware of them?

Philip Boffey: Values belong in stories, but they are extraordinarily hard to get a handle on journalistically in the space and timeframe of what reporters are usually doing. Values enter into the favorite example everyone always gives of the business person versus the environmentalist. These two are going to interpret differently the degree of health risk represented by a toxic waste disposal site or a product of some kind. Their backgrounds should be mentioned to make their biases clear. The same goes for the head of any organization that is pushing for something. But usually, science writers are faced with academic scientists, whose values are not readily identifiable. Some people will say a journalist can see a scientist's values based on where his or her funding is coming from or whether that person has ever taken money from a company or a labor union, or what she or he has testified about. But this is dangerous unless the reporter has the time to pursue the circumstances of how these different things occurred. They do not necessarily mean anything other than that the scientist was the best available expert on that particular issue. Just because the scientist was once associated with a value-laden organization does not mean that he or she is necessarily in the same camp.

Joann Rodgers: How universities and scientists deal with disclosures over conflicts of interest is definitely a value-laden area that needs more attention from the social science community as well as from journalists and scientists themselves. While it is simple to sign a form that discloses any conflicts of interest about funding, for example, it is anything but simple to get agreed-upon, meaningful disclosure language into news releases or presentations of science at meetings. There are legal, political, and financial complexities as well as the personal issue.

Stephen Schneider: Values creep into virtually everything and it is important that they be discussed in articles. As I said, even when we have objective probabilities, usually in any complex problem of interest, they get combined with aspects that include subjectivity. For a scientist, the best way to deal with a value question is to do it explicitly. Try to know what your biases are and put them in the open. Since no one can be, consciously or unconsciously, entirely value neutral, it is important to represent a distribution of opinions across a broad knowledge-based community. The problem then becomes who should be in the community whose opinions are tapped? Rarely can we rely solely on one or two sources for a balanced judgment of scientifically complex issues in which both values and uncertainty are endemic. Yet, this is typical in many media accounts.

This gets to the question of balance in reporting. Journalists are supposed to provide balance, of course, but does this mean countering the opinion of a major intergovernmental panel of hundreds of scientists with those of a few contrarian scientists, giving each equal weight in the story? In this example, a hundred-scientist, thousand-reviewer assessment of climatic change by the United Nations was often balanced in news reports by dissenting views of a handful of opponents with little guidance to the public about which group more closely represented the mainstream scientific community. There is a real question as to whether it is appropriate to balance a broad community with a few extreme dissenters unless journalists also include that the nonmainstream opinions are likely to represent a low probability case. It should not be a statement that these few dissenters are necessarily wrong, but that the bulk of knowledgeable scientists support the opposite point of view. To do that, reporters need to know a fair amount about the issue and the actors. Journalists need to find out which arguments are mainstream and which are outliers.

Getting back to values, it is very easy to dismiss people based upon the fact that they have a business or environmental perspective, or that they have been funded by the Department of Defense. Such circumstantial evidence of bias is not enough. Reporters, especially science writers, really have to do an assessment of the issues so they can get a better sense of the credibility of the arguments. Average citizens certainly cannot do it for themselves, unless they do a lot of digging.

Question: How do you cover the nature and limits of uncertainty in scientific issues where there appears to be a majority, mainstream viewpoint, but also vocal, established scientific sources whose views make them outliers on these issues?

Philip Boffey: One of the problems in journalism is to try to find what is really going on, what is accurate and which sources to trust. What makes it slightly easier in the science arena than in others is the mechanisms that are designed to both produce consensus and reduce uncertainty in science. A peer-reviewed journal gives reporters more confidence than an unreviewed source because at least someone who knew something about the subject looked at the paper. This is in contrast to material that comes in over the transom to me occasionally from individuals who have been spurned by journals, the patent office, and everybody else and want me to bring their issue to people's attention. In the scientific community, there is also the consensus panel mechanism for government agencies, which have internal staffs and processes all designed to search out what they think the truth of something is. The National Academy of Sciences does this, too, with its studies and panels. There are huge consensus mainstream organizations that are trying to define what they think the truth is. Of course, there is a second level problem in deciding whether these consensus mechanisms are operating properly. Have they gone astray somehow, have they distorted something deliberately, were the panels loaded or incompetent? Often, the journalist does not have time to investigate these questions given the constraints of daily journalism. However, these consensus mechanisms do help the journalist decide where the mainstream opinion is and how and whether to deal with outliers. Should they be part of the debate? In some issues, such as climate change, I do not feel they should be ignored because in this subject, the last major consensus report still showed there were a number of unknowns, so the situation is still fluid. However, in the debate where only a handful of people claim that the HIV virus is not causing AIDS, I feel there is enough evidence to ignore their viewpoint. Years from now, I may regret this if the outliers turn out to be right, but there comes a practical point where you say, the consensus is here and I am going to ignore the outliers.

Joann Rodgers: Sometimes deadlines and other journalistic pressures make it difficult to handle these situations. Any public information officer will tell you that reliability is often defined by journalists as some combination of accessibility and familiarity. It is a very practical consideration. In the daily fray of having to cover stories quickly, success may be defined by whom reporters can get to fastest, who is familiar, who has not lied to them in the past, or who at least will quickly tell them three other people in the field to contact. Often, there is no time to look at consensus organizations or get to a database. Journalists often say that they make five phone calls and whoever gets back to them first gets their attention. This is just a recognizable fact of life.

Stephen Schneider: Scientists worry about outliers too. Students, in particular, worry that their positions might be wrong because, with highly uncertain science and a wide range of subjective probability, the outliers could be right, even though there is little chance of this in each specific case. Scientists are often nervous about dealing with the media, particularly concerning the reputation issue.

But, in science, rewards do not come from predicting what turns out by luck to be the right answer. Credibility comes from whether you have dealt with the scientific process as best you could given the empirical and theoretical information at the time. I would much rather be wrong for the right reasons then right for the wrong reasons. One columnist writes about how I talked about global cooling rather than global warming in the early 1970s. But this was when we had no idea about how widespread the distribution of aerosol particles was around the globe. These particles reflect sunlight and cool the earth. We admitted our lack of information at the time, of course. Now, we know suspended particle hazes are regional and our old global-scale calculations were not realistic. However, the columnist and others say that I am not very credible talking about warming today because I was discussing cooling back then. But what I and others said then was the right thing given the information at the time.

It takes careful reporting to find out whether the discussions at the time were based on what scientists could know and whether caveats were applied to their findings. It is a high risk for scientists to get in the media game and it is a gamble that most do not choose to take. When students ask me how to deal with the media, I always say there are two choices: Do it a lot or not at all. If scientists work with the media a lot, what they say and how it gets reported average out. Some stories will make you look foolish to your colleagues while others will make you look better than you deserve. Occasional service as a media source is a lottery with your reputation, a gamble that many scientists, especially young ones, are unwilling to take. And in science, your reputation governs grants, promotions, and prizes.

Part II

Science in the Public Arena

Chapter 6

Popular Beliefs, Media, and Biotechnology*

Susanna Hornig Priest

Susanna Hornig Priest studies the formation of public opinion on "high technology" issues, with special emphasis on the media's role. An associate professor of journalism, Priest also directs the Center for Science and Technology Policy and Ethics at Texas A&M University. She holds degrees in anthropology, sociology, and communication. Her research interests and publications also include studies on the place of science and scientific information in contemporary American society.

For the nonscientist, evaluating scientific information (such as data on uncertain but likely risks) has much in common with buying a used car.[1] As wary consumers, we need both technical and social information. We think it is important to have technical data on the car's gas mileage, its history of ownership and use, its age, engine performance, mechanical condition, and so on. Yet we also want social information, such as what kind of reputation the seller, the manufacturer, and the specific make and model have; who the sellers are; and why they want to sell the car (why they might, for example, be anxious to sell). In short, we want to know whether information is being hidden—or

---

*This chapter is a revision of one published earlier as CBPE Discussion Paper 95-12, Center for Science and Technology Policy and Ethics, Texas A&M University. My research on media representations of biotechnology, on which this chapter is based, has been supported by the Center, the Institute for Biosciences and Technology of which it is a part, and the Texas A&M College of Liberal Arts. This research has also received significant financial support from the National Science Foundation, Ethics and Values Studies program.

[1] I am indebted to Paul B. Thompson, former director of the Texas A&M Center for Science and Technology Policy and Ethics and currently Joyce and Edward E. Brewer Professor of Applied Ethics in the Department of Philosophy, Purdue University, not only for suggesting this "used car" analogy, but also for stimulating my thinking, over the past 6 or so years, about many of the issues raised in this chapter.

hyped! The less comfortable we are with the task of assessing the technological evidence, the more stock we must put in evaluating the social evidence. However, few of us are such masters of internal combustion technology that we would fail to be equally concerned with these issues of social trust.

So it is with uncertain science, when consumers of news reports (and of the other forms of media in which scientific claims appear) are often forced to choose among competing expert perspectives in the face of limited technical literacy. These choices are not matters of evaluating technical evidence so much as they are matters of evaluating the trustworthiness and expertise of scientists and scientific institutions.

For example, the active manipulation of genetic material—of agricultural species, even of people—can be framed as the latest in a long series of benign applications of scientific knowledge, the newest chapter in a story that began with the selective breeding of plants and animals—or perhaps earlier, with the first appearance of medicine, representing the marriage of human curiosity and a humane desire to reduce suffering. Alternatively, genetic engineering and other forms of biotechnology[2] can be seen as the ultimate Frankensteinian threats to life as we know it, conjuring up images of monstrous combinations of disparate living parts, of ecosystems laid waste by the invasion of new and unaccountably more aggressive species, and of designer babies whose gender, color, and IQ are made up to parental specifications. In this interpretation, interest in human genetic engineering appears to spring less from humane concern than from a desire to eliminate imperfections (real or perceived) and breed Supermen. Similarly, some may see interest in agricultural bioengineering as springing less from a desire to eliminate human hunger than from corporate profiteering and an irresponsible impulse to tinker.

Neither of these ways of interpreting genetic engineering is without foundation. Some genetic disorders, such as Tay-Sachs disease, can have such tragic consequences that thinking people might reasonably question whether children with these conditions should be born, but they also must ask what limits should be put on the uses of genetic information. The impact of science is to some extent what we make of it.

The goal of this discussion is not to try to make known the future direction genetic technologies might take—a task that I, at least, am certainly not

---

[2]*Biotechnology* refers to any technological application of biological knowledge, from wine and cheese making to gene therapy. (Sometimes biotechnology also refers to mechanical devices, such as prostheses, that are designed to imitate biological forms.) *Genetic engineering*—the active manipulation of DNA, sometimes across species—is probably the most controversial form of biotechnology.

qualified to undertake, and that I would argue is impossible anyway. Rather, the goal is to ask how media coverage might best (that is, most constructively) cope with the existence of such radically different interpretations. However, this second question turns out to be inseparable from the first, unanswerable one.

The genetic science most likely to be defined as news is what Latour (1993) called *emergent* science, science whose truth has not yet been settled by consensus, either scientific or public. Indeed, one of the key problems in science journalism generally is that it is almost always such emergent science that is considered news. In such contexts, it is by definition not adequate to report the beliefs of scientific experts as fact; the science itself is uncertain, and its social implications even more so. Much of the unease of the scientific community with mass media coverage of science is likely attributable to unarticulated, perhaps only half-realized dissatisfaction with journalists' obsession with reporting "objective" facts in cases in which the facts have not yet been established.

PREMISES

I begin with three assumptions, each of which I recognize is questionable to one degree or another. The first is that the future impact of genetic engineering is unknown, or uncertain, even among those scientists who are engaged in its development. This is, on the one hand, a scientific future—bounded primarily by the limits of understanding and technique, but it is also a social future in which the enthusiasm, the concerns, and the goals—benevolent or not—of nonscientists may be as important an eventual determinant of direction as the limits of science itself. Good science and useful technology are built in part on serendipity; final outcomes are never known, and it would be naive to suggest (in this post-Three Mile Island, post-Chernobyl, post-Bhopal, post-Challenger, arguably postmodern world) that these outcomes are always and necessarily good.

Some might claim that science itself is always benign; only its application as technology produces failures, the oft-encountered genetically-modified-creature-escapes-from-the-laboratory theme notwithstanding. Yet it also would be naive to claim that technological interests do not color the scientific future, determining as they do the willingness of government and industry to fund particular research initiatives and not others. Indeed, the very terms genetic *engineering* and bio*technology* serve to underscore the economic and political relationship between genetic science and its envisioned applications, whether serving humanistic objectives or less lofty profit-seeking ones. At any rate, neither the specific knowledge that scientific inquiry will bring us, nor what its specific applications as technology might be—let alone the eventual social importance of that technology—is fully knowable in advance. Journalism about science needs to recognize these limits.

The second assumption is that social—that is, public—control over the general thrust and direction of genetic research is not necessarily a bad thing. This is, of course, a political position, but I think it is a political position compatible with the ideals of democracy—and with the current turn toward public, or civic, journalism. Both the price tag and the other impacts (both risks and benefits) of genetic engineering, for better or for worse, will be borne by all members of society—although perhaps not equally, as the environmental justice movement has called to our attention. Thus, society at large has a legitimate stake in evaluating both the feasibility and desirability of the directions this work does—and does not—take.

No scientist appreciates people he or she considers uninformed taking up the question of the ultimate worth of that scientist's work. The entire social structure of science rests on the tradition of peer review, of cautious, reasoned evaluation performed only by those whose own work can pass equivalent scrutiny. Yet democracy rests on the notion that public policy is undertaken with the consent of the governed, although the manner and the extent to which the general public should participate in the nitty-gritty detail work of policy formation, especially in technically complex areas, is an uncertainty in its own right. If science is to be publicly funded rather than serve as an activity of the independently wealthy (who, centuries ago, practiced science primarily to satisfy their own curiosity rather than to enhance the general social good or garner profits), we must find a way to create democracy for science. That is, science must be accountable to the broader democratic society.

These new calls for accountability in research should not be limited to concerns about doctoring data or abusing lab animals, the impropriety of which is generally obvious. The calls should extend, as well, to questions about the wisest use of public resources. This is a much more difficult notion of accountability. How should we choose between feeding children who are hungry today and developing, on a long-term basis, more nutritious and reliable food supplies?

The third assumption, I believe, should be less controversial than the first two. It is that public decisions are best made on the basis of broad public discussion, that is, by a public that is informed rather than a public that is either ignorant or propagandized. The reason this should be less controversial is that it is quite simply in everyone's interests that this be the case. It is clearly in the interests of democracy. It is also in the interests of science and even of the corporate promoters of new technologies. "Opinions" distilled on the basis of a quick glance, so to speak, at the issues are likely to be fickle ones. These opinions are the ones that opinion polls so often glean. On the other hand, support (and, yes, opposition) generated on the basis of more extensive education and active involvement in examining the issues is likely to be more enduring. Here, education cannot be taken as a gloss for propaganda, however; it means letting the public in on the perils as well as the promises of new research frontiers.

I assert here that public opinion about science, like public opinion about other political issues, is formed most meaningfully in what is sometimes described as *public space*, that is, as a result of open and informed interpersonal discussion among citizens. This notion of public debate is reminiscent of the Greek democratic ideal (its elitist limitations included). It can be understood partly in terms of the physical sites in which it is likely to take place. Italian coffee houses, Irish pubs and, at least in the romanticized recent past, American barber shops and beauty salons come to mind as examples of places where people actually talk, face-to-face, about the news of the day. Urban planners consider whether and how they can create meaningful, aesthetically appealing public spaces; here, the role of these spaces in facilitating democratic debate may be secondary to their other purposes.

Meanwhile, at least in the modern United States, the mass media are now very often a substitute symbolic site for this public debate activity (Gumpert & Drucker, 1994) rather than simply a source of fuel for it or of information and reports about it.

For political theorists and social philosophers, this notion of public space is closely related to Habermas' idea of the *public sphere (die Offentlichkeit)*, a concept also related to communication. Habermas distinguished between the earlier, largely manipulative function of public communication characteristic of the premodern world (from theater performance to church ritual to early forms of news that told subjects what rulers wanted them to hear) and an idealized vision of communication's role in the contemporary social order as a vehicle for facilitating public talk among citizens (Peters, 1993).

Whether the Internet will effectively substitute for either the town hall or the talk show for this purpose is a question on which the jury is still out; important issues of equity in Internet access loom on the public horizon. However, my analysis of the appropriate role of media assumes, with Habermas, that the stimulation of active, informed discussion and debate is preferable in democratic societies to the manipulation, however effective, of passive audiences, even "for their own good." It is not at all clear whether there are any reasonable grounds for journalism about science to be somehow exempt from such considerations.

This third assumption, then, has direct implications for what media coverage of science should be like: It should encourage such discussion by opening up new issues and alternatives to public view rather than presenting only received wisdom, even that received from the community of scientists about scientific issues.

At least one caveat applies here, however. Champions of the idea of representativeness in government might point out, with considerable justification, that making public policy for science and technology (as for any technically complex sphere) requires more inquiry, information, knowledge, reason, experience, and wisdom than the average citizen can be expected to muster even in the ideal information environment. The purpose of electing representatives is so they can make the investments of time in researching problems and alternatives that all of us, individually, cannot reasonably make. Not only are the results of public opinion polls a poor substitute for the reasoned and expressed opinions of an informed citizenry engaged in open debate, but also, as a practical matter, even an informed citizenry cannot be expected to engage itself in technical policy debates in much detail.

I doubt very much, for example, if the general public really wants to be presented with the scientific evidence "for" and "against" global warming and then be asked if they think it is a significant problem or not. I think they would just as soon the experts (scientific and political) sort this out and then present them with the broad outlines of both scientific consensus and political alternatives. Yet this is not at all the same thing as saying the public should not participate in technical policy debates.

Furthermore, the existence of this tension underscores the truly critical role of science journalism in such debates. Here, journalists absolutely cannot "just report the facts" because these are in dispute. Journalists must participate in determining how many details are too many, which points represent emerging scientific consensus, which are legitimately the subject of ongoing investigation and debate, and what the full range of short- and long-term policy responses might be. Socially responsible science journalism is neither alarmist nor narcotizing, but it still needs to go beyond the presentation of "facts" to questions of reasoned interpretation.

MESSAGES AND MEDIA

These, then, are the three assumptions: Scientific futures are uncertain, the public has a legitimate stake in defining public policy for science, and this role is better filled by an educated than an ignorant citizenry. On this basis, we can define public discussion of the uncertain future of genetic engineering and public involvement in determining at least broad areas of research emphasis as good things; we can then use this framework to begin to evaluate media coverage (see Evans & Priest, 1995).

Empirical evidence suggests that the general public will ask questions about ethics, social impact, and the regulatory environment whether or not these questions are raised in media coverage (Priest, 1995) and that news coverage does not always do enough to respond to questions of this type (Priest & Talbert, 1994). News accounts that "sell" science (Nelkin, 1995) fail to meet these needs.

It is important to recognize that there is a convergence of strategic and ethical objectives involved here. Open public discussion of the broad range of sociopolitical and ethical issues associated with genetic engineering is a good (that is, an ethical) thing for society. In addition, it is also in the interests of those with an identifiable stake in the promotion of biotechnology, lest it go the way of the multibillion-dollar Texas supercollider Congress killed in 1993, the space program, or nuclear power.

Background attitudes that question how science and technology are used and controlled are important predictors of risk perceptions (Hornig, 1992). These attitudes are not going to go away because media accounts ignore the questions they imply. Where do these attitudes come from? Of course, they may come, in turn, partly from news—but not so much from individual news accounts that might produce, magic-bullet style, particular predictable reactions. Rather they come from news as a steady diet over a lifetime that builds on whatever childhood education and socialization have begun and on the attitudes and beliefs that pervade the general culture.

In media studies, it is easy enough to overestimate the cumulative, as well as the short-term, effects of media messages. The news stream is only one component of a much broader information environment in which individual human beings, members of a persistent culture and (typically) of many intersecting subcultures, selectively choose and actively process what messages they will attend to. This information environment is made up of marketing messages as well as objective journalism, of fictional entertainment as well as factual news, and of material intended to educate as well as to report.

Popular beliefs about science—in this case, about genetics—that seem to come from the general culture rather than from anything learned in school or adopted from media messages are also a part of this information environment and can be expected to contribute in an active way to the interpretation of new information. If people believe that IQ or criminality is strongly hereditary, or that dinosaurs could be recreated from fossil DNA, then these beliefs will color their responses to new information. Clear lines are not drawn between one kind or source of information and another; for better or for worse, what the public knows about DNA will be derived from the evidence in well-publicized trials, such as the 1995 O. J. Simpson murder case, as much as from high-school biology lessons.

We might, then, begin to think in terms of an "information climate" in much the same way that public opinion specialists speak of the "climate of public opinion," meaning the general social mood, historical context, and cultural milieu in which particular new events and new pieces of information are interpreted to form new opinions, ideas, or beliefs. This information climate comes from many different sources; it is not limited to what is taught or intended as a science lesson.

In what follows, I present some examples of how marketing messages, educational programming, science fiction, and ambient popular (or *ethnoscientific*) beliefs about genetics and genetic engineering all contribute to the context in which news about the future of genetics is understood. Sometimes these contributions are predictable, but as often as not, they can be quite contrary to our expectations.

Marketing

Genetically engineered products have begun to enter the U.S. food supply in major ways; as a result, marketers' messages have made an important contribution—and not always a particularly positive one—to the information climate for bioengineering. The genetically engineered form of *bovine somatotropin* (*bST*), a growth hormone used to boost milk production in dairy cows, received its final stamp of federal approval early in 1995 after an initially rocky reception.

It is tempting to attribute public resistance to this form of bST to its use in the production of milk, a dairy product that is almost the quintessential symbol of food purity. However, this is probably unjustified. A genetically engineered substitute for *rennet*, a substance formerly extracted from calves' stomachs and essential to cheese making, had already been in use for some time without having stirred so much as a public ripple. Tomatoes (such as the Flavr Savr), genetically engineered to have a longer shelf life, were introduced just subsequent to the appearance of bST. Although they met with isolated resistance that itself may have been the result of forces the bST controversy set in motion, their reception seemed at least relatively rosy overall.

Some of this difference may be attributable to economic realities. There was already plenty of cheap, good-tasting milk, but not necessarily an oversupply of sweet, ripe-tasting tomatoes. Some of the differences in public receptivity may reflect differential special-interest concerns. For example, animal welfare groups did not have the same motivation to protest the use of an artificial substitute for something that was once taken exclusively from butchered baby cows (bioengineered rennet, used in making cheese) as they did to question the use of an artificial hormone alleged to put dairy animals under increased chronic stress (bioengineered bST).

Nevertheless, there can be little doubt that different marketing communication strategies employed by Monsanto Corporation, bST's primary promoter, and CalGene, who created the Flavr Savr, had a substantial impact on public reception. Monsanto spokespeople branded anti-bST activists as misguided fringe groups. At the same time, they failed to address adequately the concerns of their own primary market: Dairy farmers who feared that the cost of bST along with the projected increase in total milk production would drive some of them out of business (Hornig, 1991).

The company was ordered to halt its early "educational" efforts pending completion of the regulatory review process, as marketing of an unapproved product is against federal policy. Despite an aggressive campaign aimed at producers as soon as engineered bST became legal, Monsanto representatives seemed to have had considerable difficulty overcoming their initial missteps. The company's later active opposition to product labeling took the form of notifying milk producers that labeling of products as "bST free" was not supported by FDA policy. This action could have been seen as even further defensiveness, thus compounding the problem. Apparently, the FDA did not prohibit such labeling, as Monsanto's communications were easily interpreted as implying. It began to appear as though Monsanto had something to hide.

CalGene's tomatoes, on the other hand, were voluntarily labeled and distributed with explanatory brochures that described exactly what genetic engineering was and how it had been used. The effect was to elevate the genetic science involved to a point of pride rather than allow it to appear as a deficit to be overcome. It surely did not hurt that the Flavr Savr was actually a pretty good-tasting tomato, but the kind of marketing savvy that sent a box of Flavr Savrs to a university conference on biotechnology ethics I attended several years ago (at a time when these had not yet hit the local retail market) did not hurt either.

These examples help make the convergence of interests (strategic and ethical) just mentioned more clear. Obviously, it is in the interests of those marketing these new foods to communicate more proactively about the genetic techniques used to create them. At a minimum, even if better communications had no chance of eliminating opposition to bST from either farmers or consumers, this would have been obvious sooner, before the investment in development had gone too far to halt.

In the long run, trying too hard to push a new technological product against opposition is only likely to exacerbate suspicions about the sources of these messages. Such an action can fuel existing fears that science and technology are not always wielded in the public interest. It is therefore better marketing, as well as better democracy, to talk openly about risks, benefits, and even the often overlooked question of the social distribution of those risks and benefits (an issue that both CalGene and Monsanto avoided, as far as I know). This is the kind of information climate in which responsible and informed consumer choices are most likely to prevail, and it is those kinds of choices that are most likely to contribute to a stable market.

But what is the role of science journalism in cases like these? Despite journalists' protestations, much reporting, including much science journalism, originates as press releases, from coverage of press conferences, or as a result of other active interventions by sources, not as editors' or journalists' independent good ideas. For biotechnology in particular, local news coverage has been heavily dominated by industrial and university sources anxious to promote their products (Priest & Talbert, 1994). University sources—and many times sources in industrial research firms as well—are likely to be seen as scientific sources, even when the spokesperson is not a scientist.

Because science is supposed to be both objectively factual and operating in society's best interests, I suspect that journalists may be considerably less likely to question their scientific sources' motives than they would be if they were covering, for example, a business or a political beat. Journalists need to ask themselves the same kinds of critical questions about subsidized science news that they would ask about news of other types. In addition, they need to remember that the ethics of technology are complex and uncertain, with eventual outcomes and impacts often unknown and unknowable. However, such outcomes and impacts are hardly irrelevant nor are they likely to be uninteresting to readers.

Science Fiction and Science Fact

Enter *Jurassic Park*. This genre of science fiction grates on the nerves of more than a few scientists. It is inaccurate. It is misleading. What is perhaps its worst sin of all, it questions the benevolence of science and the wisdom of genetic engineering.

But wait! Isn't this exactly what we have suggested good science journalism should be doing? Raising touchy questions about the social and ethical dimensions of scientific endeavor, such as the eventual uses and impact of genetic engineering, before the science itself is in place? Suggesting to audiences of nonscientists that envisioning the directions, for better or for worse, that science and technology might eventually take can be interesting, rewarding, even important?

Precisely so. So why the furor? Scientists, of course, work hard to separate fact from fiction and are trained to be scrupulous in avoiding statements not supported by direct empirical evidence. Most scientists live up to their teachers' expectations in these respects, the odd case of trumped-up prospects (cold fusion, gold from base metal) notwithstanding. So it is not surprising that they find unsettling the popular treatments of science that deliberately go beyond the facts. It is unlikely, though, that the roots of scientists' unease with popular science fiction end there.

The film *Jurassic Park* raised very pointed (and not at all groundless) questions about what could go wrong in the very real world with genetic engineering projects. Technologies (in this case, actual life forms) might be developed that are beyond our power to fully control; our own human arrogance might blind us to this possibility. Greedy, even unbalanced, individuals might circumvent safeguards for personal gain or for the satisfaction of their own warped egos. Corporate interests might encourage us to rush into operation technologies that have not yet been fully tested.

This film's message is not about how easy it would be to recreate living dinosaurs for our own amusement out of antique DNA. Rather, it is about the dangers inherent in the commingling of corporate, personal, and scientific interests. These are very real dangers for real science, including—maybe even especially—genetic engineering.

Perhaps we need not be terribly worried about these outcomes; perhaps existing safeguards are sufficient after all. Nevertheless, these themes represent real fears that exist out there in the culture, not things this fictional portrayal manufactured out of "whole cloth." The issues are not made more trivial by their appearance in a fictional format. They may actually be made somewhat less threatening by the (reasonably obvious) fantasy setting in which they are raised, but they are certainly interesting points. It may be that here science fiction has succeeded in bringing popular attention to science policy questions, where science journalism itself (and the scientific community, for that matter) has largely failed.

Bioengineering yesteryear's dinosaurs is not really made to seem immi-
nent by the appearance of such a film. The genre is unmistakably fiction,
even though the questions raised are serious. Ironically, we must turn to
educational television and the PBS *NOVA* series to find a less ambiguous
case of confusing futuristic vision and scientific fact. Elsewhere, I have
written about the tendency of this award-winning series to mystify science
in the name of popularizing it and to dramatize the mundane pursuit of
laboratory truth in order to draw and hold audiences, an imperative no less
applicable to U.S. public television than to other forms of commercialized
visual entertainment (Hornig, 1990). Let me also take this opportunity to
state that *NOVA* undoubtedly does some good, important work. It has not won
its awards accidentally.

What did *NOVA* do in the wake of *Jurassic Park,* however? Brilliantly,
NOVA's producers apparently perceived that the film had created what is
sometimes called a *teachable moment* for genetic science—a window of
opportunity characterized by heightened public interest in genetic engineering's feasibility and meaning. So they produced a show of their own on what
it would really take to pull off the film's fictional feat. The producers (Dugan,
1993) interviewed, in turn, specialists in reconstructing DNA patterns from
fossil materials, in raising rare birds from eggs, and so on, up to and including
paleoecologists who speculated on the environmental needs of recreated dinosaur species and the extent to which the present-day environment might be
modified to meet them.

Each of these specialists dwelled on the overwhelming obstacles to solving
his or her own small piece of the "let's make a dinosaur" puzzle. Each stressed
the seeming impossibility, certainly the complexity, of the task. Yet by stringing
the comments of all these experts together, *NOVA* certainly managed to leave
the impression that all of the knowledge we would need to accomplish this feat
is either currently available or soon will be. Such knowledge awaits only the
vision and genius of whoever is smart and powerful enough to pull it all
together. This *NOVA* piece also managed, for the most part, to avoid dwelling
on the really tough ethical questions: What new environmental damage might
be wrought; who would pay for the venture and who would benefit; and what
are the limits on our rights to manipulate animal DNA?

Was *NOVA* wrong to seize this opportunity to educate the American public
about genetics? Absolutely not, and to do so effectively probably required at
least judicious use of "high drama." Let's remember, though, that the science
policy questions raised in *Jurassic Park* are also important, perhaps equally or
even more important, components of science literacy. For better or for worse,

science fiction is going to continue to contribute (along with science fact) to the information climate in which the work of science journalists is received.

Popular Beliefs

Journalism is not written on a blank slate but inscribed as one component in a complex information environment. At the same time, the people who compose journalism's audiences are hardly blank slates to begin with themselves. Were there no mass media, in other words, there would still be folk beliefs about science. Neither science journalism nor education, let alone a movie, book, or a television show, is interpreted independently of the context of preexisting belief.

For many of us, science itself is a belief system. To make this claim is not to assert that science is unreliable or its results untrue. It is merely to point out that members of the scientific community specifically, and the college-educated population more generally, accept scientific results because they believe in the scientific method and the general integrity of the community of scientists. If we read that medical researchers have found a new substance in food to be of nutritional value or to contribute to the prevention of disease, we may be a bit cynical about accepting those results at face value pending their confirmation in other research. We do not feel compelled to observe or oversee that research personally or to gather our own collaborative data, however, and in the end, we accept the consensus of the community of nutrition researchers.

This is so commonplace for us as members of the so-called educated elite that it seems odd even to be pointing it out, but I draw attention to the existence of these beliefs *as beliefs* in order to underscore the point that they are just that. We largely take science on faith and our beliefs here are not necessarily fully shared.

Mention popular culture about science to many folks and the image conjured up is one of supermarket tabloids making outlandish claims about aliens from outer space or reappearances of the dead. I have my doubts about how many readers of these claims take them literally and how many people pick up the tabloids while waiting in interminable grocery lines just to satisfy themselves that they are saner than many of their fellow human beings. Perhaps, like I do, they try to ferret out the usual nugget of probable fact over which the tabloid web has been spun, or they simply seek reassurance that the demarcation line between the worlds of fact and fantasy has not, after all, moved as a result of the introduction of incontrovertible evidence of alien abduction. (I sometimes watch *Unsolved Mysteries* and *Sightings* for similar reasons.)

Let's nevertheless assume that at least some readers take these publications and their contents at face value. However, just as mainstream journalism is not written on a blank slate, neither is tabloid journalism. Essentially, both the more outlandish claims of the tabloids and the information in more mainstream accounts must echo preexisting beliefs (perhaps thereby reinforcing them, it is true) in order to be accepted. No amount of exposure to claims about space aliens will make me believe in them, although under some circumstances I might eventually come to believe that most others believe in them.

All of this is by way of explaining what I mean when I say that part of the ambient information climate is popular belief and that these beliefs exist independently of mass media accounts. Medical beliefs (chicken soup will cure a cold), environmental beliefs (recycling will "fix" the "problem"), social beliefs (two-parent families are necessary to raising healthy children), and so on do not necessarily come from the media.

Political leaders may use the media to call attention to themselves and their stances on issues that they believe will appeal to their constituencies by drawing on these underlying beliefs ("welfare should be abolished"). Such actions momentarily highlight one set of the beliefs and perhaps partially reshape them to a new purpose, but the broad outlines of the beliefs on which these arguments play are preexisting. Religious beliefs are largely ignored by the media, who fear appearing partial on the subject no matter what they might choose to report. Yet, such beliefs obviously persist, and belief in science itself, although regularly propped up and perhaps even shaped in important ways by media accounts, is not an effect of the media any more than disbelief in science should be seen as a media effect. Both are largely the results of growing up in particular cultural and socioeconomic environments.

Popular beliefs about genetics are no exception. Whether people believe in the heritability of successfulness or criminality, for example, does not seem to follow from their exposure to media explanations of these things, but from their reliance on personal (family, e.g.) sources of information (Priest & Taylor, 1995).

Our culture is obsessed with biological explanations for our own social nature (Nelkin & Lindee, 1995). The foundation of the information climate for genetic science is popular belief in the heritability of various human characteristics and the related popular notion that "blood is thicker than water." We believe in the importance of biological heritage. This is inseparable from both our belief in, and our positive and negative responses to, genetic engineering. Is it okay to "mess around with" this heritage, or not?

This is an area that deserves more serious attention, but beliefs in the certainty or uncertainty of genetic fate may well be bound up with beliefs in such things as individual free will, the relation between hard work and achievement, and the existence of childhood genius. Such cultural beliefs are an important part of the broader context in which new information will be understood.

THE RELEVANCE OF CULTURE

So far, this chapter has considered biotechnology only in the context of the information and public opinion climate of the United States. The interplay of culture, politics, and science may be easier to see outside of what will be—for many readers—this taken-for-granted cultural context. According to one recent report, United Kingdom food retailers have refused to use U. S. soybeans in products carrying their labels because U. S. suppliers have declined to try to separate genetically engineered soy from the nonengineered product (Bentley, 1996); Monsanto was accused of trying to sneak its product in unnoticed. Meanwhile, in the United States, Food and Drug Administration (FDA) policy has been to regulate "product," not "process." In other words, if the end product of genetic engineering is not known to be unsafe and cannot be distinguished from a natural (nonengineered) variation, no one need know the difference.

The United Kingdom's public caution might reflect higher sensitivity to possible consumer concerns, resentment of perceived duplicity, distrust of big business, or the voice of experience with *Mad Cow disease*.[3] Whatever the reason, it clearly reflects a different political–cultural climate from that typical of the United States. In addition, Canadian officials were widely reported to have responded to an offer of "research funds" from Monsanto, made during a period when bST regulation was being debated there, as an attempted bribe. Somehow it is difficult for me to imagine quite the same interpretation of an otherwise similar chain of events emerging in the United States, where bST milk, largely unnoticed, is now routinely a portion of our food supply. Not incidentally, perhaps, Monsanto has finally acquired a majority stockholder stake in CalGene ("Monsanto takes," 1996).

---

[3]*Mad Cow disease* refers to Bovine spongiform encephalopathy (BSE), a condition causing brain deterioration in cows. Controversy over BSE has undermined public confidence in the beef supply, especially in the United Kingdom. The question of its transmissibility to people has also been controversial, although BSE does appear to be related to kuru and to Creutzfeldt-Jakob disease in humans.

These relatively minor rivalries and quarrels within the developed world are, of course, only one part of a bigger picture. The countries of the so-called less-developed or Third World are anxious for technologies that offer hope of feeding escalating human populations, yet they often lack both the research and the regulatory infrastructure to manage agricultural biotechnology. The Third World is clearly disadvantaged in this game. The altruistic motivations of many agricultural researchers in the developed world notwithstanding, these countries' dependence on imported technology is likely to increase.

It is now almost commonplace to point out that the scientific and technological know-how of laboratory-based First World science does not always transfer successfully or appropriately to farming systems in different cultural, political, geographic, climatological, and ecological contexts. Today's international trade rules open the door for multinational corporations to own patent rights to the genetic structure of indigenous species, an issue that received much attention from politicians and journalists in India but scant notice—perhaps not surprisingly—in the United States (Krishnakumar & Priest, 1995). Will Western science truly be the ongoing gift of the West to the East, of the North to the South? Alternatively, will it be another instrument of economic domination?

SO WHAT?

These complexities do not lead to simple conclusions about how news accounts should describe the promise of science that is still uncertain. When *Newsweek's* Sharon Begley (1995) reported that the Human Genome Project was in danger of failing to fulfill its perhaps overhyped promise, she was making a valid observation, but she was also ignoring the role of science journalism in generating the hype. If only breakthroughs are considered news, public disappointment with the real progress of science is almost inevitable, a problem we have recognized for some time but have hardly been able to solve (Friedman, Dunwoody, & Rogers, 1986).

Science journalism does not create a belief in science, but it can certainly nurture one, in the sense that communication researcher George Gerbner and others argued that television violence cultivates a belief in the pervasiveness of real-world violence (Gerbner & Gross, 1976). For better or for worse, science journalism can overstate or understate the ultimate potential—for good or for evil—of the uncertain promise of genetic engineering. Panacea or Frankenstein? Which will it be? It is hardly an issue that journalists are trained to analyze.

Indeed, going beyond the facts of science will be difficult for some well-trained science journalists and offensive to some well-trained scientists, but we need to make public policy for science in a world in which the future is, as always, only a dream. To do so democratically, we must dream together. Today's visions have a way of becoming tomorrow's realities. Science fiction may serve a serious social purpose.

Science's uncertain future needs to be presented as just that, the unknown and unknowable that we must nevertheless consider, lest it arrive before we are ready. If we are to continue to invest (socially and psychologically, not just economically) in this future, we must do so in full knowledge that its hazy outlines will always be only dimly visible from our vantage point of the present. If it fails us, let it fail on its own terms, not in terms of the expectations we have unreasonably imposed on it. If it creates new hazards for us, then let them be a cost we have considered. Otherwise, the price of future science is likely to be seen as too expensive, in terms of both dollars and dangers.

REFERENCES

Begley, S. (1995, October 9). Promises, promises. *Newsweek, 126*(15), pp. 60–62.

Bentley, S. (1996, August 23). Genetic soya excites wrath of food sector. *Marketing Week, 19*(22), p. 19.

Dugan, D. (1993). The real Jurassic Park (D. Dugan, Director). In D. Dugan (Producer), *NOVA*. Boston: WGBH Educational Foundation.

Evans, W., & Priest, S. (1995). Science content in social context. *Public Understanding of Science, 4*, 327–340.

Friedman, S. M., Dunwoody, S., & Rogers, C. L. (1986). *Scientists and journalists: Reporting science as news*. New York: The Free Press.

Gerbner, G., & Gross, L. (1976). Living with television: The violence profile. *Journal of Communication, 26*(2), 172–199.

Gumpert, G., & Drucker, S. (1994). Public space and urban life: Challenges in the communication landscape. *Journal of Communication, 44*(4), 169–177.

Hornig, S. (1990). Television's *NOVA* and the construction of scientific truth. *Critical Studies in Mass Communication, 7*(1), 11–23.

Hornig, S. (1991). *Monsanto Corporation and bovine somatotropin: A case study in failed public relations*. Center for Biotechnology Policy and Ethics, Texas A&M University College Station, TX. Discussion Paper CBPE 91–10.

Hornig, S. (1992). Framing risk: Audience and reader factors. *Journalism Quarterly, 69*, 79–90.

Krishnakumar, A., & Priest, S. (1995). *News of genetic controversy in India and the United States: International newspaper coverage of biodiversity, intellectual property rights, and GATT*. Center for Biotechnology Policy and Ethics, Texas A&M University College Station, TX. Discussion Paper CBPE 95–7.

Latour, B. (1993). *We have never been modern*. Cambridge, England: Harvard University Press.

Monsanto takes majority of CalGene (1996, August 5). *Chemical Marketing Reporter, 250*(6), p. 7.

Nelkin, D. (1995). *Selling science: How the press covers science and technology* (Rev. ed.). New York: Freeman.

Nelkin, D., & Lindee, M. (1995). *The DNA mystique: The gene as a cultural icon*. New York: Freeman.

Peters, J. D. (1993). Distrust of representation: Habermas on the public sphere. *Media, Culture and Society, 15*, 541–571.

Priest, S. (1995). Information equity, public understanding of science, and the biotechnology debate. *Journal of Communication, 45*, 39–54.

Priest, S., & Talbert, J. (1994). Mass media and the ultimate technological fix: Newspaper coverage of biotechnology. *Southwestern Mass Communication Journal, 10*(1), 76–85.

Priest, S., & Taylor, K. (1995). *The double helix and the popular imagination: Fatalism and certainty in public understanding of genetics*. Center for Biotechnology Policy and Ethics, Texas A&M University College Station. Discussion Paper No. CBPE 95–10.

Chapter 7

The Never-Ending Story of Dioxin

Sharon M. Friedman

Sharon M. Friedman is the Iacocca Professor and director of the Science and Environmental Writing Program at Lehigh University in Bethlehem, Pennsylvania. In addition to coediting **Scientists and Journalists: Reporting Science as News** *with Sharon Dunwoody and Carol L. Rogers in 1986, she is coauthor of* **Reporting on the Environment: A Handbook for Journalists** *and* **Risk Communication Manual for Electric Utilities.** *Her research focuses on how scientific and environmental issues are communicated to the public. Widely published on mass media coverage of a variety of scientifically uncertain topics, Friedman has served as a consultant to the President's Commission on the Accident at Three Mile Island and the United Nations Economic and Social Commission for Asia and the Pacific. She has conducted numerous workshops in Asia to train environmental journalists.*

Dioxin: The most deadly chemical ever made. Spread widely across the globe, it is being stored in human and animal fatty tissues causing numerous major and minor health effects.

Dioxin: Cancer-causing agent that contaminated Times Beach, Missouri, and led to the town's evacuation. People living near the Love Canal in Niagara Falls, New York, also claimed that its presence in basements and surrounding property caused numerous health effects.

Dioxin: Toxic contaminant in Agent Orange, the defoliant sprayed on vegetation in Vietnam. Some Vietnam veterans and their offspring said it gave them a litany of health problems. Vietnamese citizens blame Agent Orange for severe birth defects and other maladies.

Dioxin: One of the most powerful of the so-called endocrine disrupting chemicals. Some scientists believe it has caused reproductive problems and lowered immune responses in humans and a wide variety of mammals, birds and fish.

Each of these statements is a matter of scientific and public dispute. Despite more than 25 years of study by hundreds of scientists, and studies costing millions of dollars, the dangers of dioxin[1] are still a matter of great contention.

Some scientific questions can be answered easily within a few years, achieving consensus within the scientific community. However, the question of dioxin's toxicity is not one of them. For it and for other complex scientific controversies, consensus may not be reached even after many years. Lack of scientific consensus can result when scientists do not have knowledge—for example, when they do not know how a chemical or group of chemicals affects humans at the cellular level. It also can result from differing interpretations of the knowledge they do have or from both factors. In particular, scientific controversies about issues such as dioxin that span decades are problematic because they evolve. Throughout their evolution, these controversies often appear to become more rather than less uncertain, taking twists and turns with new discoveries or differing interpretations of highly complex data.

Tracking a long-term controversy such as dioxin is difficult enough for scientists who spend years studying the issue. For journalists, keeping abreast of all of the evolving scientific data and arguments is an almost impossible task because they must keep track of a wide range of other scientific and environmental news, not just one issue. Even if reporters keep up to date on a long-term controversy, space or air time limitations restrict their ability to provide context and background about it. At best, they report highlights or a digest of the action. As a consequence, the public reads and hears about long-term controversies in bits and pieces based on a new report, a new theory, or some other newsworthy event that grabs the media's attention. Such sporadic coverage heightens the uncertainty already attached to the issue, often confusing the public, which wonders why different theories or points of view exist.

Dioxin, in particular, has become a symbol of long-lived controversy and uncertainty—"toxic terror" to some and "overblown hyperbole" to others. The chemical came to the American public's attention in the late 1960s and 1970s, linked to a litany of now-famous environmental controversies—Love Canal, Agent Orange, and Times Beach. These are among the most significant events or issues in the history of the American environmental movement.

---

[1]*Dioxin* is a general term that describes a family made up of many chemicals. The most potent is 2,3,7,8-tetrachlorodibenzo-p-dioxin or 2,3,7,8-TCDD. The EPA uses *dioxin* in its draft reassessment report to refer not only to TCDD, but to every other polychlorinated dibenzodioxin and polychlorinated dibenzofurans as well (EPA, 1994b). It also classifies polychlorinated biphenyls (PCBs) as dioxins because of "structural similarities and the assumption that they are all toxic by the same biological mechanism" (Hanson, 1996, p. 22). The term *dioxin,* used in this chapter, unless otherwise noted, represents the whole family of chemicals.

Journalists eagerly chronicled these long-lasting sagas, devoting many pages of newspapers and magazines and hours of broadcast coverage over the years to tell the story of dioxin and those whose lives had become intertwined with it. Throughout this coverage, scientific uncertainty played a role in how the media unraveled the story. In the early years—the mid-1960s to the 1980s—the media appeared to have little doubt about dioxin's dangers. However, in the early 1990s, they increasingly focused on scientific uncertainty, leading to disputes among journalists about what information to report, what sources to quote, and how to write about the complicated science involved. In 1994, the issues of scientific uncertainty became even more clearly delineated in media coverage of a reassessment of dioxin's toxicity done by the U.S. Environmental Protection Agency (EPA).

To try to understand how well the media covered the long-term and complex dioxin issue, this chapter looks at snapshots of journalistic activity during three time periods. In the first period, from mid-1960 to the late 1980s, I examine media coverage of dioxin in *The New York Times* plus some other coverage viewed as problematic by reporters and communication researchers. In the second period, from 1991 to 1994, I explore scientific and journalistic disagreements over dioxin and the role that scientific uncertainty played in these disagreements. In the third period, from 1994 through 1995, my focus is on the release of the draft dioxin reassessment report by the EPA and its public and scientific review.

PERIOD ONE: EARLY MEDIA COVERAGE

During the early years of dioxin coverage, the media's focus on "disasters" such as Love Canal, Times Beach, and Agent Orange, helped increase public fear of chemical pollutants and their health effects, which led to stringent governmental regulations and urgent clean-up actions.

In this period, there seemed to be little uncertainty about dioxin. Both journalists and the sources they quoted strongly described dioxin as the most toxic chemical ever known. For example, a 1982 *New York Times* article related, "Dioxin has been demonstrated in animal tests to be the most acutely toxic compound made by man, according to the Environmental Protection Agency. Chronic exposure is associated with a broad range of serious health effects, including cancer" (Biddle, p. A17).

Not only was much of this coverage certain and strongly worded, but there was also a great deal of it. Communication researcher John Palen (1993) reported that *The New York Times* alone printed more than 700 articles on dioxin or related issues between 1964 and 1988. The main topics covered by *The New York Times*, he said, were defoliation in Vietnam and its effect on the war's phaseout; a chemical plant explosion at Seveso, Italy, which released a toxic cloud of dioxin; litigation by Vietnam veterans who believed they had been adversely affected by exposure to Agent Orange; and the evacuation of Times Beach, Missouri. An onslaught of dioxin coverage occurred in 1983, according to Palen, as "the Missouri and Agent Orange stories came together to generate a firestorm of controversy" (p. 3). That year, *The New York Times* alone ran 191 dioxin stories, but after an out-of-court settlement of the Agent Orange suit, coverage began to drop. By 1988, only 10 stories appeared in *The New York Times* on dioxin (Palen, 1993).

Although most of the coverage of these dioxin events showed a clear concern for human health effects, occasional critiques of the state of the science began to appear. In 1983, for example, an in-depth article in *The Washington Post* questioned the confused state of scientific knowledge about dioxin, pointing out differing scientific views about its dangers even then (Earley, 1983).

Dioxin media coverage also received criticism. In 1983, science reporter Paul Hayes of *The Milwaukee Journal* wrote that the media coverage of dioxin was hysterical and unsophisticated; he charged that the dangers of dioxin were "overstated" and "unwarranted." "Is dioxin deadly?" he asked. His answer: "Yes . . . for guinea pigs. . . and as far as is known now, not for humans" (Nelkin, 1995, p. 57).

Hayes was not the only one who thought dioxin media coverage had become hysterical. In 1983, the House of Delegates of the American Medical Association (AMA) passed a resolution that accused the media of making dioxin the subject of a "witch hunt" through "hysterical malreporting" that, through ignorance, damaged the lives of residents of contaminated areas. However, the AMA soon backed away from the "imprudent language" in its resolution (Peterson, 1983).

Whether Hayes and the AMA were correct about the hysterical nature of the dioxin media coverage, the sheer number of dioxin articles, according to sociologist Dorothy Nelkin (1995), helped give birth to public *chemophobia*, with dioxin serving as a symbol for all toxic chemicals. The media documented people's fears about toxic chemicals anecdotally through numerous victim stories. In these stories, people related that they and others in their families or towns had been exposed to toxic chemicals and that this exposure had led to cancer, other serious illnesses, and even death.

Public fears of chemicals also showed up in public opinion polls and studies by social scientists, such as Nancy Kraus, Torbjorn Malmfors, and Paul Slovic (1992), who concluded that the public appeared to equate even small exposures to toxic or carcinogenic chemicals with almost certain harm.

One consequence of this public fear and its media portrayal was a demand for more and tougher federal environmental regulations and clean ups. As a result, the EPA developed strict regulations on dioxin emissions to air, water, and land. In 1985, the EPA reassessed 2,3,7,8-TCDD, the most potent form of dioxin, and classified it as a probable human carcinogen based on animal data. In 1988, the EPA reassessed dioxin again, but this time its independent Science Advisory Board (SAB), which reviewed the study, suggested that the agency develop new methods for estimating human exposure to dioxin and for relating exposure levels to health risks (Schierow, 1995).

PERIOD TWO: SCIENTIFIC UNCERTAINTY AND THE JOURNALISTIC DEBATE

Following a decade when dioxin toxicity was seen as a near certainty and tough regulations were the rule, the 1990s brought growing controversy and uncertainty both in dioxin science and in media coverage. Affected industries began to chip away at regulations with reinterpretations of scientific data and even won some converts among environmental journalists.

In 1990, softening the strict dioxin government regulations became the focus of "a well-financed public relations campaign by the paper and chlorine industries," according to *The Wall Street Journal* (Bailey, 1992, p. A1). This campaign helped to create significant levels of uncertainty among some scientists, journalists, and government leaders, which led to a third EPA reassessment of dioxin. Two industry trade associations, the American Paper Institute and the Chlorine Institute, sponsored the campaign. They "aggressively promoted two pieces of evidence suggesting dioxin" was less dangerous than previously thought (Bailey, 1992, p. A1).

The first piece was a reanalysis of a 1978 study, on which all dioxin regulation had been based. Using newer technologies, the reanalysis found only half the number of cancer tumors caused by the chemical in rats than in the original study. The paper industry used this evidence to label dioxin a "weak carcinogen" (Bailey, 1992, p. A1).

The second piece of evidence grew out of a dioxin conference attended by many of the nation's leading dioxin experts. It was sponsored by the Chlorine Institute at the Banbury Center in Cold Spring Harbor, New York. One main focus of the conference was a discussion of how dioxin binds to a molecule called the *Ah receptor*, a protein that resides in human and other vertebrate cells. This discussion led to speculation about evidence of a threshold, or level, below which dioxin would not be harmful (Roberts, 1991).

The Banbury conference discussions, along with the 1988 SAB recommendations to look for new methods of measuring dioxin exposure levels in humans, led EPA Administrator William Reilly to announce, in April 1991, that the agency would once again reassess dioxin. The study was supposed to take only 1 year.

As the media covered these new developments, the public began to read and hear more about the uncertainties surrounding the chemical. For example, after the Banbury conference, the Chlorine Institute sent out a widely disseminated press packet including what it called a "consensus summary" that had not been reviewed by participants and misrepresented their conclusions. It said that the meeting reinforced the notion that "dioxin is much less toxic to humans than originally believed" (Roberts, 1991, p. 866). This information was widely discussed in the scientific and general media, giving a false impression of near scientific consensus on downgrading dioxin's toxicity.

Journalists also began to give more prominent coverage to scientists who questioned the degree of dioxin's toxicity. One prominent scientist who created a media furor was Vernon Houk, Director of the Center for Environmental Health of the Centers for Disease Control and Prevention (CDC) in Atlanta and one of the officials who had recommended the Times Beach evacuation. In August 1991, he told reporters that, given today's knowledge of dioxin, the evacuation of Times Beach was probably unnecessary.

Because most people had taken it on faith that dioxin was extremely toxic and needed to be heavily regulated, the growing uncertainty over its health effects created doubts not only about dioxin, but also about the EPA, environmental regulation, and science itself. The media reflected the public doubts. Editorials castigated the EPA for wasting taxpayers' dollars on unnecessary clean ups. They also criticized scientists for not making up their minds. A 1991 article in *Time* declared, "This kind of waffling [about the Times Beach evacuation] only reinforces public skepticism about the credibility of scientists, who seem to change their mind with bewildering regularity whether the subject is the danger of dioxin or the benefits of oat bran" (Gorman, 1991, p. 52).

Backlash and the Journalistic Debate

Scientific uncertainty about dioxin was not only troublesome to scientists and the public, but it also had an unanticipated effect on environmental journalists. It helped foster a serious disagreement among reporters about how dioxin in particular and environmental issues in general should be covered. Various environmental reporters appeared to choose sides in the scientific debate—if not directly in print, at least in their assumptions about the issue. Some supported those skeptical of dioxin's dangers, seeing little value in animal testing applied to human situations and believing that EPA's regulatory action level for dioxin was far too stringent. Others defended the science that had already condemned dioxin as a deadly chemical, seeing the questioning of its toxicity as motivated more by political attempts to soften regulations than scientific evidence.

The journalistic debate over dioxin was also catalyzed by a larger environmental backlash in the nation led by politically conservative organizations and individuals who argued, among other things, that the nation suffered from too much environmental regulation and its costs were far too great for the benefits received. Sponsored by a variety of industries and private land use advocates with interests in mining, timbering, and grazing, groups such as Wise Use advocated major changes in federal environmental laws.

Reflecting on backlash views, some reporters began to ask "tough questions about the effectiveness of the nation's environmental laws" (Carmody, 1995, p. 41). However, their questioning did not stop at environmental laws; they also began to query environmental journalism practices.

Chief among these critical journalists was Keith Schneider, then an environmental reporter for *The New York Times*. He told media critic David Shaw of the *Los Angeles Times* that he developed a new perspective on reporting environmental issues after the 1989 "media circus" caused by charges from an environmental organization that Alar, a growth regulator sprayed on some apples, caused cancer in children (Shaw, 1994a, p. A31). Schneider described his new approach by saying he was asking some pertinent questions about American environmental policy, such as:

- Are rules for cleaning up toxic wastes raising risks to public health in many instances instead of lowering them?
- Are the levels of dioxin most Americans are exposed to as dangerous as other environmental risks, like sunbathing?

- Has the United States spent too much energy worrying about pesticide residue in food and not enough on the much larger pesticide exposures regularly endured by millions of farmers and farm workers?
- Is more and "tougher" regulation truly the answer to solving problems associated with managing household and industrial wastes? Or is such a policy targeting rural America for new dumps, incinerators, and waste treatment plants? (Schneider, 1993b, pp. 1, 6)

Schneider's perspective drew criticism from many of his environmental journalism colleagues and environmental organizations, but drew praise from smaller numbers of journalists, many industries, and more conservative elements in the environmental arena.

Although other reporters, such as Boyce Rensberger of *The Washington Post,* Gregg Easterbrook, formerly of *Newsweek,* and John Stossel of *ABC News*, were also criticized for their coverage of various environmental issues, Schneider became a central figure in both the environmental backlash and the journalism debates. In part, this was because of the highly influential nature of *The New York Times,* whose stories are frequently carried in other newspapers or used by broadcast stations. More important, however, was the fact that he raised serious questions about whether environmental journalists were favoring environmental organizations as sources and whether these reporters were asking the right questions about issues. His coverage of dioxin, in particular, crystallized the journalistic debate.

Dioxin Coverage in *The New York Times*

Schneider's dioxin articles were usually long, well-documented, and included a number of viewpoints, although he frequently gave more space to antiregulatory sources than did other reporters. His writing from 1991 through 1994 suggested that the EPA had overreacted to dioxin and that the chemical probably was not as dangerous, particularly as a carcinogen, as scientists had thought.

Typical of his articles was one on August 15, 1991, which was headlined "U.S. Backing Away From Saying Dioxin Is a Deadly Peril." In it, Schneider reviewed scientific evidence used by the CDC's Vernon Houk and others to cast doubt on the carcinogenic nature of dioxin. Not typical, however, was an analogy he used in the first paragraph of the story, which drew a firestorm of criticism. He wrote, "Exposure to the chemical, once thought to be much more hazardous than chain smoking, is now considered by some experts to be no more risky than spending a week sunbathing" (p. A1). This article was widely reprinted in the nation's media and many publications incorrectly attributed the sunbathing analogy to government scientists.

The source of this important analogy became an issue in the journalistic debate. Schneider had credited anonymous experts. Freelance environmental writer Vicki Monks (1993), however, revealed in *American Journalism Review* that Schneider told her that he and his editors developed the analogy after they reviewed charts of risk factors for other hazards. According to Monks, Schneider said he had checked the comparison with Houk and two other epidemiologists. In another version reported by environmental journalist Kevin Carmody (1995) in *Columbia Journalism Review*, Schneider said the analogy was primarily the opinion of Houk, who later repudiated it as misleading.

Arguing Over the Science

However, this analogy was not the main reason that Schneider and other environmental journalists clashed over dioxin coverage. The journalists argued over the scientific uncertainty surrounding dioxin by trading blows over the quality of scientific sources they quoted and the various scientific reports they cited, seemingly trying to convince one another of the rightness of a particular point of view. Much of the argument among scientists was rooted in uncertainty over extrapolation from animal and cellular studies, threshold versus non-threshold effects, differences in computer models used to produce and analyze data, and different philosophies about levels of public safety. Reporters debated whose scientific interpretations were correct and which risk numbers or characterizations were more valid.

For example, Monks, in her *American Journalism Review* article, used an EPA scientist to dispute Schneider's interpretation of the science. There is "no scientific basis for suggesting that dioxin is less dangerous than previously thought," the EPA scientist was quoted as saying. Monks (1993) also asked how dioxin could be less dangerous when some scientists were finding possible noncancer effects of dioxin on the immune and reproductive systems "even at the minute levels in the general population" (p. 19).

In another example, Rae Tyson (1993), then an environmental reporter for *USA Today*, charged that Schneider had "relied on some questionable science to prove his point" (pp. 7–8). To counter this questionable science, Tyson cited a July 1993 study by the Institute of Medicine that concluded that "dioxin (in the herbicide Agent Orange) was linked 'to a range of health problems,'" as well as a number of other recent studies that had identified serious health risks (pp. 7–8).

Schneider responded to Tyson's charges by citing other scientific studies and standards. He pointed out, "In 1991, the World Health Organization officially set a new, higher limit for the amount of dioxin it considered safe for people to ingest daily. That level was 1,600 times higher than the level set by the EPA" (Schneider, 1993a, p. 5).

He rebutted Monks' charges by arguing that her *American Journalism Review* article was "largely based on an exceedingly narrow view, which she tries to legitimize by quoting experts representing one side of the dioxin issue." Schneider said Monks had missed one of the most important points in the dioxin debate—"how much weight to give animal data"—since there is a "disagreement among scientists on what the animal studies mean for people" (Schneider, 1993a, p. 5).

Basic to this journalistic disagreement was the quality of the sources used, the manner in which scientific uncertainty was presented, and the assumptions the journalists themselves made about dioxin's dangers.

Consequences of the Journalistic Debate

The journalistic argument over how to cover the uncertain science of dioxin probably made readers and viewers even more confused about the chemical, the health effects of chemical pollutants in general, and the degree of government regulation necessary to control such pollutants. Although *The New York Times* declared that dioxin was no more dangerous than a week's sunbathing, other newspapers said it was still as deadly as ever, particularly because of suspected noncancer effects on the immune, reproductive, and developmental systems.

Was the highly influential *New York Times* correct in casting doubt on the dangers of dioxin and were other publications and newscasts scaring people needlessly? A few media critics began to assert just that. For example, media critic Shaw (1994b) wrote a long, three-part series for the *Los Angeles Times* called "Living Scared: Why Do the Media Make Life Seem So Risky?" He devoted a half-page article (1994a) to Schneider's views on environmental journalism and the debate over his controversial coverage of dioxin. Editorials in various publications, including the journal *Science* (Abelson, 1993, 1994), echoed concerns about media scare tactics. ABC television correspondent John Stossel (1994) criticized media coverage of environmental issues, including dioxin, in a joint prime-time program and a special edition of *Nightline* called

"Are We Scaring Ourselves to Death?" that aired on the same night in 1994. Three years later, Stossel (1997) again attacked media coverage of dioxin, in particular, and environmental journalism, in general, in his ABC special on "Junk Science."

The journalistic debate over dioxin from 1991 to 1994 and its coverage created doubt in some people's minds about the credibility of environmental journalists and the techniques they use to cover stories. During this time Schneider argued that many of his journalistic opponents favored environmental sources and were not objective. His critics retorted that he favored industry and politically conservative sources. The argument polarized the environmental journalism community and perhaps led some editors and news directors to doubt the community's veracity.

To be sure, the environmental debate also had its positive effects: It made environmental journalists reexamine their beliefs, their writing philosophies, and their portrayal and quotation of sources. Such self-evaluation helps strengthen relatively new fields, such as environmental journalism, as they mature. As will be shown, it also may have helped tone down some of the more sensational subsequent dioxin stories and led to improved coverage.

PERIOD THREE: THE MEDIA AND THE EPA DRAFT REASSESSMENT REPORT

The history of the EPA's draft dioxin reassessment report has two important chapters. The first was the release of the draft itself in 1994. The second was the draft's review by the EPA's independent SAB, which had to approve it before it could become final and serve as the basis for further government regulation. Possibly reflecting lessons learned during the journalistic debate period, media coverage of the release of the draft report appeared to be more careful than earlier coverage. However, general media coverage of the SAB review—which sought changes in important parts of the draft report—was almost nonexistent, although it was heavily covered by the trade and scientific press.

The Draft Dioxin Reassessment Report

The draft report was an important document for the EPA, the affected industries, and the public. In particular, the EPA had a very complex series of points to get across to the public. The agency made special efforts from 1991 on to keep the reassessment process open and visible to the public, media, and scientific communities through public meetings and workshops where scientists reviewed draft documents (EPA, 1994a). There was some media coverage of almost all of these activities, especially in 1992.

Other interested parties also tried to capture the media's attention while trying to put their own spin on the draft report's findings, particularly as the release of the document drew near. According to one reporter, many U.S. industry associations and businesses "besieged reporters with news releases downplaying the damaging effects of dioxin" (Bronstein, 1994). Environmental groups and coalitions held dozens of news briefings around the country. For example, Sierra Club activists held more than 50 press conferences throughout the United States on September 13, 1994, the day the draft report was released. They called for a phaseout of the industrial processes that produce dioxin (Sierra Club, 1994).

What the Draft Report Said

The draft reassessment consisted of six volumes totaling more than 2,000 pages (EPA, 1994c). It was divided into two major parts, the Exposure Assessment Document and the Health Assessment Document. It reaffirmed the EPA's 1985 assessment "with greater confidence" that dioxin was a proven animal carcinogen and a probable human carcinogen. The draft reassessment also declared that, at some doses, dioxin exposure could result in noncancer health concerns in humans, including developmental and reproductive effects, immune suppression, and disruption of regulatory hormones (EPA, 1994a, 1994b).

The draft report identified medical and municipal waste incinerators as the major dioxin sources in the environment. However, officials noted that they did not have sufficient information about emissions from known sources and requested additional data from industry and other groups.

The report explained that the pathway for exposure to dioxin for humans is primarily via airborne dioxins that settle on plants and are then passed on through the food chain and deposited in fatty tissue (EPA, 1994a, 1994b).

How the Media Covered the Report

The media covered the draft report during two major periods in 1994. In May, *The New York Times'* Keith Schneider once again played a controversial and influential role, scooping the competition with a leaked summary of the risk characterization chapter from the EPA's draft report. His article was controversial because it emphasized dioxin's noncancerous effects and down-played its cancer-causing potential. This was clearly evident in the headline, "Fetal Harm is Cited as Primary Hazard in Dioxin Exposure." In his first paragraph, Schneider (1994a) made his point:

> In a report on dioxin, a group of scientists at the Environmental Protection Agency has concluded that cancer is not the most serious health hazard at common exposure levels. Of greater concern, the report said, are subtle effects on fetal development and the immune system that may be the result of very low levels of exposure. (p. A1)

His article became quite influential because it was widely reprinted or quoted by other media outlets. Most emphasized Schneider's point of view that cancer was not the main problem with dioxin, casting doubt on long-held public views about dioxin's cancer-causing properties.

Although highlighting new findings about noncancer effects may have been appropriate, Schneider's characterization of noncancer effects as more worthy of concern than cancer effects was inaccurate, according to a leading EPA scientist working on the report (Shaw, 1994a). Some journalists also appeared to disagree with Schneider's view and wrote very different interpretations of the leaked chapter. For example, those at *The Wall Street Journal* wrote that the EPA report "will find 'there is no evidence that dioxin is any less harmful than previously thought...,'" and that the draft report "will reaffirm that dioxin poses a cancer risk to humans" (Noah & Aeppel, 1994, p. A16).

The second major coverage period began when the EPA released its draft report on September 13, 1994. Once again, there was a leak, this time to *The Washington Post*, which published a front-page story on September 12th. This article's lead paragraph said, "The Environmental Protection Agency has concluded in a long-awaited study that dioxin—a class of potent chemical compounds that works its way into fish, meat and dairy products—probably causes cancer in humans" (Lee, p. A1).

The Associated Press (1994a) also wrote a story about the report on September 12th. A version of the story appearing in the *Chicago Tribune* started this way: "Exposure to dioxin, even at minute levels, poses cancer risks and wider health concerns than previously suspected including possible damage to the immune and reproductive systems, concludes an Environmental Protection Agency study" (p. 4).

National Public Radio's *Morning Edition* broadcast a discussion about the draft report on September 12th, featuring four prominent members of the dioxin debate, as did *CNN News* that evening. Other media outlets, not so fortunate to have advance information that day, ran prerelease stories outlining what to expect from the report, quoting both environmental and industry experts.

The New York Times did not publish a story on September 12th and ran an Associated Press story headlined, "E.P.A. Affirms Health Dangers From Dioxin" on September 13th. Its lead paragraph was more conservative than the one that had appeared in the *Chicago Tribune:* "In a draft report, a Federal agency has affirmed the health dangers from exposure to the chemical dioxin, but held back from declaring it a known cause of cancer in people" (Associated Press, 1994b, p. A14).

This article was followed up with a longer one by Schneider (1994b) on September 14th, which continued to emphasize the view that dioxin was not as dangerous as people thought. His lead was more cautious than those of other reporters: "Calling the potential risk to human health from dioxin worrisome but significantly less than that posed by smoking, the Environmental Protection Agency said today that it was ready to take steps to reduce the chance that people would be exposed to harm from the toxic chemical" (p. A15). Schneider reported that the EPA called dioxin a probable human carcinogen, but he put that fact in the fifth paragraph of his story, which was a lower placement than that found in most other stories about the report.

This time his story had little influence on the rest of the media. Most reporters put the EPA's view that dioxin was a probable human carcinogen high in the story and also paid attention to the noncancer effects and its presence in the food chain. Four other reporters used the smoking comparison—which was in the EPA report—but they put it quite low in their stories. So, in two major instances in 1994, different interpretations of the EPA's findings by Schneider and journalists from some of the nation's other major newspapers gave the public a somewhat contradictory picture about the EPA's overall findings on dioxin's dangers, particularly those related to cancer.

Quality of the Newspaper Coverage

A content analysis of 36 newspaper articles and 4 editorials or columns about the release of the draft report, plus a review of magazine, wire service, and broadcast coverage in the Lexis–Nexis database,[2] showed that some articles

---

[2]Using the terms "dioxin and reassessment report or study or review and date = September 1994," I found 123 newspaper articles in the Major Papers category of the Lexis–Nexis database. This category included 39 major U.S. and 19 foreign newspapers in the spring of 1997. After a review to remove irrelevant or foreign articles, I downloaded 66 U.S. articles for further study. From these, I eliminated 9 letters to the editor and 17 articles or editorials that were not on the topic. Some articles regarding dioxin and the draft reassessment report might have been missed if they were not located by Lexis under the above key words.

were superficial and predictable, given past coverage of dioxin and other risk topics. Surprisingly, however, some aspects of the coverage improved over earlier stories, perhaps indicating that reporters had absorbed some of the points made in the journalistic debate in the early 1990s. Forty-five percent of the articles included more than two paragraphs explaining the potentially cancerous effects of dioxin, whereas 35% did so for the effects of dioxin on the immune, endocrine, and reproductive systems. The articles carefully treated dioxin concerns to avoid unnecessary public panic about dioxin's presence in the food chain. No article sensationalized the food aspect. Most named beef, fish, chicken, and mother's milk as possible dioxin sources, but they also included a statement from an EPA official that the benefits of a balanced diet outweighed dioxin's risks.

Most articles mentioned the tentative nature of the EPA draft reassessment report, a departure from the May 1994 coverage on the leaked chapter. The most frequent comments were that it was a draft or that it would undergo scientific review or public comment.

Almost two thirds of the articles included concerns, questions about, and criticism related to scientific uncertainty issues, even if they did not go into detail about them. The majority wrote about data gaps in the report and the agency's need for further information, which EPA officials themselves had pointed out in both a news release and at a news briefing. Other articles discussed disagreements about interpretations of the scientific data in the report from both the environmental and industrial sides. Greenpeace, for example, was quoted as saying that the EPA had neglected dozens of dioxin sources and underestimated actual emissions (Knickerbocker, 1994). The most commonly reported industrial complaint was that the EPA was overstating the science when it inferred that health effects would occur in humans (Schneider, 1994b).

There was good balance among sources used by reporters, which is not too surprising because of the aggressive "spin control" activities pursued by diverse and numerous interested parties. This balance was a considerable improvement over past scientific and environmental coverage in which government officials had been far more heavily quoted than other sources, and statements made by environmental sources often had outnumbered those made by industry representatives (Friedman, Villamil, Suriano, & Egolf, 1996). In contrast, 70% of the reassessment articles included statements from all three groups—EPA officials, environmentalists, and industry spokespersons.

In treating issues of scientific uncertainty highlighted in the report, the newspapers also did somewhat better than expected, given previous studies of media coverage of risk issues. Key scientific questions in the report were discussed in a large percentage of the articles, including where dioxin in the atmosphere comes from, how it is transported and deposited, how much dioxin is present in food sources; and how much risk dioxin poses to humans—both for cancer and for its effects on the hormonal, immune, and reproductive systems—given current amounts of dioxin found in people's bodies. Even the question about how well data from animal tests applied to humans was briefly discussed in almost half of the articles. However, the more technical issues, such as what types of models should have been used in the risk characterization and the EPA's use of a controversial technique to handle a multichemical approach, received little or no coverage. Clearly, these last subjects were not easy for reporters to understand and explain.

Coverage in Other Media

Unfortunately, general magazines, television, and radio did not do as well as newspapers in covering the draft report. Only two general magazines, *Time* and *Newsweek*, ran articles about the draft report, compared to heavy coverage in scientific, environmental, or technical magazines or journals. Local broadcast coverage consisted of brief one- or two-line items, with strong language and few caveats, containing no discussions of scientific uncertainty or mention that this was a draft report. A typical news broadcast said, "A new federal EPA report out tomorrow raises concerns that humans may be hurt by dioxin at very low levels" (WNBC-TV, 1994). National television network coverage was sparse. NBC appeared to be the only major network that mentioned the draft report, with anchor Tom Brokaw (1994) reading two sentences about it. The *MacNeil/Lehrer News Hour* on PBS (Warner & Lehrer, 1994) also gave the draft report only brief play. A longer story appeared on CNN (Barger, 1994) and was very strongly worded—bordering on the sensational—about dioxin's health risks, again with no mention that this was a draft report.

The best broadcast coverage appeared on National Public Radio, which aired two stories. Both balanced their sources, explained many of the controversial points about the EPA's findings (including arguments over threshold levels and animal studies), and noted that the report would require further peer review (Harris, 1994).

The Science Advisory Board Review and Its Coverage

As noted earlier, the release of the draft report was not the end of the dioxin reassessment process. The EPA held a series of public meetings for comment and then submitted the draft report to its SAB in December 1994. The SAB appointed 39 outside scientists to a review committee, which met for 2 days in May 1995 to hear briefings by EPA staff and public comments on the EPA's reassessment.

The SAB review committee released its report in September 1995. Although it commended the EPA for doing a "very credible and thorough job" and generally approved of the Exposure Assessment Document and the first seven chapters of the Health Assessment Document, it did not endorse the last two chapters (EPA, 1995).

Its problem with chapter 8 on dose-response was the EPA's reliance on a particular type of model, called a *linear nonthreshold model*, for estimating cancer risk. The review committee suggested that alternative risk models be evaluated that posed little increase in risk at very low levels of dioxin exposure. There also was concern about whether dioxin-like compounds other than 2,3,7,8-TCDD were likely to increase human cancer incidence.

Chapter 9, which summarized the previous chapters and characterized the risk, seemed to create the most problems for the review committee. The committee felt that this chapter had not been as thoroughly peer reviewed as the other chapters and that it had a tendency to overstate the possibility of the danger from dioxin (although several members of the committee disagreed with this statement). The committee pointed out that important uncertainties associated with the EPA's conclusions were not fully identified and that the characterization of the noncancer risk was not performed in a way that could lead to meaningful analysis of risk management alternatives (EPA, 1995).

The review committee asked the EPA to rework these two chapters, have them peer reviewed, and then bring them back for final review. When all this is accomplished, the EPA will issue its final dioxin reassessment report. As of January 1999, the EPA projected a 1999 release.

Although coverage of the draft dioxin reassessment report was fairly extensive in 1994, coverage of the SAB review was almost nonexistent in the general media in 1995, despite three major news opportunities: the public hearing in May, the release of the report in September, and a Congressional hearing in December.[3] There were some news reports, a few op-ed articles, and at least

---

[3]These findings are based on searches in the Lexis–Nexis database using the Major Papers, Papers, Wires, Magazines, and Scripts categories, with the search terms described previously plus other much broader search terms. A search on other databases was also done. Finally, *The New York Times, The Washington Post, The Wall Street Journal, Time,* and *Newsweek* were reviewed during the months of May, September, and December 1995 in microfiche and actual copies to make sure articles were not being missed by the database searches.

one editorial about the May 1995 open meeting, most of which emphasized comments that were critical of the draft report and challenged the science employed in it. For example, an op-ed piece in *The Wall Street Journal* concluded that "EPA's research was policy or politically driven" (Kelly, 1995). An editorial in *The Detroit News* (1995) charged that the EPA had:

> misconstrued scientific data to magnify the health threat of dioxin, a byproduct of fundamental industrial processes. In a harsh attack on agency credibility, a scientific advisory panel recently rejected as deceptive EPA's conclusions about dioxin risks. The agency's latest attempt to subvert science only strengthens the case for federal regulatory reform. ("More lies," p. A10)

The editorial's vitriolic tone drew several protest letters to the editor. So did the op-ed piece in *The Wall Street Journal,* including one from the SAB chairperson responding to the charge that the EPA's decisions were not based on sound science by calling the charge "misguided and misleading" (Schierow, 1995).

Yet, beyond this minor tempest, the SAB review received little coverage. Only a few newspapers, including *The Columbus Dispatch, Bangor Daily News,* and *The Washington Times,* appear to have discussed what the SAB had to say. The United Press International wire service briefly mentioned in a longer story on dioxin that the SAB had "confirmed the draft report's conclusions" but "had not yet reached consensus as to the EPA's analysis of health risks" (Kaiser, 1995). Both Greenwire and PR Newswire carried stories about the SAB report, but few newspapers appeared to have picked them up. In contrast, SAB activities were carefully detailed in numerous technical magazines and newsletters for scientific and industrial stakeholders.

Unfortunately, members of the public—also stakeholders in the dioxin debate—did not find out from the mass media what the SAB said about the quality of the EPA draft report and whether its findings were valid. Given that the SAB review probably will force changes in the EPA findings that the media so readily trumpeted in September 1994, the lack of general media follow-up did not serve the public well.

The Contradictory Media Performance

The response of the media to the draft reassessment report and then to the SAB review appears contradictory. Media coverage of the draft report's release was indeed careful and balanced, but there were few follow-up stories about the SAB review to continue to keep readers informed about the situation. These actions appear puzzling, but they can be explained.

The improved coverage of the draft report could be related to three factors in addition to the influence of the journalistic debate of the early 1990s. First, the report's major findings were leaked in May so there were no startling new developments. Because many environmental journalists were already familiar with the complex issues involved, it may have been easier for them to write more careful stories.

Second, EPA officials made an effort with reporters to prevent public panic and point out the data gaps and the need for additional information. The agency also tried to ensure, according to an EPA press officer, that reporters would not assume that the downplayed cancer effect reported in May in *The New York Times* was the "sum and substance of the report" and that the word *draft* was not ignored (L. Hester, personal communication on January 22, 1996). Judging from the articles reviewed, the EPA accomplished its goals and helped provide more effective and less sensational coverage.

Third, the aggressive behavior of industrial and environmental information sources provided additional information to help journalists understand the different viewpoints about some of the complex scientific issues in the report.

In contrast, the lack of coverage of the SAB report could have been because the issues were "too complex and tentative," according to an EPA official who was designated to work with the SAB (S. Rondberg, personal communication on January 22, 1996). Another EPA employee suggested that perhaps editors did not give reporters the opportunity to follow up on the draft report, noting this is "symptomatic of the media's decreasing interest in environmental journalism" (L. Hester, personal communication on January 22, 1996).

Of course, the draft reassessment report and its SAB review were not the only dioxin stories being covered during this period. Hundreds of other dioxin stories appeared in newspapers throughout the United States and in at least 10 other countries. Many of these stories trumpeted the dangers of dioxin contamination and told of scientific disputes over its health effects, adding to the public uncertainty about the chemical.

There is little doubt that dioxin will remain in the news in the future both by itself and as part of the larger debate on endocrine-disrupting chemicals, continuing to create uncertainty, controversy, and fear among the public. Of course, another potential newsmaker will be the EPA's final dioxin reassessment report, which, as of this writing, has taken more than 7 years to appear.

CONCLUSIONS

Although dioxin is important as an issue in its own right, it is also representative of other long-term uncertain scientific concerns. In such issues, scientific knowledge changes: It expands and evolves over time. As scientific methodology improves, scientists know more about what they do and do not know.

Unfortunately, covering long-term issues in which the science is uncertain and keeps changing is not the media's forte. This dioxin case study has shown that the media had serious problems covering long-term aspects of this issue. True, reporters told people about short-term events such as the evacuation of Times Beach or the results of the Banbury dioxin conference and their coverage improved somewhat with the release of the EPA's draft reassessment report. However, most journalists did not help readers and viewers understand the more technical elements of the dioxin reassessment, including the difficulty scientists have in determining safe dioxin exposure levels or the many different factors that are involved in determining levels of risk. Rarely did they tell people how much knowledge scientists lacked about some of the elements in the risk estimate equation.

Such problematic media coverage has repercussions not only in the case of dioxin, but also in other long-term uncertainty issues. Coverage of uncertain science that only provides highlights or centers on events and leaves out context tends to lead people to expect black-and-white answers to complex questions. Are they and their families in danger or not? Is a particular food or drug good or bad for them? Is a new technology the answer to their prayers or the beginning of a nightmare? Because of the uncertainties inherent in the scientific process, answers to such questions are usually tentative and colored in shades of gray. However, many journalists do not convey the gray, tentative nature of science. Because media stories usually provide little continuity over time, people do not see the evolution of the science. As a result, some people question both the veracity of science and the government regulations based on it.

Some news organizations have sought a better way to cover long-term, complex issues by putting more in-depth information on their World Wide Websites. For those people who have access to the Internet, these enhanced media resources can provide more information, explanation, history, context, and perspective, as well as links to related sites, to help them better understand complicated and evolving science. However, websites are an imperfect solution because many people might not have the time or the desire to look up additional information, believing that the whole story should appear in print or on the air. Then there is the important question of the accuracy and potential biases of websites and not all Americans have Internet access. Among those who do not are people in economic classes that often have the most at stake in environmental debates.

Other solutions for more effective coverage of long-term uncertain science besides the imperfect Internet must be sought. Two solutions stand out as important. First, scientific and other organizations need to provide more and better explanations, in addition to contextual information about uncertain science issues, so that journalists can better understand and subsequently explain them in their stories. Concerted explanatory efforts by the EPA and various interest groups appeared to contribute positively to the coverage of the dioxin draft reassessment report. However, such information would best serve the public's needs if it did not have a great deal of spin.

The second important solution would be for editors and news directors to become more innovative in the way they cover stories about long-term uncertain science. Instead of treating them as everyday, discrete stories keyed to events, they should consider longer, more feature-oriented approaches that would provide room for explanations and context. Many more well-illustrated, in-depth series of articles on long-term, uncertain scientific issues are needed. That several recent ones have won Public Service Pulitzer Prizes should encourage more efforts.[4]

Media organizations could also duplicate for other uncertain subjects the innovative approach attempted in the fall of 1997 by *The New York Times,* with its unprecedented coverage of climate change issues. Concentrating on detailing and explaining the scientific, political, economic, and social ramifications of the issue, the newspaper published more than 200 articles that mentioned the subject between September and December. It also published a 12-page separate Sunday section devoted to the United Nations Conference on Climate Change in Kyoto, Japan ("Global warming, 1997"). The sheer quantity of stories, if nothing else, drew readers' attention to this uncertain issue in a new way, indicating its growing importance to the country and the world.

Such innovative efforts need to continue and grow. The media must recognize the obstacles inherent in covering long-term scientific issues, such as dioxin, and find fresh approaches to them. Only in this way will they provide coverage that allows the public to understand the evolving nature of uncertain science.

---

[4]Recent series on long-term uncertain issues that won the Pulitzer Prize for Public Service in 1997, 1996, and 1992, respectively, are "Oceans of Trouble," *The Times-Picayune,* New Orleans, LA; "Boss Hog," *The News and Observer,* Raleigh, NC; and "Sierra in Peril," *The Sacramento (CA) Bee.*

ACKNOWLEDGMENTS

Sincere thanks are owed to my coeditors for their valuable comments. A medal is owed to Kenneth A. Friedman, who read and helped edit many drafts of this chapter. Thanks also to Megan Fitzpatrick, Amy Mizoras, and Brenda Egolf for their help with coding and preliminary analysis of the 1994 draft dioxin report coverage.

REFERENCES

Abelson, P. H. (1993, July 23). Toxic terror: phantom risks; two books balance the debate on environmental hazards (editorial). *Science, 261,* 407.
Abelson, P. H. (1994, August 26). Chlorine and organochlorine compounds; EPA Ban (editorial). *Science, 265,* 1155.
Associated Press. (1994a, September 12). Dioxin dangers may be worse than suspected. *Chicago Tribune,* p. 4.
Associated Press. (1994b, September 13). E.P.A. affirms health dangers from dioxin. *The New York Times,* p. A14.
Bailey, J. (1992, February 20). How two industries created a fresh spin on the dioxin debate. *The Wall Street Journal,* p. A1.
Barger, B. (1994, September 12). EPA study warns of dangers of dioxins for humans. CNN News Transcript #875-6.
Biddle, W. (1982, December 16). Toxic chemicals imperil flooded town in Missouri. *The New York Times,* p. A17.
Brokaw, T. (1994, September 12). *The Nightly News.* NBC.
Bronstein, S. (1994, September 13). EPA agrees: Dioxin likely causes cancer, birth defects. *The Atlanta Journal-Constitution,* p. A5.
Carmody, K. (1995, May/June). It's a jungle out there: Environmental journalism in an age of backlash. *Columbia Journalism Review,* 40–45.
Earley, P. (1983, February 27). Dioxin is still a mystery: A $33 million decision despite scientific confusion. *The Washington Post,* p. B5.
Environmental Protection Agency (1994a, June). *Estimating exposure to dioxin-like compounds,* Volume 1: Executive Summary, Review Draft.
Environmental Protection Agency (1994b, August). *Health Assessment Document for 2,3,7,8-Tetrachlorodibenzo-p-Dioxin (TCDD) and related compounds,* Volume III, Review Draft.
Environmental Protection Agency. (1994c, September 13). *EPA calls for new dioxin data to complete reassessment process* [news release] R-219.
Environmental Protection Agency. (1995, September). *Reevaluating dioxin: Science Advisory Board's review of EPA's reassessment of dioxin and dioxin-like compounds.* Document # EPA-SAB-EC-95-021.
Friedman, S. M., Villamil, K., Suriano, R., & Egolf, B. (1996). Alar and apples: Newspapers, risk and media responsibility. *Public Understanding of Science, 5,* 1–20.

Global warming: A preview to the Kyoto Conference. (1997, December 1). *The New York Times*, pp. F1–12.

Gorman, C. (1991, August 26). The double take on dioxin. *Time*, 52.

Hanson, D. (1996, January 1). Dioxin reassessment eyed by House panel. *Chemical & Engineering News*, 22.

Harris, R. (1994, September 12). EPA takes second look at dioxin. *Morning Edition*, National Public Radio. Dioxin remains a danger in the environment. *All Things Considered*, National Public Radio.

Jackson, T., Marshall, B., McQuaid, J. & Schleifstein, M., (1996, March 24-31). Oceans of trouble (8-part series). *The Times-Picayune*. [Online]. Available: http://www.pulitzer.org/year/1997/public-service/works.

Kaiser, J. (1995, May 18). Toxic chemical travels in wind. *UPI Washington News*.

Kelly, K. (1995, June 29). Cleaning up EPA's dioxin mess. *The Wall Street Journal*, p. A16.

Knickerbocker, B. (1994, September 21). Exhaustive US report on dioxin satisfies few in scientific debate. *The Christian Science Monitor*, p. 2.

Kraus, N., Malmfors T., & Slovic, P. (1992). Intuitive toxicology: Expert and lay judgments of chemical risks. *Risk Analysis, 12,* 228–229.

Knudson, T. (1991, June 9-13). The Sierra in peril. (5-part series). *The Sacramento Bee.* 6/9, p.A1; 6/10, pp. A1 & A10; 6/11, pp. A1, A12-13; 6/12, pp. A1 & A9-10; 6/13, pp. A1 & A15-16.

Lee. G. (1994, September 12). EPA study links dioxin to cancer; Report stops short of calling chemical a known carcinogen. *The Washington Post*, p. A1.

Monks, V. (1993, June). See no evil. *American Journalism Review,* 18–25.

More lies from EPA [editorial]. (1995, June 9). *The Detroit News*, p. A10.

Nelkin, D. (1995). *Selling science: How the press covers science and technology* (Rev. ed.). New York: Freeman.

Noah T., & Aeppel, T. (1994, May 11). Politics & policy: EPA reaffirms health hazards posed by dioxin. *The Wall Street Journal*, p. A16.

Palen, J. A. (1993, February). *Dioxin in the news.* Paper presented at the annual meeting of the American Association for the Advancement of Science, Boston.

Peterson, C. (1983, July 1). Imprudent language: AMA backpedals on dioxin. *The Washington Post,* p. A1.

Roberts, L. (1991, February 22). Flap erupts over dioxin meeting; Participants angered over industry trade group's press release misrepresenting their views and research findings. *Science, 261,* 866.

Schierow, L. (1995, October 24). *Dioxin: Reassessing the risk. Congressional Research Service Report.* [Online]. Available: http://c3.org/library/crsdioxin.html.

Schneider, K. (1991, August 15). U.S. backing away from saying dioxin is a deadly peril. *The New York Times*, p. A1.

Schneider, K. (1993a, September). Debating dioxin [letter to the editor]. *American Journalism Review,* 5–6.

Schneider, K. (1993b, Fall). Toxic debates. *SEJournal, 3,* 1, 6–7.

Schneider, K. (1994a, May 11). Fetal harm, not cancer, is called the primary threat from dioxin. *The New York Times*, p. A1.

Schneider, K. (1994b, September 14). E.P.A. moves to reduce health risks from dioxin. *The New York Times*, p. A15.

Shaw, D. (1994a, September 11). Controversial stories go against the grain. *Los Angeles Times,* p. A31.

Shaw, D. (1994b, September 11–13). Living scared: Why do the media make life seem so risky? [three-part series]. *Los Angeles Times.*

Sierra Club. (1994, November). *Club calls for dioxin phaseout* [Online]. Available: http://www.sierraclub.org/planet/199411/alert-dioxin.html.

Stith, P., & Warrick, J. (1995, February 19-26). Boss hog: North Carolina's pork revolution (5-part series). *The News and Observer* (Raleigh). [Online] Available URL: http://www.nando.net/sproject/hogs/hoghome.html.

Stossel, J. (1994, April 21). Are we scaring ourselves to death? ABC New Special and *Nightline* Special: Are we scaring ourselves to death: The people respond. ABC, Victor Neufeld, executive producer.

Stossel, J. (1997, January 9). Junk Science: What you know that may not be so. ABC News Special, Victor Neufeld, executive producer.

Tyson, R. (1993, Fall). Controversy has up and down sides. *SEJournal, 3,* 1, 7–8.

Warner, M., & Lehrer, J. (1994, September 13). *The MacNeil/Lehrer NewsHour* Transcript #5053. PBS.

WNBC-TV, (1994, September 12). 11 p.m. news. New York.

Chapter 8

An Uncertain Social Contract: The Case of Human Resources for Science

Daryl E. Chubin

*Daryl E. Chubin is division director for research, evaluation, and communication in the Directorate for Education and Human Resources of the National Science Foundation (NSF), currently serving as senior policy associate in the National Science Board Office of NSF. A former university professor, he served in 1997 as assistant director for social and behavioral sciences in the White House Office of Science and Technology Policy, and continues to teach university courses in public policy. He has written or coauthored six books, including **Rethinking Science as a Career: Perceptions and Realities in the Physical Sciences.***

SETTING THE CONTEXT

The Big Crunch

The scientific research community of the 1950s and 1960s was the beneficiary of peacetime prosperity and uninterrupted growth in federal funding. Science's social contract, fueled by the Cold War, was good for America's economic growth and for science, but it was too good to last. The research community, which had had fewer researchers and research universities, ample job opportunities, little international competition or doubt about U.S. research performance, and entrusted the judgment of scientific merit to expert peers, became, by the late 1970s, bigger and more diffuse. After 20 years of enormous postwar expansion of academia and the creation of corporate and government research laboratories all around the United States, the federal government could no longer meet scientists' expectations of sustained funding without sustained evidence of benefit to the nation's security, productivity, and quality of life.

Physicist David Goodstein (1995) called this change the *Big Crunch*. For scientists, and the policymakers who sought their advice, the vision of government as benefactor contained in *Science—The Endless Frontier* (Bush, 1945/1960) included unlimited expansion of the human resources for science, technology, and the U.S. workforce. By the early 1990s, however, American universities were importing students in record numbers, conferring PhDs in seemingly saturated fields, creating a temporary class of postdoctoral researchers, and pretending that all was well. It was not. This chapter suggests what went wrong, how the social contract between science and government was rendered, if not obsolete, then certainly dysfunctional by world events and an unwitting conspiracy to produce more of the same. It suggests, however, that the contract can be renegotiated. New human resources can be produced and utilized to support not only scientific research, but also a national workforce and global economy that values uncertainty as a reality of modern life and rewards those who are versatile enough to help explain it as part of their scientific work.

Political scientists Radford Byerly, Jr. and Roger A. Pielke, Jr. (1995), each of whom has Washington, DC policy experience, recently examined the government–science relationship further and concluded that:

> the social contract governing U.S. science is an obstacle to needed changes in science policy. This policy cannot realistically justify large science budgets. . . . The postwar ecology of science isolates research from both practical applications and the very environment which today presses it to demonstrate efficacy with respect to the solution of practical problems. This pressure stresses the structure of postwar science policy, creating the crisis. . . . Under democratic accountability, science is consciously guided by society's goals rather than scientific serendipity. Good science is necessary but not sufficient; association with a societal goal is required. . . . Reliance on an outdated social contract leads to a loss of faith in science and a subsequent loss of political support. (pp. 1531–1532)

The key words here are *budgets*, *demonstrate*, *accountability*, and *support*. Each is fraught with an ambiguity or imprecision—linguistic, if not scientific, uncertainty—that begs for elaboration and illustration by measurement. *Science—The Endless Frontier* (Bush, 1945/1960) also rationalized the creation of the NSF, codified the delegation of funding advice through peer review to scientists, and created a context of authority. That authority today is under siege as the federal government struggles to control the budget deficit, reduce the national debt, and rein in discretionary spending. In such an environment, there is a premium on reducing uncertainty in the sense of ambiguity just described, especially over investments with distant horizons such as science and technology. Living with uncertainty is not the same as doing something about it. How scientists describe and justify the latter, this chapter argues, may go far to influence federal investments in science. To quote Byerly and Pielke (1995) again, "The Bush contract is postwar public policy, not natural law" (p. 1532).

Demonstrations of returns on investment—the latest instigated by the Clinton–Gore reinventing government theme of the 1992 campaign, sanctioned as policy by the Government Performance and Results act of 1993, and punctuated by the 104th Congress' Contract With America—are now linked to agency budgets (Council of Economic Advisers, 1995). In the absence of measurable returns in the short run, or effective lobbying to fill the gaps in expectations unmet, crises of confidence in social institutions (but especially those in the federal sector) develop.

Under deficit control, agency research and development (R&D) budgets are in jeopardy, their missions questioned. Although scientists protest that science is the future, most citizens wonder how much science the nation can afford. The research and innovation spawned in what former federal budget chief and science commentator William Carey (1988) called the *sandbox of the laboratory*—whether the disease-centered intramural variety at the National Institutes of Health (NIH), a Department of Energy National Laboratory, or an NSF Science and Technology Center located at a research university—is "very much in the hands of communicators—of science writers and reporters. They are a breed of science watchers, and the last thing in science's interests is to patronize or condescend to them" (p. 144). Scientists have done just that, either warily approaching or spurning altogether the soapbox of politics and the mass media.

Unmasking the Myths

The consequences of such behavior in a culture that reveres, or, at least, notices the soapbox are serious but predictable. Pollster Daniel Yankelovich (1984) reminded us more than a decade ago that

> The "social contract" has allowed science to pursue long-term fundamental questions and to build slowly . . . its new knowledge. Science has been able to do this in the context of a society such as ours, which in most domains is impatient, excessively pragmatic, and thinks only in the short term. (p. 11)

Today, this presentist mentality is communicated daily from the soapbox of the print and electronic media. Uncertainty is the foe of such coverage. Science, however, springs from a mythology of long-term social benefit, of confidence in the exploration—with public funds, no less—of the uncertain, and of the unknown.

This mythology was recently expressed by physical scientist cum policy analyst Daniel Sarewitz in *Frontiers of Illusion* (1996). Five myths capture the uneasy relationship between science and government, Sarewitz said, and "modern science and technology policy is therefore founded upon a leap of faith" (p. 10). It is this leap of faith that exposes the pervasive uncertainty that the practitioners of science, technology, and government all confront. To paraphrase Sarewitz, these are the five myths:

1. *Infinite benefit:* More science and more technology will lead to more public good.
2. *Unfettered research:* Any scientifically reasonable line of research into fundamental natural processes is as likely to yield societal benefit as any other.
3. *Accountability:* Peer review, reproducibility of results, and other control on the quality of scientific research embody the principal ethical responsibilities of the research system.
4. *Authoritativeness:* Scientific information provides an objective basis for resolving political disputes.
5. *Endless frontier:* New knowledge generated at the frontiers of science is autonomous of its moral and practical consequences in society. (pp. 10–11).

Whether in the sandbox, on the soapbox, or on the trip from one to another, uncertainties abound. How they are presented, negotiated, and interpreted—in technical communities, in the policy arena, and in the political process—is the dance linking science and government. One British radio astronomer-editor-commentator put it this way:

> It seems that the "old," positivistic image of science, as an abstract, timeless search for irrefutable facts—ending the pain of uncertainty, the burden of dilemma and choice, separable from "society," and leading inexorably to technical innovations for the good of all—exhibits an apparently puzzling tenacity. But it should not surprise us that this is so. The old ideology underpins many of our most respected social institutions, and to doubt *their* credibility would be to lose one's social nerve. So long as the state remains the main provider of research finance, scientists themselves will hold fast to the old picture, as it has earned them, in times past, access to the political arena and to the resources that they need. It is therefore difficult for them to drop the claim that they bring only a

consensual certainty to bear when they find "facts" or offer advice, difficult to come to terms with any public admission that they, too, have to reconcile observations and values in reaching their judgment. (Edge, 1995, p. 18)

The themes of this chapter, then, are clear: The myths that mask the uncertainty of science are an ideology and rhetoric that have served scientists since the end of World War II, when the federal government pledged "sand" for the sandbox known as The Endless Frontier. The *soapbox* is a budgetary tool that determines how what is produced in the sandbox will be interpreted, and scientists must skillfully use the soapbox to inform various audiences through gatekeepers and policymakers who influence investments in the sandbox. Yet, each of these themes also poses dilemmas for science. Two are addressed here:

1. How can the uncertainty that scientific knowledge represents—the revision of earlier truths—be seen as an asset to policymaking where the uncertainty is assumed and itself a justification for public funding?
2. How can science, and specifically the need to replenish the U.S. workforce with new scientists, become more "citizen friendly" (Roy, 1991)—accessible, well-reported, intelligently criticized, and, for the most part, celebrated as a national good?

UNCERTAINTY FROM THE SOAPBOX

The Politics of Budget Talk

Some would say that the federal budget is the root of all uncertainty in science. To expand this argument: Without sufficient resources during the coming year and the foreseeable future, the creativity of scientists cannot thrive.

Research programs do not adhere to annual cycles or come to fruition on predetermined timetables. "In the long run . . ." is an expectation that a social good will derive from investing in R&D or just research. The problem with such claims is that the future of science devolves to budget talk. It elevates one externality, as economists would say, as the cause of all that is good or bad about science. What agencies plan or investigators do all becomes contingent on the budget.

No social institution, of course, is exempt from the political economy of the nation. So while I do not subscribe to budget talk as the cause, I recognize it as an undeniable part of scientists' rhetoric. Debating the percentage decrease in the R&D portion of the federal budget caused by deficit reduction by the year 2002 has occupied much of the policy discourse in the last 2 years, with the President's Science Advisor suggesting that next year's numbers are more telling than 5-year projections and the Republican Congress insisting that their proposed cuts are more responsible than the Democrats' ("The Budget Blues," 1996). Despite partisan differences in extrapolating the amount and kind of incursions into the discretionary budget, the outlook for federal R&D is, at best, uncertain. Consider these numbers: In FY 1995, the $1.5 trillion federal budget was apportioned as follows: 15% for interest on the national debt and 50% for entitlement programs such as Medicare and Social Security. That leaves 35%, which was split almost evenly between defense and domestic discretionary funding. The latter amounts to about $270 billion; in the main science appropriations bill alone, NSF and NASA compete with the Department of Housing and Urban Affairs and the Department of Veterans Affairs. Uncertainty? How much can the nation afford to make R&D a funding priority (Domenici, 1996)?

Analysis and Irreverence

Nevertheless, scientists need to separate the politically driven from the rest. Where can science assert its authority and where must it acknowledge a lack of control? Others exercise political hegemony over the budget. Must they also control interpretations of value and payoff from discretionary investments such as science? Interestingly, scientists have not helped their cause by doing what they presumably do best—analyzing returns on investment. Indeed, science for the most part has eschewed such analysis, except for the macroeconomics of economist Robert Solow and economic historian Nathan Rosenberg, as well as the microeconomics (at the level of industries and firms) of economists Richard Nelson and Edwin Mansfield. There is precious little to combat claims that the nation cannot afford increased investment in R&D (for a review, see National Science and Technology Council, 1996).

   It is as if scientists take the social investment in science to be self-evident and, after pronouncing it so, wait for others to nod in agreement and hastily ante up. Yet, science is both politically inexpedient and risky as investments go. Thus, scientists as citizens and as members of professional associations should consider courting local media through a strategy that reports ongoing progress in their federally funded research projects rather than through haphazard and frenzied appeals around budget authorization and appropriation hearings. Budget politics must be put in perspective, not as the cause, but as the context. Treating the budget as an episodic or annual necessary evil reinforces bad habits, drives science away from its strength in analysis, and drives it toward the very presentist mentality that reduces its value to that of just another interest group. As posed by our first theme mentioned, what makes science special—and potentially an asset to policymaking—is its irreverence for what is known, its indulgence of tentative public knowledge, and its love of uncertainty. Those are the very characteristics that should increase investment in science and the knowledge it produces—if scientists can ever figure out ways of explaining that link and expressing it in compelling language.

For now, scientists may be their own worst enemy. Journalists do not get it right because scientists do not make the case (Friedman, Dunwoody, & Rogers, 1986; Nelkin, 1995). This is addressed later. For now, there are more pressing questions: one of leadership and one of what can be called *public science literacy*.

COURTING A CONSTITUENCY

Leadership

Any gap between science and the public can be assigned to the discourse and the interest in changing it. Attitudes alone are not at work here. Although scientists point to widespread science illiteracy in the general population (see "Science Observer," 1988), does that translate into no votes or a lack of public support for what scientists do? Seven of 10 Americans consider the benefits of science greater than its risks, a trend that has been stable for nearly 20 years (Miller, 1992; National Science Board, 1996). They hold scientists in high esteem, yet to most, science is a black box. So the linkage between perception and support is complicated by intervening variables. Foremost among them is leadership.

More than 10 years ago, Miller (1983) studied 287 science policy leaders and found "a woeful lack of interest in mobilizing the 'science-attentive public'" (pp. 41–43). By his definition, the science-attentives have a self-defined interest in science and technology (S&T) issues, are knowledgeable about S&T, and engage in a regular pattern of information acquisition such as reading newspapers and science magazines or watching television shows such as *NOVA*. During the long postwar period, science leaders turned to their own members for support rather than trying to mobilize these millions of private citizens interested in science.

When resources were plentiful, this strategy made sense. Even 10 years ago, however, ignoring the 10% of the U.S. adult population self-defined as "well informed about science and technology" could be considered a mistake (National Science Board, 1996, chap. 7). Miller (1983) found that a tiny fraction of the attentive public had contacted a public official on a science-related matter. This inaction, however, was not caused by a lack of concern, Miller reported, but by a lack of information about what the science leadership would like them to do. The polled leaders confirmed that they thought it best to go it alone.

These findings, themselves not widely reported, are provocative because they challenge the notion that a *science-attentive public* (who, building on Miller's definition, is sensitive to science issues and seeks information from various sources) must necessarily be *science literate* (understanding scientific relationships and able to apply scientific concepts in new contexts). The *science-interested public* (those who claim to be curious about discoveries and new technologies) is estimated to be closer to 40% of the adult population (National Science Board, 1996). This is a significant number because it represents a sizeable constituency. It seems that faith in the Vannevar Bush approach to science policy lulled the science leadership, buoyed by uninterrupted federal funding, into becoming inattentive to the broader public. Only one in five leaders polled by Miller (1983) reported an effort to inform the general public on S&T matters, with those in the university sector least likely to have done so.

Citizen-Friendly Science

The residue of this failure to enlist public support for science is evident today. If leadership is expected to convert interest into action through information, then science and the public—both the *science-attentive* and the *science-interested* (defined by Shamos, 1988, as those who appear to appreciate rather than understand science)—have been ill served. As Prewitt (1982) put it,"Instead of asking what the public knows or should know about science, we might ask what the scientists know or should know about the public"(pp. 5–6). One striking finding was that the views of a sample of scientists and of science-attentive nonscientists in 1980 were remarkably similar on science policy issues (pp. 10-11).

Because public opinion is crucial to the governing process—some would say to a fault now that opinion polling has become the politicians' thermometer—these findings on the relation of leadership and information in a participatory democracy provide long-dormant support for a renegotiated social contract between science and U.S. society. The general public is not attentive to science, but it is interested and positively disposed to it. Most of all, it recognizes that science is, as Prewitt (1982) concluded, "of public consequence" (p. 13). Science matters. How to mobilize this sentiment is a strategic task for science—its leaders and rank-and-file alike. To Yankelovich (1984),

> Upgrading the political literacy of scientists [is] . . . a prerequisite for two-way communication. . . . Sooner or later, the decisions that determine our survival must be endorsed by the American electorate. In this critical but noisy process, science can play many roles. It can, for all practical purposes, be absent as an effective influence, or it can be reduced to the presentation of technical testimony that trivializes the role of science. It can be muffled, confused, and naive—or, it can make itself heard on the side of sanity and wisdom. Unfortunately, the lesser alternatives are likely to prevail unless science as an institution seizes the initiative in changing its unwritten contract with the rest of us. (p. 12)

WHY SCIENCE MATTERS—THE CASE OF UNCERTAINTY OVER CAREERS IN SCIENCE

Whether the issue is the addictive potential of tobacco, the urgency of global warming, the reliability of DNA fingerprinting in court, the propriety of data handling and record-keeping by researchers, or the alleged oversupply of PhD scientists, uncertainty reigns. Put another way, scientific authority is in question. Consider the role of scientists as expert witnesses. Eighty-six percent of the civil cases in the U.S. legal system feature expert witnesses, an average of four per trial. An NSF-supported study shows that:

> When testimony was given in complex language, jurors were more likely to form judgments based on the credentials of the expert rather than the validity of the testimony. Experts who are paid highly, and whom jurors assumed testified frequently, were considered "hired guns" and were regarded less favorably, regardless of their testimony. . . . In an effort to validate the claims that are in dispute, a rising number of expert witnesses are being used in any given case, and sometimes they contradict each other. In this demanding and sometimes confusing environment, jurors use peripheral factors, in addition to the testimony itself, to make their decisions. (Hanson, 1995, p. 3)

Out of the artificial environment of the courtroom, peripheral factors abound. Blaming the media for undermining the public perception of scientific authority is one tactic that scientists take. Claiming an antiscience bias is another. Instead, I suggest that the media, which, of course, are as diverse as the scientific community in style, specialization, and quality, are in control of the public communication process. That said, how can scientists shape their messages not just to influence the budget process, but also to explain what the support of science—and the role of analysis by relevant authorities—means to society?

One example of the way Sarewitz's (1996) myth of authoritativeness became entangled in scientists' efforts to shape messages is the checkered history of the projected supply-and-demand imbalances among PhD scientists. Scientists are fond of saying, "You can never have too many scientists." Employment markets often speak to the contrary, making forecasts of too many or too few new scientists an occupational hazard. As higher education analysts Hartle and Galloway (1996) put it:

America never seems to have the "right" number of scientific personnel. In the late 1950s, as the United States chased the Soviet Union into outer space, it was clear that the nation had too few scientists to meet the demand, so policy makers sought ways to increase the supply. Their solution was the passage of the National Defense Education Act, which—among other things—expanded the National Science Foundation and authorized a wide array of science programs. Enrollments in graduate education boomed. . . . But by the mid-1960s . . . the national birth rate had peaked and . . . the nation was on track to producing far more PhDs than it could eventually absorb. . . . By the mid-1970s . . . there came to be a surplus of PhDs. (p. 27)

Labor economists have realized that imbalances are simply part of a boom-or-bust cycle that is wrenching to the individuals involved and a stern warning to students who follow that the market is changing. Often, shortages in some fields mean surpluses in another. Such market adjustments, combined with demographic bumps in birth rates, surges in faculty retirements, and influxes in immigrants, can change employment prospects in the time it takes to earn a PhD in science, typically less than 7 years. This makes career planning perilous at best. To make matters worse, in the late 1980s, NSF circulated a working draft of a study (Policy Research and Analysis, 1989), begun in 1985, but never published, predicting a huge shortfall in science PhDs by the turn of the century. By 1990, the undersupply scenario had gained wide currency, termed a *national crisis in the making* by the incoming president of the AAAS (Atkinson, 1990).

For most of the current decade, anguish over PhDs in science—who they are, how many in which fields, and what their career prospects are—has continued to grow. The reasons, however, attest as much to deceit and suspicion of abuse of authoritativeness as to inherent uncertainty in predicting demand for scientists.

Although official Washington, DC and the scientific community warned of shortfall, new PhDs, especially in the physical sciences, encountered few jobs both in and out of academia.

The clash between a forecasted glut of opportunity and the reality of scarce positions caught the eye of the Committee on Science, Space and Technology (U.S. House of Representatives, 1992). A hearing raised the specter of uncertainty over sufficient science personnel as a ruse for increasing the NSF budget. The shortfall methodology was assailed as flawed by witnesses from other federal agencies and independent scholars. Subsequent editorials declared "Scientist Shortfall a Myth" (Rensberger, 1992) and "Top Graduates in Science Also Put Dreams on Hold" (Kilborn, 1993). Soon after this miniscandal, two colleagues and I began what would be a 2-year study of careers for physical scientists (Tobias, Chubin, & Aylesworth, 1995). We talked to scientists of different generations, fielded three surveys, and concluded that people—science's most important product—tend to be treated more as an afterthought than a resource amenable to public policy intervention. How science has grappled with this issue, its fallout, and its public portrayal in the mass media and the science press is itself a case study in gap-filling, how mythology perverts uncertainty from something empirically shaky to something else politically charged and policy sensitive.

First, there is the gap between the nation's need for science-trained professionals and the current diminished demand for PhDs. Second is the gap between the breadth and depth of graduate education, a sentiment expressed in congressional testimony by then-NSF Director Neal Lane (1995), who wondered why "a society so broadly based in science and technology managed to define so narrowly the role and responsibilities of scientists and engineers within its midst" (p. 1). Third is a growing generation gap between senior scientists who have enjoyed fruitful careers in research and new PhDs who are encountering a glut of competitors and an insensitivity among policymakers and the doyens of their disciplines about their plight.

Anecdotal evidence from recent graduates in science makes clear that even for the best trained in the physical sciences, career expectations are that of a sputtering launch and a cloudy future of depressed opportunities for scientists narrowly specialized and oriented to exclusively research-centered work. A National Academy of Sciences' report, *Reshaping the Graduate Education of Scientists and Engineers* (1995), acknowledged problems in doctoral training and job prospects (a significant acknowledgment by those whose careers were launched during the Bush-inspired social contract era).

What, then, needs to be done and who should take the lead? The graduate faculty, professional societies, and the federal government all have roles to play.

Some adjustment of our graduate education models and practices is in order. The burden is on universities, but couching the issue as the overproduction of PhDs will not help. The issue is what those new scientists are equipped to do. The need for more versatile PhD scientists oriented to all sectors of the economy is stark.

How can professional societies and the science leadership help? Calling for more funding feeds the perception that more PhD researchers are needed. Yet, how does that square with the paucity of opportunities for physical scientists and mathematicians? Contradictory messages mobilize neither the public nor budget-conscious policymakers.

Human resource development and utilization belong at the center of science policy formulation. This country needs a human resource policy for S&T that harmonizes the demographics of its student population with the demands to train foreign talent. We currently are equipping the globe with PhDs. This is both good and bad. In the short run, we welcome foreign nationals into our graduate schools—some would say at the expense of U.S. minorities and women. This is a public relations nightmare and shortsighted at best (Finn, 1995). We antagonize our citizens, deter their participation, and at the same time, fuel the indignity over PhDs who stay and compete for jobs or who return home and staff our competitors in the global technological marketplace. Some would say we are mistreating the next generation. Both U.S. preeminence and the support of science by a public that sees science as further detached from what they or their children can do, and benefit from, will suffer.

Immigration policy, however, supports the preferences of graduate departments of science and engineering. This is not just a matter of turning off the international student spigot. America has a long tradition, epitomized by those seeking political asylum and the opportunity to do science during World War II, of welcoming emigres to its scientific laboratories. Foreign scientists have helped the United States retain its preeminence in scientific discovery, (as the national distribution of Nobel laureates clearly attest).

Despite the need for an overall human resource policy, the scientific community (with few exceptions) has been peculiarly silent on the lack of market opportunities for new PhDs. The discourse is still narrowly focused on the numbers—the language of oversupply—instead of the composition of the future S&T workforce. In addition, all the ingredients for strife between groups are present in the categorical comparisons: opportunities for the foreign-born instead of the native-born, advantages for the senior investigators while the professionally young grow indignant, suspicions that women are interviewed as tokens for scarce academic positions while men who studied under the great men at the top 20 research universities have the inside track. Why is science leadership silent? Is it denial, ambivalence, or the magnitude of the issue? This is not about opportunity alone, but about how to reconstruct the system after the Big Crunch.

Denial and ambivalence will undermine any new social contract, not just between science and government, but also between science and society. While budget uncertainties—the cause—beleaguer all parts of the R&D system (from funding agencies to university producers to industry and academic consumers), the need to sustain doctoral education and viable career prospects in science must be communicated candidly, wisely, and empirically. This is the meaning of *citizen-friendly science* posed at the outset: a way to understand the role of uncertainty in the fortunes of 21st century science. Instead, we get gloomy journalistic prognoses like this one, under the headline "Surplus in Science," which appeared in *The Washington Post*, "The economy of science and engineering is poorly understood and marked by egregiously erroneous forecasts of surplus and shortage in times past. But it's hard to avoid the feeling that a major mess is shaping up without anyone knowing what to do about it." (Greenberg, 1995, p. A25)

Consider the range of reactions to this story: The general public will pay no attention; the science-interested will be curious about the surplus (is it real and if so, why no action?); the science-attentive will worry about how to combat it; and scientists will bemoan the effects of the headline on budgets for NIH and NSF (whose annual appropriation was being held hostage at the time of the Greenberg story just cited). What escapes most accounts is the reluctance of senior faculty researchers to surrender control over doctoral research assistants and postdoctoral fellows. Meanwhile, neophytes cling to hopes of a career as they wallow in an endless job application process or jump at the precious part-time or soft-money teaching or research position.

From a policy perspective, uncertainty demands more than agonizing in public. After investing heavily as a nation through research grant-financed assistantships, as well as fellowships and traineeships, we squander many of these technical resources by providing too few alternate pathways for applying the skills and cultivating the opportunities—there are no guarantees—for career development. Is misinformation or inclination to blame? How can the damage be repaired and cadres of scientists salvaged in the national interest? The answers may reside in some strange places, but surely science and policy authorities can do better to find them. Explicitly tying uncertainty to action or inaction would demonstrate that uncertainty has a role in the discourse over policymaking as well as in the public's appreciation of the process.

According to Atwell (1996), to some:

"the current mismatch between doctoral education and the number and kinds of jobs available for new faculty members is at the root of many of the serious problems facing colleges and universities. And smug complacency about the quality of our doctoral programs inhibits our ability to respond to the need for change" (p. B4).

To others, a federal human resource development policy would:

recognize that people are not a mere byproduct of investment in science and engineering; they are the product—a precious and renewable resource at that. Whatever the policy and its dimensions, it must be comprehensive enough to encompass issues of composition as well as number . . . . Illuminating the dilemmas of immigration, underrepresentation, and market uncertainty together is a federal responsibility, even if formulating solutions is not. (Chubin & Tobias, 1996)

FINAL THOUGHTS ON UNCERTAINTY

Consult any dictionary, ancient or abridged editions, and you will find that synonyms for the word *uncertain* imply a lack of predictability. That which is *uncertain* is doubtful or problematic; it often involves danger through an inability to predict or place confidence in the unknown. In the relation of science and government, and the unwritten contract that binds these two institutions, uncertainty is axiomatic.

This chapter argued, following Sarewitz, that from the time of *Science—The Endless Frontier*, mythology has shrouded the uncertainty in politics of budget talk and the portrayals of science in the sandbox, where researchers prefer to stay, to the soapbox, where their spokespersons—leaders of the community—must venture to remind the citizenry that investing in the sandbox assures democracy (as well as a quality of life) and future prosperity in a world lacking in predictability. In the end, the human resources attracted to and prepared for careers in science must fulfill the social contract and cope anew with the uncertainties of science, government, and the unknown.

To return to the questions posed under the two themes of this chapter, one can offer these final thoughts, first as bumper stickers, then as prescriptions:

1. *Leaders must lead.* They must do more politicking and do it better. Transparently political acts acquire the whiff of entitlement and treatment based

on factors other than those on which the institution of science has thrived—expert judgment, competition, and merit. Nevertheless, science leadership would do well to court the media, to invest in specialists who understand it, can marshal its forces, and turn its power to serve science for the public good. This requires behaviors to ensure a more accessible, citizen-friendly science. The task of explaining one's science could be approached much as a research problem: planned, cost-estimated, and monitored for effectiveness. It is time for science to conduct a set of field experiments on its success in connecting with the public—communicating, informing, motivating, responding—in various ways.

2. *More of the same will not suffice.* New cohorts of scientists must become more adept at interacting with the media and various nonscientific audiences. This is what Lane (1996) called *civic science.* Cultivating it is a matter of will, not capability. For decades we have been told that scientists are smart enough to do anything, and do it well. Can graduate training, then, become cross-training (Tobias et al., 1995), sufficiently diversified to require coursework in public communication (verbal and written), in management, in teamwork, in pedagogy—in short, in all those things that smart people are expected to do well but who do not or cannot without formal instruction?

3. *Employ assets strategically.* The uncertainty that scientific knowledge represents can be an asset to policymaking and itself a justification for public funding of science, but some bad habits, indeed aversions, must change. Without narrowing the cognitive distance between scientists and various publics—the value of uncertainty, of continued inquiry, of support for probing what is unknown—will never be appreciated. Uncertainty, like scientists, is a social good because it reveals that society has a deep abiding need to analyze, to know, to plan, to anticipate the future—both the intended and unintended consequences of public policies. That is why the demise of the congressional Office of Technology Assessment by the 104th Congress was so odious. It was symbol manipulation of the first rank, asserting that federal policymakers can select their uncertainties or choose to deal with only some. Rendering budget uncertainty a known commodity in a 7-year timeframe became the overriding policy goal. Other uncertainties were subordinated, as if one can put on hold the rest of the world. Is it not folly to think that balancing the budget will make all other social goods attainable?

4. *Beware of myths.* Scientists—enamored of the myths of infinite benefit, unfettered research, accountability (only to one another), authoritativeness, and the endless frontier—buy into the faulty logic of the cause when they reduce all of science's ills to fiscal security. Science after the Big Crunch demands more ingenuity, a political literacy, and an organizational consciousness about

uncertainty. It demands using the soapbox, but it also demands inviting the public into the sandbox. How can we alert the citizenry—policymakers, the attentive, the interested, and the indifferent alike—that science is the institution with the most relevant expertise about the future? Effective answers will subsume the key question: How can science become more citizen friendly—accessible, well-reported, intelligently criticized? Only when scientists and journalists succeed in citizen friendliness will science, for the most part, be celebrated as a national good.

ACKNOWLEDGMENTS

I am grateful to the editors, especially Sharon Friedman, for comments on earlier versions. The views expressed here are the author's own and do not reflect those of the Office of Science and Technology Policy or the National Science Foundation. This chapter is dedicated to the memory of two whose careers revered and revealed science in different ways, Carl Sagan and William Carey.

REFERENCES

Atkinson, R. C. (1990, April 27). Supply and demand for scientists and engineers: A national crisis in the making. *Science, 248,* 425–432.

Atwell, R. H. (1996, November 29). Doctoral education must match the nation's needs and the realities of the marketplace. *Chronicle of Higher Education,* p. B4.

The Budget Blues—Outlook on Future Civilian R&D Funding (I) (1996, September 5). *FYI, The American Institute of Physics Bulletin of Science Policy News,* No. 130; fyi:@aip.org.

Bush, V. (1945). *Science—the endless frontier: A report to the President on a program for postwar scientific research.* Washington, DC: United States Office of Scientific Research and Development. (Reprinted by the National Science Foundation, 1960).

Byerly, R., Jr., & Pielke, R. A., Jr. (1995, September 15). The changing ecology of United States science. *Science, 269,* 1531–1532.

Carey, W. D. (1988). Scientists and sandboxes: Regions of the mind. *American Scientist, 76,* 143–145.

Chubin, D. E., & Tobias, S. (1996, March 29). The forgotten component of science policy. *Science's NextWave,* [Online]|. Available: http://www.nextwave.org/.

Council of Economic Advisers (1995). *Supporting research and development to promote economic growth: The federal government's role.* Washington, DC: Author.

Domenici, P. V. (1996, September 6). The reality of science funding. *Science, 273,* 1319.

Edge, D. (1995). Reinventing the wheel. In S. Jasanoff, G. Markle, J. Peterson, & T. Pinch (Eds.), *Handbook of science and technology studies* (pp. 3–23). Thousand Oaks, CA: Sage.

Finn, R. (1995, November 27). Scientists' heated debate on immigration mirrors issues argued throughout U.S. *The Scientist, 9,*(23), pp. 1, 8–9.

Friedman, S. M., Dunwoody, S., & Rogers, C. L. (1986). *Scientists and journalists: Reporting science as news.* New York: The Free Press.

Goodstein, D. (1995, September–October). Peer review after the big crunch. *American Scientist, 83,* 401–402.

Greenberg, D. (1995, December 6). Surplus in science. *The Washington Post* , p. A25.

Hanson, M. (1995, December). Expert testimony: "Just the facts." *NSF Features,* p. 3.

Hartle, T. W., & Galloway, F. J. (1996, September–October). Too many PhDs? Too many MDs? *Change,* 27–33.

Kilborn, P. T. (1993, June 6). Top graduates in science also put dreams on hold. *The New York Times,* pp. 1, 30.

Lane, N. (1995). Testimony before Appropriations Committee, U.S. House of Representatives, 104th Congress.

Lane, N. (1996, February). *Science and the American dream: Healthy or history?* Paper presented at the annual meeting of the American Association for the Advancement of Science, Baltimore.

Miller, J. (1983).*The American people and science policy.* New York: Pergamon.

Miller, J. (1992). *The public understanding of science and technology 1990.* Report to the National Science Foundation.

National Academy of Sciences (1995). *Reshaping the graduate education of scientists and engineers.* Washington, DC: National Academy Press.

National Science Board (1996). *Science and engineering indicators—1996.* Washington, DC: National Science Foundation.

National Science and Technology Council (1996, July). *Assessing fundamental science.* Washington, DC: Office of Science and Technology Policy, Committee on Fundamental Science.

Nelkin, D. (1995). *Selling science: How the press covers science and technology* (Rev. ed.). New York: Freeman.

Policy Research and Analysis (1989, April 25). *Future scarcities of scientists and engineers: Problems and solutions.* Washington, DC: NSF Working Draft.

Prewitt, K. (1982, Spring). The public and science policy. *Science, Technology, & Human Values, 7,* 5–14.

Rensberger, B. (1992, April 9). Scientist shortfall a myth. *The Washington Post,* p. A1.

Roy, R. (1991, January 25). "Citizen–friendly" science [editorial]. *Science, 251,* 362.

Sarewitz, D. (1996). *Frontiers of illusion: Science, technology, and the politics of progress.* Philadelphia: Temple University Press.

Science observer: How much science does the public understand? (1988). *American Scientist, 76,* 439–463; (Unsigned editorial)

Shamos, M. H. (1988, October 3). Science literacy is futile—Try science appreciation. *The Scientist, 1*(18), p. 9.

Tobias, S., Chubin, D., & Aylesworth, K. (1995). *Rethinking science as a career: Perceptions and realities in the physical sciences.* Tucson, AZ: Research Corporation.

U.S. House of Representatives (1992, April 8). *Projecting science and engineering personnel requirements for the 1990s: How good are the numbers.* Committee on Science, Space and Technology, Subcommittee on Investigations and Oversight, 102nd Congress, 2nd Session.

Yankelovich, D. (1984, Fall). Science and the public process: Why the gap must close. *Issues in Science and Technology,* 6–12.

Chapter 9

Reporting on the Changing Science of Human Behavior

Deborah Blum

*Deborah Blum has written about primates, sex, and a variety of other scientific topics during her Pulitzer Prize-winning career as a journalist. Until 1998, she was a full-time science writer for **The Sacramento Bee;** she now teaches at the University of Wisconsin-Madison, where she previously earned a master's degree in the science writing program. She is the author of two books, **The Monkey Wars** and **Sex on the Brain,** and coeditor of **A Field Guide to Science Writing.***

I had forgotten Eddie Finney. He belonged to a few grim and exhausting weeks from long ago. There he had stayed and I had not missed him. Until, almost 20 years later, I began working on a series on the biology of behavior. Then, right in the midst of interviewing scientists about violence, he came back, from some dark corner of my mind. I could see him again with that half-smile on his face, sitting in the courtroom, his feet up casually on the wooden defense table. He would wink at me every morning, clearly amused by little Miss Prim and Proper, the brand-new reporter cautiously inspecting the murderer.

Eddie Finney was not the first killer whose trial I had covered, but he was—and remains to this day—the most terrifying I have encountered, the only person I have ever met who seemed ice-cold indifferent all the way through. It was that quality of icy self-absorption that suddenly became real again, as I listened to scientists trying to explain the brains of murderers. The discussions were mostly clinical: days of discussing enzymes and neurotransmitters, hormones and brain structure. Yet, Eddie Finney was there too, to remind me that chemistry is not enough, that there are limits to the ability of science to define humans, for better and for worse.

He was 20 years old at the time of trial, the son of a maintenance worker in the small Georgia town where I worked. His parents came to court, dressed like churchgoers, every day. They sat numbly, talking to no one, just listening. Here is what we all heard: Finney and a friend, Johnny Westbrook, had visited an upper-class neighborhood looking for yard work. They were hired to come back the next day by a widow, whose yard stretched across a green and shady half acre. She was 70 and I have wondered sometimes what she said, what she gave away in that first too-trusting conversation. Did she say something such as "I'm a widow, I live alone, I can't handle the yard work myself?" Because when they came back the next day, they came prepared. They brought a gun.

They forced her into the house, robbed her, tied her to her bed, and took turns raping her and having snacks in the kitchen. She finally got out the door and ran screaming for help to her next-door neighbor and best friend, a woman of about the same age. It was evening by then; her friend was just starting dinner. The beginnings of a meatloaf were out on the counter when her husband later came home. By all accounts, the would-be rescuer ran out of the kitchen still wearing her little checked apron. They slammed the gun into her head, ripped up her apron, and used it to bind both women's hands. Then, they took the widow's car and drove out into the country, into a neighboring county, down a dirt road, into the shadows of a forest popular with deer hunters.

They had the gun, of course, and it was loaded. Yet, it turned out in the trial, Eddie Finney thought that was too quick a way to kill, too boring. The women were beaten with boards taken from a deer stand used for hunting, and then, just to make sure, he jumped up and down on their chests. I will tell you only that the resulting autopsy evidence at the trial was so grisly that jurors were physically sick.

The bodies were left in the forest. The car was abandoned by some railroad tracks. Both men had records. There were fingerprints in the car and spatters of blood and the killers were stupid and flashy with newly stolen cash and jewelry. They were arrested within days on suspicion of murder. Suspicion only because no one knew where the bodies were or if the women were alive.

It came out at the trial that the police had asked Finney to help them find the women. For a running joke, he had directed them all over central Georgia. They begged him, for the families' sake, to tell the truth. Finally, bored with the game, he led them to the bodies. It appeared that he considered the trial entertaining as well. He sat back every day, feet up, smiling at the crowd. The only people he ignored completely were his parents, as if they would have been a bad audience.

I have come to suspect that his lawyers must have hated him, to let him behave like that in the courtroom, instead of insisting that he present the image of a nice, quiet boy. It was the only criminal trial I have covered in which a primary suspect seemed so happy to be there, as if it were all a show and he were the star. In a way, he was right; the drama centered on him or at least what he had done. In closing arguments, the district attorney brought a heavy board, a deer-stand board. First, he spoke of how many bones had been broken in the killings; then, he smashed the board against the floor. "Ask yourself this," he said to the jury. "If this isn't a death penalty crime, what is?"

It was a long time before I could hear a cracking sound—a car backfire or a thunderstorm—without thinking of murder. I was glad to leave it behind. It was three jobs, a move across country, graduate school, and a career shift to science writing before I really thought about Eddie Finney again. I had been working at *The Sacramento Bee*, as a science writer, for more than 10 years when I decided to do a series on behavioral biology. One of the blessings of working at a fairly large regional paper is that there is time and money to do in-depth work. Also, *The Sacramento Bee*'s editors really believe in reporting on complex issues. I had worked on a host of challenging projects since I had been there. Let's face it: Behavioral biology was a perfect fit with the notions of complex and challenging.

What I wanted to tackle, actually, was the so-called nature versus nurture debate. I like to do stories that emphasize the connection between research (which people tend to place on some abstract plane) and real life. I had noticed what I thought was an interesting pattern at several meetings of the American Association for the Advancement of Science. At one meeting, there had been a host of presentations on the biology of behavior. In the next, in 1995, there were just as many presentations warning of the ethical risks and dilemmas for scientists involved in that field. Both aspects interested me: the apparent heating up of the research and the corresponding coolness of the response. And the science continues to heat up: the 1996, 1997, and 1998 meetings were packed with straight-ahead behavioral biology.

I was intrigued by this wavering between enthusiasm for the science and moral queasiness. This kind of beginning—simple curiosity—can sometimes feel almost too open-ended as a beginning to a project. Some reporters prefer to establish their line of sight early, deciding up front, for instance, to write a series on corruption in science. I prefer to explore, to leave open, the possibility of changing my mind. To step back briefly, I once did a series on space-based weapons that began with the premise that California scientists were helping design tomorrow's wars. The final product, though, was about the fact that they were designing very expensive weapons that did not work. I reached that conclusion about 3 months into the investigation, forcing me to refocus my articles.

Obviously, there are risks to open-endedness. If you sell a proposal on pure interest and no evidence, then you have no idea if the rabbit is actually in the hat. You may pull out the world's most boring series; in the weapons series, I was starting to wonder if I would have a story at all. It gives a nice, panic-driven edge to the reporting, of course, but I would not recommend it as policy. Most in-depth projects demand some serious advance exploration.

Among other things, feeling your way through a project demands a great deal of time. It took 8 months, to produce the biology of behavior series, "Only Human," which ran for 4 days in late 1995. Saying that you want to write about human behavior is almost like saying that you want to write a series about the universe. The options stretch into infinity. I spent almost 2 months doing preliminary interviews and reading through journals before I decided on a focus or point of view.

Having mentioned some of the drawbacks, in this case—in a research realm that made even researchers uneasy—I think a slow exploration was the right approach. I investigated and eventually discarded some very borderline science because I had gained enough depth of understanding to do that. I was also able, to consider how best to approach an evolving science, to give readers a sense of the continuum, how the field had changed, and how it might continue to do so. All of that—curiosity, open-mindedness, a sense of science in motion, allowance for error—becomes essential when covering an uncertain science.

Scientists by no means understand the biology of living behavior, of humans, or of any other animal. They have pieces of the puzzle, but they are not even sure how to order those shapes. In this sense, behavioral biologists are only part of the research crowd. Incomplete understanding, evolving knowledge is the rule for many disciplines. I was reminded of this recently when doing a series of climate stories, just as a series of storms poured untold and unwanted water all over northern California, causing disastrous floods. As I queried meteorologists on the hows and whys of bad weather formation, Kelly Redmond, a forecaster with the National Weather Service's Climate Prediction Center in Reno, Nevada, finally said to me: "Here's what it's like. You're standing in front of a giant painting. And you can see a rooftop here, a tree branch there, maybe even a few streets. Some of it is in beautiful detail. But mostly the painting is blank, unfinished. And yet, from those few finished parts, we're trying to see the picture" (personal communication on January 8, 1997). Science writers, too, need to get a sense of that unfinished painting, and I hope that we are learning how important it is to convey that sense of work-in-progress. Our readers, listeners, and viewers should know that uncertainty is a normal part of the process of science.

It is also true that this very open-ended nature makes it easy for people with strong biases (and this includes researchers) to use those pieces of scenery to create a picture they want to see. They may imply the simplicity we seem to want and when the subject is human behavior, simplicity can be dangerous. People may suggest that certain individuals, or groups, are born bad, stupid, or unnecessarily.

So, the uncertainty factor in behavioral biology, as in most science, is not unusual. What separates it from some other sciences are the many ethical dilemmas attached to it. It is not just that there is a potential to do harm; the science has already been used to do so. In the first half of this century, a cadre of scientists argued for the concept of bad seeds and inheritable criminal tendencies. Understanding of behavioral genetics was even sketchier then. Yet, the scientists persuaded lawmakers that they had the full picture. Some 60,000 Americans (all poor, all powerless) were involuntarily sterilized under laws duly created. The American laws later became the model for the Nazi eugenics program. The shadow of that vicious period of eugenics remains with us today, and there are those who still argue that the issues are too dangerous to be discussed. Some newspaper readers made this point: Maybe the science is good research, but it is hurtful by suggestion. Let's leave it alone.

I do not believe in that. I do not believe that we rid ourselves of risks by pretending they are not there. Instead, at least in this case, I believe that if newspapers can help readers better understand the science involved, those readers will be less easily duped by those who seek to misuse the research. I am not arguing that every person needs to be educated to the point that he or she can conduct gene-mapping surveys. We do not all need to be scientists; we all need a basic understanding of the process.

Science evolves, it changes, and it may make mistakes. Researchers, we hope, take care to correct their errors. This is normal process; this is not aberration. What field of human endeavor is error-free? Good science writing, if nothing else, gets that concept across. I would like to believe that readers of my stories would laugh if someone tried to persuade them that we know that one gene can make an entire group of people stupid.

Finally, although the human drama of behavioral biology makes it different from, say, condensed matter physics, that tension is something of a gift to journalists. It allows us to raise the potentially boring issues of scientific process, uncertainty, method, and credibility in a compelling way. In a subtle way, it is (yes, I admit it) education, but the very drama also adds another kind of responsibility. These stories of crime or genetic threats or scientific mistakes are not merely opportunities to show off, to flash a few exciting phrases. They are real. I may talk now about the remembered horrors of the Finney-Westbrook trial, but I was still a buffered distance from the tragedy. The families of the murdered women could not bear to even sit in the courtroom with the defendants; they could not look at them. When I left to write my last story—the decision to invoke the death penalty—Eddie Finney's parents were still sitting, isolated on a wooden bench. They were weeping. When we write about how people behave—what they do to each other—we should never forgot who the story is about or why it needs to be told.

It is my firmly held opinion that a lengthy series on a controversial topic needs to be precisely focused. Otherwise, it becomes a rambling mess of scientists arguing and contradicting each other. People call this the *he said, she said phenomenon*, or sometimes the *talking heads dilemma*. No one is going to read 4 days of stories that end up as one enormous "Huh?" There needs to be a flow and a direction to a series, a point of view. I organize my stories around viewpoint; it helps me select the topics I am going to cover and how I am going to present them. Let me emphasize that this differs from parading a political bias. For example, in 1991, I wrote a series on primate research called "The Monkey Wars," which explored the ethical dilemmas of primate research. The viewpoint was this: Animal research is not just the story of a bunch of furry animals. It is about us. The research puts a light on our species—the decisions we make, as the planet's most powerful species, to use other species. Thus, every story in that series was built around a person making choices—a researcher, a surgeon, an activist.

The focus of "Only Human" was more subtle, and it was harder to find. Yet, I perceive it as so important that I have returned to it again and again as a reporter. It has kept me interested in behavioral biology long after the series ended. Doing the series changed the way I thought about the science of behavior. I began by being curious about the way biology influences behavior—and I learned that behavior influences biology. Perhaps certain hormone levels heighten a competitive attitude; perhaps seeking out competition raises those hormone levels. Perhaps a nurturing environment encourages a more stable brain chemistry and perhaps a hostile environment does the opposite.

Reporting this story taught me that biology dances with behavior. We tend to think of the debate as nature versus nurture, when there is no either-or. Who we are and how we behave is a matter of nature and nurture, and those two forces shape each other constantly. Biology influences behavior; behavior influences biology. Perhaps some genes are more influential, perhaps some environments exert more force, perhaps the fundamentals are established early, but the potential for change and response is lifelong. I think this is a message with a lot of hope, but practically, it is that constant feedback that makes analyzing a behavior so very tricky. This give-and-take between what we inherit and what the world provides us is somehow very difficult to hammer into the public consciousness.

Although the series explored those questions by looking at various behaviors, at intelligence, and at sex differences, I am going to continue here with a focus on violence only. Let us ask what creates a killer. Is it some internal biology, is it environment and circumstance, or is it some combination of the two? Can you answer those questions in any realistic way? We can generalize, announce safely that some scientists suspect some criminals possess a biology that predisposes them to violence. That is easy and that is safe, but let's make it specific, personal. Are killers, like Eddie Finney, born that way, set on that path before their first breath? There are those who believe this is true.

Yet, can you imagine any credible scientist picking up a newborn and labeling that baby a future murderer? If you insist on nature versus nurture, then you are trapped between that and the alternative. Is the killer created out of bitterness and cruelty and whatever twists a person into something lethal? How do you determine that? Who is to blame? Even my belief—that it is both nature and nurture—does not eliminate those issues. Again, it is the explosive potential of such questions that makes covering the uncertainties in behavioral biology so different from those in other sciences.

Having said that, I know there are very good scientists who argue that some criminals—not killers, necessarily—are shaped primarily by biology. One of the foremost of these is Robert Hare, a psychologist at the University of British Columbia. Hare has devoted his career to studying psychopaths (sometimes called sociopaths). He describes them as so chilly in their reactions that they sometimes seem not quite human. They are separated from the rest of us by a matter of temperature. Quoting him here, "I think sometimes of a continuum from water to ice. Liquid water and ice have the same components but they are very different, aren't they? And these guys are the ice" (Blum, 1995, p. A1).

Hare is the developer of the renowned *Psychopathy Check List (PCL),* used to diagnose psychopaths and also used as a measure of other troubling tendencies, such as antisocial behavior. The PCL is solidly mainstream. Many prisons use it as a predictor of which inmates will return (high scorers routinely come back). Most people, in fact, most criminals, do not get very high scores on the check list. Yet, those who do, Hare argued, are born psychopaths. It matters not how kind the home, how friendly the environment, he said; a psychopath is born so disconnected from those around him, he can never be brought truly into the family circle. Hare claimed to have used the PCL to identify psychopathic tendencies, and emotional coldness, in children as young as 6 years old.

Psychopaths are not necessarily murderers. What they are, Hare said, is totally self-absorbed, each a sun in the solar system around him. They are solely directed toward getting exactly what they want, resentful of anyone who gets in their way and they will do what is necessary to reach their goal (Blum, 1995). Thus, some become con men, thieves, rapists, or killers. Often, they are not arrested for the same crime twice. They tend to regard both people and laws that interfere with their goals as irritants and obstacles. They do, however, learn to fake reactions, according to Hare. They become expert at pretending concern or compassion and, he added, they become expert at fooling prison psychologists.

In one startling series of tests, Hare and his colleagues compared the brains of diagnosed psychopaths with a control group. All had a criminal record; the control group tended to be mainly people with a history of minor drug abuse. The scientists were strictly interested in emotional response. They sat each participant in front of a computer screen that flashed a series of words: some nonsense (xyzubl), some neutral (table), and some loaded (death). They got the same reaction from every member of the control group: When a word like *death* appeared on the screen, the regions of the brain associated with emotional processing flashed to brilliant life. Interviews showed that people in the control group tended to associate the word with someone they cared about and had lost, but that did not happen with the psychopaths. There was no emotional connection. The parts of the brain associated with affection and grief stayed dark. Their brains processed death as something neutral.

Hare said that when he first showed the images to neuroscientists they suggested the equipment was not working properly. "And then they asked me, are these really human brains?" he said (Blum, 1995). He came to believe that emotional response is essential to a rational human response and that these brains are truly dysfunctional. He suspected that the chemistry or structure that isolates the emotional regions of the brain, that blocks caring for others, forms at a very young age, perhaps even in infancy. From this point, he argued, environment is irrelevant. No loving home or giving family can alter it, neither can punishment. He argued that diagnosed high-end psychopaths should be isolated from all other prisoners and held for life. He spoke of working with one psychopath in a Canadian prison who asked for help in getting a different prison job. Hare was unable to help. Later, Hare had some work done on his car in the prison auto shop where the man still worked. On the way home, the brakes failed. The brake line had been cut.

Could he prove his suspicion that the inmate was responsible? No. "But people ask me if psychopaths feel anything when they kill," he said, "and the answer is no. To them, it's like a chess game. The only point is—are they winning?" (Blum, 1995).

At this point, Eddie Finney suddenly clicked back into my mind. I could not return to Georgia past, bearing a Robert Hare with me, and have Finney officially diagnosed. Yet, he fit Hare's descriptions so well; I wondered what Finney's brain would have looked like in response to the word *death,* and because the trial was suddenly so real again, I found myself wondering about his parents, who seemed so nice and so sad, and about their son, who seemed to have treated murder as a form of personal entertainment.

Could I argue myself into believing that he was always that way, untouchable by kindness? In the realm of psychopathy, there are scientists who counter Hare's argument. They agree that once created, a psychopath is fixed, ego-centered to a degree that most of us cannot conceive and that those emotion-dead brains are real. Yet, they do not agree on what created them. There are scientists who will still argue that nurture/environment/conscious choice is all that exists. We can be taught self-absorption by example; a child can be isolated enough by the cruelty of his parents or the hostile setting of his life that his brain develops an emotional numbness in defense.

It turns out that a cold response to others is an unusually interesting example. For instance, Bruce Perry, a neuroscientist at the Baylor University School of Medicine in Houston, has studied children who grow up in high-crime, inner-city neighborhoods. He spent the early 1990s, for instance, focusing on Chicago public housing, infamous for such cases as a 5-year-old boy killed by two 10-year-olds because he refused to steal candy for them.

Perry's (1997) investigation focused on two major neurotransmitters in the brain, noradrenaline and serotonin. *Noradrenaline* is one of the body's prime alarm responses; it tenses muscles, speeds the heart, and prepares for quick reaction to danger. *Serotonin* is the opposite, inducing a calming response, a slower, more thoughtful reaction. We each inherit a certain baseline level of these neurotransmitters and they tend to balance. People with high noradrenaline run lower in serotonin, and they seem to end up in trouble more often.

Yet, Perry's work, with children of a threatening world, shows that constant threat can change that balance. Keep the pressure on, keep the state of alarm constant enough, and the body will eventually reset in self-defense. (The opposite is also true: Children born jittery with high noradrenaline will calm down with loving treatment.) A small subset of these children go further. After too long a period in which noradrenaline keeps their hearts beating extra fast, their bodies heated with nerves, they literally cool down. In response to danger, their heart rate slows, and their skin cools. This group, he said, becomes predatory.

There is a curiously complementary study by a pair of psychologists at the University of Washington in Seattle, looking at wife beaters. These researchers, John Gottman and Larry Jacobsen, asked men convicted of spousal abuse to recreate arguments with their wives only verbally, while hooked up to monitoring equipment. Most of the men went hot with anger as the words flew, but again, a small group went cold. They turned out to be the most vicious and most violent. As they became angry, as they prepared to retaliate, their hearts also slowed. They became cooler, more deliberate, more calculating. "Like pythons, waiting to strike," Jacobsen said. He believed that reaction was probably created by their childhoods, the kind of self-defensive beginnings that Perry charted.

If there is a consensus, it is that there is something in a person's original biology—perhaps in genes, perhaps from an early injury to the brain—that may predispose the person to react in a certain way. In other words, put a child with a certain vulnerable biology into a poisonous environment and he or she may indeed grow into a predator or, perhaps, a psychopath. There may also be, as Hare suspected, a select few who are so strongly predisposed that almost nothing will alter the developmental path. I mean that in both positive and negative ways. There are also children who build strong and decent lives out of the worst possible beginnings. Perry and many others commented on this as well, noting the resiliency and hopefulness of some children. Perry said that some of the children he studied hold onto a single act of kindness for years; it gives them hope.

It is into this complexity that the science seems to be going, trying to chart that ever-shifting balance between genes and environment, biology and behavior. Does that promise an end to uncertainty? Hardly. Did I realize that I would grapple with all those issues when I took up this particular series? Hardly. Nor did I realize how intensely readers would grapple with those same issues. In this area, as much as any I have ever covered, readers take the stories personally. They see themselves mirrored; they see people they know. They react not with interest, but with emotion. The series won national reporting awards. It also provoked the most intense response of any series I have written. I spent hours talking to local community groups, doing radio interviews, answering letters, and dealing with a small but furious picket line protesting the very existence of a biology of violence.

Many readers called me, some angry, some fascinated, and some who just wanted to talk about their lives. One caller was an attorney, a friend to a woman with a troubled son. The son was creepy, she said. They suspected that he had killed some animals. He seemed to hurt other children for fun. He had no sense of other people's rights or privacy. If he was visiting and he wanted to open drawers and cabinets and boxes, he did. He had rummaged through the lawyer's house. "He doesn't respond to what you say," she said. "He's not there." She read the story I had written about psychopaths and even as I thought of Finney, she and the mother thought of the 12-year-old boy. The mother had called the sheriff's department at one point, convinced her son was eventually going to do something terrible. We cannot do anything if he has not done something against the law, they told her. Wait and watch.

It is very difficult for journalism, a profession that adores the simple answer, to do watch-and-wait stories. It is frustrating. Yet, I think, that notion contains one of the realities of covering uncertainty in science. Science will change; our understanding will change, and what we write must provide that sense of motion. We have yet to report on the end of a story. Rather, as Kelly Redmond suggested, we are illuminating landmarks in a living landscape (Blum, 1997, p. A1).

Behavioral geneticists continue to find genes related to behavior, but if you read the fine print, their influence is sometimes no more than 10%. It is easier to trumpet the discoveries—and those stories may get better play—but we serve neither science nor ourselves when the retractions, clarifications, and qualifications come later. In practical terms, journalists need to do their homework, to find a comfort zone in writing about a changing science. All of us could do better in getting across the notion of scientific process.

We also need to recognize that an uncertain science is not a wrong one. Behavioral biology seems solid in its overall concept: That is, genes influence behavior. But how much? A major uncertainty is how to translate that knowledge to an individual. The specific questions are hard to answer: What made Eddie Finney a murderer at age 20? Will the young boy I mentioned go the same way? Even if you knew that the potential was there, could you really predict those particularly heartless murders that I described earlier? Even if we could give a probability—say, 60% likelihood—of someone becoming an aggressive adult, what would we do about it?

As a hypothetical example, let's say scientists identified and could manipulate the genes that control noradrenaline levels. We know that noradrenaline can be associated with an aggressive response. Would we argue to modify all high-level types into more docile levels? What if noradrenaline is also related to an adventurous spirit, to exploring, to risk-taking in a healthy way? So, that much might depend on childhood, family, school. At what point would you declare a child a risk? Would you just watch and wait?

These are not just hypothetical questions, of course. They are political questions, even civil rights questions. They come up because, as we have discussed, there is a difference between studying the biology of behavior and studying the structure of clouds. People read between the lines on stories like these and, in that open space, they add all their own fears and concerns. There is room to appreciate uncertainty simply because it is also uncertain what we would do with the knowledge if we ever possessed it.

REFERENCES

Blum, D. (1995, October 19). Natural born killers are more than a movie title. *The Sacramento Bee*, p. A1.

Blum, D. (1997, January 9). Wall of high pressure keeping storms away. *The Sacramento Bee*, p. A1.

Hare, R. D. (1996). Psychopathy: A construct whose time has come. *Criminal Justice and Behavior, 23*, 25–54.

Kiehl, K., Smith, A., Forster, B., & Hare, R. D. (1996). Protocol for a functional MRI study of semantic and affective processing. *British Psychology Journal* (Special issue on international perspectives on issues in criminological and legal psychology), *24*.

Perry, B. (1997). Memories of fear: How the brain stores and retrieves physiologic states, feelings, behaviors and thought from traumatic events. In J. Goodwin and R. Attias (Eds.), *Images of the body in trauma*. New York: Basic Books.

Chapter 10

Science in the Public Arena: A Panel Discussion

Dianne Dumanoski
William H. Farland
Sheldon Krimsky

*Dianne Dumanoski, a freelance environmental writer and coauthor of **Our Stolen Future**, is an award-winning former environmental reporter for **The Boston Globe** and a former Knight Fellow in Science Journalism at the Massachusetts Institute of Technology. She worked in television as a reporter and producer before switching to print journalism, where she pioneered coverage of emerging global environmental issues.*

*William H. Farland is a biologist and currently director of the Environmental Protection Agency's National Center for Environmental Assessment. He is leading the EPA's multiyear effort to reassess the effects of dioxin and related compounds, which reflects his long-term career commitment to develop national and international approaches to the testing and assessment of the fate and effects of environmental agents. He is a member of the editorial board for the journal **Risk Analysis**.*

*Sheldon Krimsky, a professor of urban and environmental policy at Tufts University, has focused his research on the links between science and technology, ethics and values, and public policy. He has served on the board of directors for the Council for Responsible Genetics. He has written extensively on evaluating and communicating risk, including his fifth book, **Agricultural Biotechnology and the Environment: Science, Policy and Social Values**.*

Question: If you could draw lessons from how scientists and journalists handle uncertainty, what would they be?

Dianne Dumanoski: One lesson I have drawn is that reporters sometimes bring assumptions to stories about uncertainty, and these assumptions usually are unarticulated, unexamined, and even unconscious. Much of the back and forth in environmental reporting has to do not only with what scientists say, but also with judgments that reporters make about uncertainty based on their own assumptions. For example, one reporter, when writing about the global warming controversy, juxtaposed data taken from land surface temperatures with satellite data. Because there was not complete agreement between the two, he concluded there was uncertainty about global warming. Based on that conclusion, he asserted that scientists and others who suggested that it was time to act now on global warming were being emotional. That he did so was based on his assumption that people who wanted action did not have enough scientific support for their position. There also was another assumption buried in the story, which was that if governments or society wait 5 years to take action, scientists are going to know appreciably more.

I challenge these assumptions. It is not necessarily emotionalism to make the judgment that one wants action now. This judgment has to do with how one perceives risk. If a person perceives that we are fiddling with the controls in the fish tank and we are the fish in that tank, he or she might believe, in a conservative and rational way, that it is better to act now rather than wait to see what happens.

Is the second assumption that somehow we are going to know more later on a safe assumption when it comes to complex science involving global systems? We will know more, but will we be any more certain? And what will be the quality of what we will know? Most likely, we are going to be making these environmental decisions in the face of evolving science, uncertainty, and scientific ignorance, which is hardly ever discussed.

Scientific ignorance sometimes brings many surprises. Many of the big issues we have reported on involve scientists quibbling about small degrees of uncertainty. For example, at the beginning of the debate on ozone depletion, there were arguments about whether the level of erosion of the ozone layer would be between 7% or 13% within 100 years. Yet, in 1985, a report came out from the British Antarctic survey, saying there was something upwards of a 50% loss of ozone over Antarctica. This went far beyond any scientist's worst case scenario. Such a large loss had never been a consideration on anyone's radar screen and it certainly changed the level of the debate once it was discovered. Uncertainty cuts both ways. In some cases, something that was considered a serious problem can turn out to be less of a threat. In other cases, something is considered less serious than it should be and we get surprised, such as with the rate of ozone depletion.

Dioxin is another example. In 1991, some scientists, mostly with industry backing, developed evidence that it might be less toxic than previously considered, and some influential reporters started to carry this message to the public. But then, scientists working at the University of Wisconsin found very strong effects on male rats exposed prenatally to dioxin. This experiment opened up a whole new avenue of research looking at reproductive and other effects, rather than just focusing on dioxin's carcinogenicity. Here again, new science changed the debate and showed that dioxin was still something to be strongly concerned about, despite what some scientists and reporters were saying.

Reporters need to carefully examine their own assumptions. When stories tilt toward taking action, they often downplay or fail to highlight uncertainties. Stories that tilt away from taking action tend to look only at the uncertainties and suggest that one should not act until there is certainty. From my experience covering environmental issues, environmental decisionmakers are in the same position as reporters. At some point a decision has to be made, a story has to be written. You go with what you have; it is your best guess at the moment.

William Farland: These discussions on genetic engineering, dioxin, and the nature versus nurture debate give us an opportunity to examine whether reporting in the media actually focuses on what the general scientific community thinks about an issue or whether it focuses only on opposing scientists with different viewpoints. All three of the cases had an element of coverage of dueling scientists, at least in their early stages. It is extremely important that the public get an idea of what the general scientific community thinks, what the range of opinion is around a particular topic. In the absence of seeing that, the public gets confused by dueling scientists. People also need to understand that what they might be hearing about is emerging science and that the general scientific community may not have formulated a feeling about it yet. That is an important message for journalists to get across.

I deal with risk assessment, and the National Academy of Sciences describes risk assessment as the evaluation of scientific information on the hazardous properties of agents and the types of exposure and the extent of the exposure that people get. But by its very nature, the process of risk assessment requires scientific inference to bridge knowledge gaps because, to reach conclusions in the face of incomplete information, we have to make best judgments. Risk assessment requires us to leap those gaps with the best judgments we can come up with. As we pull the information together, we talk about the strengths and the weaknesses of the data we do have, the assumptions that we have had to make in the absence of data, and the types of uncertainties that come with that process. The two types of uncertainties that we deal with are with the data themselves and with the inferences that we have drawn. Some of the uncertainties can be addressed by asking empirically about the science that we have in front of us and discussing what would be generally accepted by the scientific community. The science of risk assessment is evolving and the science that goes into risk assessment is evolving.

We then try to capture these uncertainties, assumptions, and all of the strengths and weaknesses that I have mentioned into an adequate risk categorization. The risk categorization is the product of the process of risk assessment, but it is not the whole story. It feeds into decisions made in risk management, and risk management requires us to consider social, political, and economic factors, as well as science, as we decide how we deal with or manage various kinds of risks. Unfortunately, what often happens is there appears to be a one-to-one correlation between the science, or our certainty in the science, and the approach that we have taken to a particular risk. Frequently, the media attempt to say how the EPA will deal with the risk based on the science alone, but this is premature, because other factors also play a role in risk management. Once a risk management decision has been made, if it is not a popular decision, many people's solution is that we need to go back and rethink or change the science. Yet, in fact, the decision may not have been based totally on the science at all.

The media need to better understand risk assessment and risk management processes and to deal with the issue of the personalization of risk that occurs as people read their stories about various risks. Readers and viewers need to have a sense of what risk assessment can and cannot say about individual risks versus population risks.

Sheldon Krimsky: Scientific uncertainty is a given and we are never going to eliminate it. And even when we think we have eliminated it, surprisingly as time goes on, we find that it is reintroduced. Journalists must distinguish between different categories of uncertainty when they write about science. The different kinds of uncertainty do make a difference. For example, there is the obvious conflicting data: You do one experiment, you do another experiment, and they do not match up. That is one kind of uncertainty.

Then there is the kind of uncertainty where important questions have not been asked or tested experimentally. I once did a study of the U.S. Department of Agriculture's (USDA) review of proposals for the release of genetically engineered plants into the environment. And we did an interesting thing in this study. We took all the proposals, reviewed all the assessments, and created categories by which USDA reviewers had made judgments. For example, we had a category called theory—USDA experts had made a judgment based upon pure theory. Another category was used to describe the judgments based upon new experimental data. A third category described the judgments based upon old experimental data. And then there was a category called principle of ignorance. This was for occasions when the experts made a judgment because they had not seen or heard of any hazards, so, in their terms, "we have no reason to believe that it is anything but safe." Clearly, this is another kind of uncertainty.

Then there is an uncertainty associated with different interpretations of data. You have a body of data and people interpret it differently. This happens very frequently in areas of environment and health.

Another important point I want to make is to look for the context in which the science is embedded. There is a broader context and it informs the kind of questions scientists ask. For example, it makes a difference whether the scientist is asking where is the gay gene versus where is the heterosexual or bisexual gene. All those questions define a context.

Question: Many scientific issues are long term and knowledge changes over time. Yet the nature of journalism is short term. Given reporter turnover and various journalistic constraints, do you have any coping strategies to suggest?

Dianne Dumanoski: I think it is getting increasingly difficult to do this job well, and I am not sure that I have any quick and dirty strategies. Many newspaper editors are not willing to send reporters to weeklong scientific meetings so they can learn the chemistry of the ozone hole. I had trouble getting an editor to do that 5 or 6 years ago, and I think this situation is getting increasingly difficult. There is less space, more pressure for a faster turnaround, and less investment in long investigative projects. I do not think there are any quick strategies that are going to solve that.

Certain business pressures are exerting themselves on the news business along with particular views on how to attract readers, such as with short, fluffy stories. In the science section, long investigative pieces and explorations of difficult issues, such as uncertainty, are not high on editors' lists right now. Any reporter I have talked to in the last 3 or 4 years has said something like: "You know that series I did three years ago that you liked so much? I could never get that into the paper now." Maybe the post-World War II golden age of journalism is over. I do not see these trends reversing in the short term and maybe that is going to mean that journalists have to find other avenues of communication, including the Internet and World Wide Web, although they too have their problems related to brevity and exploration of complex issues, among others.

William Farland: My response to your question would be to try to get away from writing about uncertainty issues on deadline. In truth, the nation is confronted with risk and other uncertainty issues, regardless of whether editors want to publish articles about them and whether the public wants to read these longer, complicated pieces. Often, I am very frustrated with trying to deal with a journalist who has literally 15 minutes to inquire about a complex issue. While I try to accommodate that need with the clearest explanation possible, I have always suggested that when the reporter is finished with his article, he call me back and we have a longer discussion. That way, the next time that the issue arises, he will have a base of information to use.

I have two or three reporters that I deal with fairly routinely and that is nice since they are familiar with the issues. Unfortunately, these folks change, too, as the emphasis of their particular publications waxes and wanes.

Sheldon Krimsky: It is important to keep in mind that people may not be getting their science information from newspapers but, rather, from television and other forms of communication that are replacing newspapers such as the World Wide Web or entertainment media such as movies and fictional books. Even in newspapers, if *USA Today*'s extremely short articles are the mode, can we expect newspapers to be able to present science and other complex information adequately? The sound bites of cable and network reporting and the tendency of the print media to follow that format have been destructive to nuanced reporting demanded of scientific stories.

Question: Do you think that scientists and journalists have a responsibility to empower the public so they can cope with uncertain issues? If so, how might they go about doing that?

Dianne Dumanoski: To be responsible, scientists have to understand something about journalists. I speak to scientist groups fairly often and there is, as anybody who has worked in this field knows, a conflict between scientists and journalists that really is, at its root, a clash of cultures. One of the difficulties is because scientists seem to believe that their way of knowing and doing things is the right way and that other ways are not equal or as worthy. I try to persuade them—with some difficulty—to regard the challenge of dealing with journalists as a kind of anthropological challenge. When they deal with journalists, they are working with another culture. They must understand that it plays by different rules. For example, they should know that reporters usually do not allow scientists to review their articles before they are published, particularly if the reporters are on a short deadline. Sometimes, reporters do check back with scientists to ensure accuracy of scientific information, but rarely do they allow scientists to look over or edit their articles.

There are reasons that these rules have evolved in the journalistic culture. Too often, sources want to change what they say in an interview after they have had time to think about it, and before it gets into print. This would severely affect the integrity of the story, particularly if these sources want to apply "spin control"or paper over some mistake. Sources other than scientists, including government officials—even Bill Clinton—are not able to review articles in advance of publication. It is just part of the way the media work. And if scientists want to communicate through the mass media, they have to understand its culture and learn to communicate within its rules.

Another problem for scientists is that strong peer pressure exists within the scientific community against becoming a visible scientist, one who communicates about science with the media and the public. I think the scientific community has a long way to go before it will become effective at communicating with the public.

Reporters, on the other hand, often seem reluctant to examine their own assumptions and the way they practice their craft. What are the plots of our stories and how do we deal with uncertainty? We do not want to be reflective or maybe we do not have time since we are often on daily deadlines. But I have not found it easy to engage many journalists in talking about the assumptions that inform our stories. Perhaps some feel that such discussion is threatening because they are supposed to be objective in reporting. However, I believe there is no such thing as objective journalism. There is intellectual honesty and there is fairness, but there is no objectivity. Journalists do not randomly select information that goes into their stories; they decide where to start writing and what and whom to include. Their judgments are based on assumptions, but it is very threatening for journalists to talk about these assumptions because it might show that they have a point of view on the issue. I think the journalism community has to confront this issue and, until it does, it will be difficult to have a dialogue about how differing—and unacknowledged—assumptions about uncertainty shape stories and further contribute to public confusion.

William Farland: From a responsibility perspective, the dioxin case study is a good one for talking about how one can engage the public and try to do so from both a scientific and a media standpoint. This case involves a difficult set of facts and an even more difficult interpretation of those facts that the public needs to understand and evaluate. At EPA, we tried to engage the public at the beginning of the dioxin reassessment process, which began in 1991, to ask them what they thought about dioxin. We wanted to know what they thought we should be dealing with in our reassessment and how important they thought it was that we address various issues. Later, we had these same types of meetings when we released the draft dioxin reassessment report for public comment in 1994.

The media very often responded to these public meetings by covering them and reporting about the issues that people brought up, discussing either the positives or negatives about the responses that we could or could not give. I think this media coverage encouraged other people to attend subsequent public meetings. So that is a good outcome of this activity. As we followed up with these same groups and went back to meet with them to explain our progress on the dioxin reassessment, we developed a real sense that there was some engagement there. In fact, we believe we now have a large group of people out there waiting to see what the final results of the dioxin reassessment are going to be. And I think that they will be able to interpret the results better having been engaged in the public process as we have gone along.

Sheldon Krimsky: On this question of the responsibility of science, I believe that in our country we are losing a reservoir of independent scientists because of investment in universities from corporations and because of individual en-trepreneurship. Studies done of the biomedical sciences show a field in which most leading scientists have corporate affiliations, where there is an increase in trade secrets, and, according to a recent study, an explosion of patents, gene-products, and technologies described in published works. Independent scientists are a scarce commodity. If you think about who has the freedom and independence and credibility in this country to speak out, I am afraid that members of government are limited. They just can say so much. If people are working for industry, they can say only so much because there will be repercussions. There are people in the independent sector, but they do not have the credibility. If we lose the reservoir of independent-minded university scientists, this society will be at a great loss.

The media must become aware of the financial interests of scientists. We are now living in a different world than we were 25 years ago. Scientists are funded to do risk studies by companies who have an interest in the outcome. Some of the data that are given to government agencies to make decisions come from the companies themselves, and the scientific community cannot get access to the primary data because they are protected by proprietary rights of the companies.

Today, we also see corporate-funded research even to the extent that entire university departments are funded by industry. Universities and researchers must disclose these relationships so the public has a good sense of what may even be only the appearance of a conflict of interest. This also is true for the researcher who is evaluating drugs when he has investments in the company that is poised to manufacture them. That has to be disclosed, and the disclosure provisions right now in this country are insufficient.

Increasingly, scientific journals are requiring disclosure about potential conflicts of interest to the editors of the journals. For example, the *Journal of the American Medical Association,* the *New England Journal of Medicine,* and *Lancet* request authors to disclose financial interests to editors, who, in consultation with the authors, can decide whether the interests should be published with the article. And while some government agencies require that scientists who serve on review committees or otherwise consult with government agencies disclose financial interests, the agencies often will not release that information to reporters or even to other committees of scientists advising a government organization.

William Farland: At EPA, with our Science Advisory Board, we actually ask individuals to disclose any conflicts in public, and very often that is done at the beginning of a meeting. The fact that individuals have research funded by groups that might have an interest in the issue under consideration does not impugn their integrity. Nor does it put them in a position that prevents them from functioning in the group. But it does put them in a very difficult situation in terms of perceptions about whether they are being biased in their views in the peer review. We have had people declining to serve on our peer review panels because of our disclosure practices and the perception problems they might encounter.

Dianne Dumanoski: Looking at funding relationships and potential conflicts of interest is not easy for a journalist to do. A former colleague of mine at *The Boston Globe* wrote an investigative magazine article that looked at the funding of some of the prominent naysayers in the global warming debate. It took him months to investigate the situation. He filed Freedom of Information requests and had to do all sorts of investigating, including flying to a meeting where these individuals had to testify on the record so he could actually get some of the information. The article was very informative and identified for readers which researchers were being funded by coal and oil interests. While this funding did not necessarily mean that these scientists' opinions were wrong, it was a piece of information that needed to be on the table. And such information is not routinely disclosed. This is a challenge to both the scientific and media communities. It is important not only for the global warming debate, but also for everything else that we cover.

Part III

Beyond the Basics

Chapter 11

The Importance
of Understanding Audiences

Carol L. Rogers

Carol L. Rogers is on the faculty of the College of Journalism at the University of Maryland, College Park. She is the former director of communications for the American Association for the Advancement of Science, of which she is a fellow and section officer. She has served on the board of the National Association of Science Writers and of a number of other professional organizations and is currently on the board of the Council for the Advancement of Science Writing. Her research interests include media coverage of science issues, and in particular, how audiences make sense of the messages they receive. She is editor of the journal Science Communication and coeditor, with Sharon M. Friedman and Sharon Dunwoody, of Scientists and Journalists: Reporting Science as News.

Whether you are writing a story, producing a TV documentary, developing a website, creating a museum exhibit, preparing a speech, or engaging in other communication activities, you need to consider the audience—those you hope to attract, inform, or entertain.

But here's the rub.

In spite of scores—if not hundreds—of studies over the last 40 or 50 years, audiences remain an enigma. Actually, we know a lot about the audience interest in science, and we know a lot about how science is presented in the mass media. However, we understand a lot less about how audiences make sense of information about complex scientific issues, issues in which uncertainty is a major component.

This chapter briefly explores some of what we know about audiences and mass media science information. I then listen to what audiences say about news stories on two topics in which uncertainty plays a prominent role: AIDS and global warming. Finally, the chapter concludes with some suggestions about how paying attention to what those audiences say can help journalists better meet audience needs.

BACKGROUND

We know people are very interested in science. The late astronomer and science popularizer Carl Sagan was fond of saying that children are natural-born scientists, inherently curious about the world around them and the way things work. It is the way we often encountered science in the classroom that seemed to turn many people off to science, he contended. Even so, evidence of people's interest in science is easy to come by in such things as the popularity of television programs such as *NOVA*, visits to science museums, and books about science for general audiences.

In addition, surveys reflect this interest. A recent study found that nearly 50% of Americans were very interested in science discoveries and new technologies, 70% in medical discoveries, and 52% in environmental issues. This "level of interest [of Americans in science] has remained high for more than two decades and reached a new high point in 1997" (National Science Board, 1998, p. 7-2).

People also tell us that they are interested in having science widely covered in the mass media. More than 40 years ago, a study commissioned by the NASW concluded that a "relatively large number of people" wanted to see mass media coverage of science, even though they had little science news available to them in the mass media (Survey Research Center, 1958, p. 3). More recently, a survey by pollster Lou Harris concluded that "the number of American adults who want serious scientific news is substantial" and a "majority of the public nationwide considers science news to be of equal importance to every other major area of news coverage" (Scientists' Institute for Public Information, 1993, p.2).

It may be that people say they want more science coverage in the media because they rely on such coverage to keep up with science, especially science that is new and controversial. "For most people, the reality of science is what they read in the press," according to sociologist Dorothy Nelkin (1995). She continued:

> They understand science less through direct experience or past education than through the filter of journalistic language and imagery. The media are their only contact with what is going on in rapidly changing scientific and technical fields, as well as a major source of information about the implications of these changes for their lives. (p. 2)

In fact, mass media can be especially important sources of information for unobtrusive issues, those things we do not typically encounter in our everyday lives (Zucker, 1978). Many science issues certainly fall in that category. For example, most of us are not likely to have much direct experience with such things as cloning, global warming, or endangered species. Even with an issue as seemingly ubiquitous as AIDS, more than 60% of Americans said they did not personally know anyone with AIDS, the HIV virus, or who had died from AIDS (The Henry J. Kaiser Family Foundation, 1996b). Although just over 25% of Americans learned about AIDS from family members, friends, or acquaintances and fewer than one in five learned about the disease from doctors or other healthcare workers, some two thirds of Americans said they had obtained AIDS information from television and more than one half recalled getting such information from newspapers (The Henry J. Kaiser Family Foundation, 1996c).

Yet, we do not have a very clear picture of why people attend to science information in the mass media and what they get from such coverage. For example, in the NASW survey, more than one half of the respondents said they wanted to "keep up" with things, leading the study's authors to conclude that people found science to be "very much a part of the total range of things it is important to know about" (Survey Research Center, 1958, p. 172). The study's authors observed, "Orientation to science seems to serve the broader functions of making sense of the world and helping manage one's relations to it" (p. 178).

However, general awareness apparently is not the only reason. The 1993 survey found an even more basic reason. "Public interest in news about science is not simply an idle fascination with the wonders of science," according to the Scientists' Institute for Public Information (1993), sponsor of the Harris survey. "The survey indicates that science news provides basic, functional information necessary for living in the modern world" (p. 2).

For example, Singer and Endreny (1993) reminded us that people use mass media, along with personal experience and interpersonal communication, to inform their perceptions of risk. Yet, they pointed out that communication scholars lack an understanding of the extent to which those perceptions of risk are actually shaped by the media. Their study of media coverage of hazards and the risks associated with them dealt with some 300 different hazards, including such uncertain science issues as acid rain, dioxin, AIDS, gene splicing, estrogens, and fluorocarbons.

Mass media probably play a somewhat limited role in risk judgments. Specifically, people appear to use mass media to get general information about risks. However, when it comes to deciding what they themselves should do about those risks, people are more likely to use interpersonal channels of communication, such as friends, colleagues, and others in the community (Dunwoody & Neuwirth, 1991).

We are told from numerous studies that people do not know much about science. Certainly, they seem to have a poor understanding of the body of knowledge that is science (see, e.g., the National Science Board, 1998). To cite a couple of specifics, only about 10% of Americans understand what a molecule is; only about 20% of Americans can define DNA (National Science Board, 1998).

Yet, this picture of a scientifically illiterate public stands in stark contrast to the more complex one painted by Wynne (1993) and others, who argued that one-dimensional quantitative measures fail to take into account the context-specific way that most people understand science. Specifically, Wynne said that laypeople negotiate their relationship with science in a broader, social context, taking into account "existing relationships, divisions of labour, dependency, and trust" (p. 328).

Examples of such complex understandings abound. They include studies of people's use of mathematics in settings ranging from grocery shopping to dietary calculations to home money management; surveys of residents' opinions about the safety of hazardous chemical sites near their homes; and studies of how people in certain settings, such as radiation workers at a nuclear reprocessing plant, actively chose to entrust others with the technical knowledge of radiation risks (Wynne, 1993).

Within this broader conception of what it means to be knowledgeable, we should not be surprised to find that experts and laypeople evaluate risks differently. Experts tend to focus on a narrow, cost–benefit framework in assessing risks, whereas laypersons take a wider array of issues into account. Rather than conclude that laypersons do not understand risk issues, Hornig (1993) suggested that nonexperts have an "expanded vocabulary of risk," which considers such things as availability of information and ethical considerations in addition to cost and benefit considerations.

These surveys documenting public interest in science, along with the work by Wynne, Priest, and others that explores the complex ways people understand science—especially uncertain science—serve to remind us that we often sell the public short. We might do well to heed the words of social scientist Kenneth Prewitt (1982), who argued that the "public knows more about science than scientists know about the general public" (p. 6).

It is not only scientists who do not understand the public. Journalists appear to have a very poor understanding of the public as well. One could argue that such understanding is particularly important for journalists, because their work centers on providing information to those very individuals. Yet, in fact, journalists work with "hazy and rather naive" notions of their audiences (Levy,

Robinson, & Davis, 1986, p. 227). Ask journalists about feedback from readers, listeners, and viewers; the journalists will say they rarely, if ever, get it. As journalism professors McAdams and Elliott (1996) pointed out:

> People who write tend to read more than the average person does. They are likely to be more educated, have a larger vocabulary, and a greater interest in various topics. . . . They may be out of touch with their audiences and not know truly who their audiences are. (p. 21)

It is not surprising, then, that in a study of television producers and audiences, Crane (1992) discovered that it was often difficult to find a link between what producers thought they were communicating and what the audience actually saw or interpreted from what it saw. For example, Crane found that newsroom staffs evaluated television programs by the quality of their production characteristics, such as whether the reports included live shots or how well the reporter performed, but audiences judged programs on the quality of the information presented (p. 23).

PEOPLE MAKE SENSE OF AIDS
AND GLOBAL WARMING

What can listening to audiences tell us about how mass media might better provide understandable information about uncertain and complex issues? An analysis of some of my own recent work on how people make sense of media coverage of AIDS and global warming offers some preliminary answers.

The study included a series of six focus groups consisting of adults 22 to 87 years old. None of the focus group participants had any particular expertise in AIDS or global warming. Each focus group, ranging in number from 5 to 11 people, either watched a network television news report, listened to a National Public Radio report, or read a story in *The Washington Post* about each issue.

Focus group participants, just over one half of whom were women, were recruited through fliers, newspaper ads, and phone calls. They turned out to be better educated than the population at large, with all of them having at least some college education. Many of them had advanced degrees. Therefore, although they were not representative of a more general population, their educational backgrounds should have made it easier for them to understand the mass media stories they encountered.

AIDS and global warming, as examples of uncertain science, have a number of similarities and differences that make them particularly fruitful topics to examine. In terms of similarities, although their individual histories are quite different, AIDS and global warming came to the public's attention at approximately the same time, in the early 1980s. So we have had similar timeframes in which to become familiar with the issues and develop opinions and concerns.

Also, health and environment are among those issues that are regularly included in studies of public and media agendas. Both AIDS and global warming, in particular, have been widely studied by mass communication researchers, who have examined media coverage and, in a more limited sense, audience reaction to that coverage (see, e.g., regarding AIDS: Kinsella, 1989, Konick, 1993; Neuman, Just, & Crigler, 1992; Rogers, Dearing, & Chang, 1991; regarding global warming: Trumbo, 1995; Wilkins, 1993; Wilkins & Patterson, 1991). Such studies serve to demonstrate the importance of those issues to our society and help to provide a broader context within which this study can be viewed.

On the other hand, AIDS and global warming lie at opposite ends of a spectrum that situates an immediate, personal issue, such as AIDS, at one end, and a more long-term, seemingly remote issue, such as global warming, at the other.

Furthermore, and probably most important, the problems of AIDS and global warming present different types of uncertainty, each of which, in turn, makes different demands on audiences. For example, the cause of AIDS and its mode of transmission are fairly well-understood by the scientific community and by a broader public. As this was being written, the uncertainties, in part, had to do with when to begin using the new combination drug therapies in patients, what the long-term effects of the new treatments might be, who would pay for those treatments, and what the possibilities were for the development of a vaccine.

Global warming presents a more complex picture in terms of the uncertainties, which include the amount of warming that is actually occurring, the relative contributions of human populations to that warming, the regional distributions of the global warming phenomenon, and the likely impacts of global warming on those regions.

The issues of global warming and AIDS differ in another important way. Although a consensus exists among a majority of climate scientists that global warming is occurring and that human activities are playing a role, vocal dissenting scientists highlight these uncertainties in public arenas and are regularly included in media coverage of the topic. Few contrasting voices are prominent in media coverage of AIDS.

Before turning to some of the focus group results, let's take a brief look at the two issues.

AIDS

As of December 1997, more than 30 million people around the world were infected with AIDS or the human immunodeficiency virus (HIV) that causes AIDS. At the same time, nearly 12 million people died from AIDS in the 20 years since the epidemic began (UNAIDS/WHO Working Group on Global HIV/AIDS and STD Surveillance, 1997).

In the United States alone, through June 1997, 612,078 cases of AIDS had been reported to the Centers for Disease Control and Prevention. Nearly 380,000 of these people with AIDS had died, making AIDS the second leading cause of death for individuals between the ages of 25 and 44. Furthermore, a recent study estimated that 650,000 to 900,000 U.S. residents are living with HIV infection (National Institute of Allergy and Infectious Diseases, 1997).

Although the disease that became known as AIDS has undoubtedly been around for a long time, the medical community in the United States did not become aware of AIDS until 1981. That was when two doctors from Los Angeles reported two deaths in a "bizarre outbreak of pneumonia in five otherwise healthy men" (Kinsella, 1989, p. 9).

Since that dramatic announcement, polls, studies, and media accounts have mirrored the progression of AIDS from a minor disease to a household name and an illness considered by many to be the country's number one health problem. As early as April 1987, some 70% of survey respondents said AIDS was the "most important health problem facing the United States" (Rogers et al., 1991, p. 22). Just 4 months later, surveys found that "virtually everyone (more than 99%)" had heard of AIDS. In addition, most people had some idea of how AIDS could be transmitted and what effects the disease had on people who get it (Dawson, Cynamon, & Fitti, 1987, p. 1).

In this same period, AIDS went from being a rare story in the media to the "story of the decade," as described in 1988 by Abe Rosenthal, former executive editor of *The New York Times* (Kinsella, 1989, p. 86).

Although critics charge that media coverage of AIDS was slow to get off the ground (see, e.g., Kinsella, 1989; Rogers et al., 1991), the coverage picked up steam in the mid-1980s and has been generally robust and consistent since then (The Henry J. Kaiser Family Foundation, 1996a). It is probably not surprising that AIDS coverage during the last 15 years has been heavily driven by major events, such as scientific and medical developments; coverage of prominent persons with AIDS such as actor Rock Hudson, who died in 1985, and athlete Magic Johnson, who announced in 1991 that he was HIV positive; and controversies about issues such as mandatory testing and individual privacy (The Henry J. Kaiser Family Foundation, 1996a; Kinsella, 1989; Rogers et al., 1991).

Global Warming

In December 1997, some 160 nations, including the United States, signed a landmark treaty at an international conference in Kyoto, Japan, to reduce emissions of greenhouse gases that cause global warming. The treaty still needed to be ratified by the signatories, but it represented a major step in efforts stretching back over several years to deal with what many believe is one of the world's most serious environmental problems.

Global warming is a rise in the average temperature of the Earth's climate, caused by a buildup of greenhouse gases in the atmosphere. The operative word is *average*, however, because despite the term *global*, the warming is unlikely to be uniform across the Earth's surface. In fact, significant regional differences are expected to occur in such things as temperature and precipitation patterns.

Although the history of global warming research stretches back more than 100 years, global warming really became a public issue in 1980, when *Science* magazine published an article that reported that the Earth's temperature was rising (Trumbo, 1995). Then, in 1983, a National Academy of Sciences' report said that a doubling of levels of carbon dioxide eventually would warm the Earth by 3 to 8° Fahrenheit (Environmental Defense Fund, 1995). Throughout the 1980s and 1990s, the global warming phenomenon has been a contentious issue for science, politics, and a wider public as individual scientists, nonprofit organizations, corporations, government agencies, and international conferences have focused on the issue.

As noted, most of the world's climate scientists agree that global warming is under way. However, until recently, researchers were uncertain whether global warming reflected natural variations in the Earth's climate or whether human activities were major contributors to that warming. But in the fall of 1995, the Intergovernmental Panel on Climate Change (1995), a joint endeavor of the United Nations Environment Program and the World Meteorological Organization, concluded that the observed increase in global temperature over the last century "is unlikely to be entirely natural in origin" and that "the balance of evidence . . . suggests a discernible human influence on global climate" (p. 4).

Throughout the 1980s, the public gradually became aware of global warming. By the end of the decade, 86% of poll respondents had heard of the greenhouse effect (Trumbo, 1995). At the same time, the U. S. Environmental Protection Agency ranked global climate change as one of the agency's greatest concerns, whereas in a 1990 Roper poll, it barely made it into the top 20 of the public's environmental concerns (Roberts, 1990).

More recently, the Pew Research Center surveyed public concern about environmental issues just prior to the 1997 Kyoto conference. The survey found that most Americans knew what the greenhouse effect was, but only one quarter of respondents, compared to about 30% several years earlier, said they worry a "great deal" about global warming or the greenhouse effect. However, the survey found that respondents were willing to pay more for gasoline to help reduce global warming (Pew Research Center for the People & the Press, 1997).

At about the same time, *The New York Times* poll found 65% of Americans had heard or read "a lot" or "some" about global warming. Sixty-five percent said the United States "should take steps now to cut its own emissions 'regardless of what other countries do'" (Cushman, 1997, p. A36).

Media coverage of global warming has exhibited an uneven pattern over the last 15 years or so. It increased considerably in the mid-1980s, peaked around mid-1989, and then fell off steadily during the 1990s (Trumbo, 1995). In addition, the stories reflected a "distinct coverage pattern," according to Wilkins (1993), who examined print media coverage between 1987 and 1990 (p. 76). She found that more than one half of the stories were published during warm weather months, with more than one half also tied to such political events as congressional hearings, legislation, and international agreements.

STORY CHARACTERISTICS
THAT INHIBIT UNDERSTANDING

With that as background, we can now ask what participants in this series of focus groups had to say about media coverage of the two issues. What particular aspects of the coverage posed difficulties for them in terms of understanding these stories about AIDS and global warming? What might those patterns tell us about how audiences make sense of uncertain science when they encounter it in the mass media?

In the following accounts from the focus groups I conducted, adults from a variety of backgrounds describe some of their reactions to the various media stories about these topics.

The AIDS stories used in the focus groups came out of the 11th International AIDS Conference held in Vancouver, British Columbia, in July 1996. The stories primarily reported on the success of using combination drug therapies in patients with AIDS. These drug therapies include the first AIDS drug, AZT, which hinders the ability of HIV to reproduce at an early stage in its life cycle, and the powerful *protease inhibitors*, a newer class of antiretroviral treatments that interrupt HIV replication at a later stage in its life cycle. In addition, most of the second column of the two-column newspaper story used in this study discussed the prevalence of AIDS in young gay males. Both the radio and television reports touched on the issues of side effects and costs.

The global warming stories employed in the study were based on the Intergovernmental Panel on Climate Change (IPCC) report in the fall of 1995, in which a consensus statement was approved that said there is "a discernible human influence on global climate" (p. 4). Much of the newspaper account was devoted to a discussion of the language contained in the document, with a couple of sentences explaining global warming projections at the end. All three reports included interviews with scientists involved in the international meeting that approved the report.

Regardless of whether the story was about AIDS or global warming and regardless of the medium in which the story appeared, two characteristics caused particular problems for the focus group participants as they tried to understand it: lack of information and lack of context. Story structure also posed a problem, especially in the newspaper stories. Visuals proved to be problematic in television stories. In the global warming reports, the way the story was framed appeared to inhibit understanding of the uncertainties involved. Let's take each of these in turn.

Lack of Information

One of the biggest concerns expressed by the focus group participants was that the stories lacked basic information that individuals felt they needed to understand the content. Specifically, the participants found the stories assumed levels of knowledge on the part of audiences—whether newspaper readers, TV viewers, or radio listeners—that they did not have.

Typical were the comments of one participant about the knowledge required to understand the newspaper AIDS story:

> I had to make a lot of assumptions, that it's cheaper to not use the fancy new designer drugs—and obviously I'm assuming, based on the fact that they said resistance is a problem . . . that perhaps you don't develop a resistance to some of the other options. I had to keep making all these assumptions about how the things that they stated about the new drugs . . . aren't true for some of the other, less serious treatments. And I wished they'd addressed that a little more.

Another participant, also reacting to the newspaper story, wanted a definition of a protease inhibitor:

> I have no idea what a protease inhibitor is. And I would have liked to get a paragraph or a couple of sentences about what that is. Because that would have made the article a lot more ... informative to me. It's nice to know that, in this combination, the protease inhibitor . . . is having this effect, but I don't know what that [the protease inhibitor] is and I would be interested to know that.

In discussing the radio report, one participant was even more detailed about what information was missing: "The story kind of assumed a lot. It assumed that you knew what AIDS was, how it related to HIV, what a protease inhibitor was, what AZT is, all kinds of stuff."

Participants in several of the focus groups said they wanted more information about side effects:

> I was curious about the side effects. They clearly mentioned that there were some but they didn't say what they were. These massive doses of drugs that they're discussing, there's got to be some sort of consequences, side effects.

> Well, actually, I was surprised how briefly they treated the side effects. I mean they had one person speak for, like, two seconds. . . . I think other people have mentioned that those sounded pretty bad, so I would like to have heard more about those.

Participants also wanted more information about various aspects of the cost issues associated with the therapies:

> I wondered about the cost of it. I mean, they didn't really address that.

> Well, who's going to get it [the new protease inhibitors]? Why not give it first if it seems to be so effective? You know, it is a cost issue certainly.

> Did you pick up anything about the economic aspects of this all? . . . I know that, in part, whether or not a doctor does that [prescribes protease inhibitors] depends on whether or not the patient has insurance or can afford the medication. . . . It will maybe become a case where not only are poor people more likely to become infected [with HIV] but poor people are less likely to be treated and that's sort of just really left out.

Focus group participants found what they considered important information missing in the global warming stories as well. They seemed to be looking primarily for the evidence that had formed the basis of the consensus statement.

For example, several comments surfaced regarding the TV news report on the United Nations panel's statement on global warming:

> I thought that you had to take on faith that a consensus was reached and secondly, even though the consensus was reached, it's a very complicated subject and I'd like to know exactly what the consensus was and I don't think that came across in this report.

> They cut it off, it seems to me, so quickly too. . . . I felt as though I wanted more information. I didn't really get the point. It was sort of vague.

It was not just the brevity of a typical TV news report that might have accounted for the lack of evidence in the story. The newspaper story generated similar criticism. Typical were these comments from two participants after they read the newspaper account of the issue:

> They didn't give a lot of evidence. They stated that the balance of evidence suggested there's a discernible human influence on global climate. But I really didn't get out anything where there is evidence. . . . It gave me some facts in the very last paragraph. It doesn't say where they got the facts from or anything like that.

> I believe in global warming. But, I mean, I would have liked to have seen what evidence in particular these officials looked at that was so significant that they were coming to this conclusion. And there's no sense here of knowing.

Participants also wanted to know more about the people who were involved in the United Nations statement. They especially wanted some idea of the experts' backgrounds—whether they were scientists or government officials. These comments from individuals in different groups were typical:

> A group of scientists, not necessarily . . . [as] scientists but as representatives of various different fields and also different countries, have come to a consensus. And there was no real background on who the players were, who was pushing alternate resolutions. There . . . wasn't even an awareness that there was a political aspect.

> Or even like what was the background, the professional background, of these delegates? Like I said, I'd want to know . . . was there a requirement that you have a scientist on it who is doing research as well as someone who is a policymaker. . . . Were the vast majority of these people just policymakers . . . and the report comes across their desk and they either buy it or they don't, depending on what their own positions would be, what their job security is?

Participants also wanted to know what the effects of global warming would be. They wanted more details about precisely what human activities were contributing to global warming and what steps people could take to minimize the problem.

> It's nice that the temperature is going to go up 2 to 7 degrees. I hate cold winters, but what does that mean? What's the effect? The dollar and cents would be nice or any kind of an effect.

> It would be nice if they say, okay, this is your general pattern for warming and cooling and if you throw it off this much here you're going to throw it off this much here. And that translates into x billion dollars.

> From a day-to-day way I'm going to live my life, this doesn't tell me anything. This doesn't tell me if my putting my can in the recycle bin does anything. They don't say what discernible human influence is. I mean, what have we been doing? Have we stopped using aerosol and has that worked? I don't know.

A close look at these comments highlights several different problems with content—or lack of content—in the stories that inhibited audience comprehension of the uncertainties involved. In the AIDS stories, for example, audiences wanted more explanation to enable them to make sense of the information. They needed to know the basics about the drugs being discussed and the relation between AIDS and HIV. Equally important, two issues that were especially significant to the focus group participants and which they discussed at great length—side effects and costs—were barely mentioned in any of the reports.

As for the global warming reports, the focus group participants also wanted more basic information, in this case, more detail about how the experts came to know about the human influence and where the facts came from. They wanted to be let in to the decision-making process. Furthermore, they wanted to know more about the experts themselves in order to evaluate their credibility. They were unwilling to take the people featured in the stories at face value. In addition, although one of the stories mentioned that there was uncertainty about the issue, the focus group participants commented that the story provided little information about the nature of that uncertainty.

Lack of Context

Repeatedly, focus group participants expressed frustration with the lack of context provided in stories. With both AIDS and global warming, they wanted to know where this new information fit into the bigger picture of what came before and what was next. Without such context, they had difficulty making sense of the information and deciding just how important it was in the larger scheme of things.

Typical was one comment on the TV news report about the new AIDS therapies:

> But there was no very good sense of how important it really is. . . . There's no sense of what was the last, sort of big step, how far do you have to go and how important is this really.

Newspaper stories fared no better. One participant specifically criticized the newspaper story because it provided "no clear context," whereas another participant just expressed exasperation:

> I was a little frustrated when I got to . . . sort of the end of the first half of it and it was talking a great deal about what all the new drugs could do and made only a passing reference to how that related to some of the other treatments and I didn't know. I found myself wanting them to throw in a couple of lines somewhere.

Another participant, also commenting on the newspaper story about the new AIDS therapies, said, "I felt like they only gave part of the information. You weren't sure what the implications were."

Focus group participants raised similar issues about the global warming coverage:

> It's not clear whether they're saying that the global temperature overall could rise 7% or 7 degrees or whether some areas are really going to get hit hard, whether there is going to be 2 degrees in some areas and 5 in others, and 7 in others and also it's considerably lower than earlier estimates partially because of preventative actions already taken by governments. That sentence could be so much more informative. I mean, that really could have been expanded into another paragraph to tell, okay, what were the earlier estimates and also which of these preventative actions actually work.

Another participant felt it would have been useful had the TV news report on global warming related the phenomenon to other weather events:

> I also have some knowledge of previous weather conditions that made me wonder why those previous weather conditions were not covered in this story to put it in some context, like the dust bowls of the '30s. Stuff like that. I mean, you know, do you just kind of throw out all previous experience?. . . I found myself really just kind of growing less interested in the story because it seemed to have nothing but the visuals after a while. It was just kind of a statement, you know, these scientists have concurred but no reasoning, no back up, no justifications.

Focus group participants were clearly struggling to make sense of these stories, but the stories did not provide the context that enabled them to do so.

The participants wanted to know how the new information was related to other things; for example, they wanted to be able to relate global warming to previous weather patterns. Some of the missing context had to do with the uncertainties inherent in the issues themselves. With AIDS, for example, that missing context included information about the long-range effects of the medications. With global warming, it included the implications for the planet and the people on it.

Story Structure

We might expect newspaper stories, especially those in papers such as *The Washington Post*, to be somewhat long and complex. However, participants in both focus groups that read the newspaper stories said the AIDS account was particularly difficult because of the two very different aspects of AIDS it discussed. As several participants explained:

> I guess one of the big questions is why would they throw that last bit in. I mean, they were talking about the three-combination drug thing, which in itself is very interesting but then they . . . started talking about the different behavioral aspects of transmission. . . . It really seemed like a different article and it didn't seem to me to be [a] coherent article altogether.

> In my head these were two different articles and whether they would come together I don't know. . . . both of them, both halves of the article are definitely advancements in terms of treating HIV and AIDS, whether it be education of the gay community or scientific advancement or treatment. So are they related? I don't know. . . . So both of them to me were interesting to know. I just don't, it is really odd the way they put them together.

The concerns readers expressed about the AIDS newspaper report are especially interesting because the story is written as a typical meeting story. It follows the journalistic convention of the inverted pyramid structure; that is, it features the most important news first—in this case, the combination drug therapies, and includes other information if space permits. Yet, what might make perfect sense from a journalistic perspective did not appear to help readers comprehend this complex issue.

Although participants had fewer problems with the structure of the radio reports, the radio AIDS story presented difficulties. For example, commenting about the AIDS radio report, one participant said there were "too many points." Another participant expressed frustration that the radio story contained "all these different things and they didn't really . . . wrap it up."

Visuals

Visuals can be an effective way to help audiences understand complex topics. TV news reports can be expected to excel on this score, but the focus group participants had some problems with the visuals in both the AIDS and global warming stories.

Participants said the visuals in the AIDS story distracted them from the story's content and, in some cases, contradicted the narration.

> But I mean everybody looked healthy, and happy, and playing. I mean, I just don't get it. Actually, I didn't even know that was a Third World country for a second. It looked like it was a slum in America, the outside shot.

> I thought there was a certain amount of irony in the visuals. One of the visuals was Abbott Laboratories and the drug companies are the object of protest of many of the AIDS activists because of the price of the drugs and that was one of the disadvantages that was pointed out in the whole story. So I think there's a certain amount of irony in using that as a visual.

Participants raised even greater concerns about the visuals in the global warming report. Some of the participants felt the visuals were deceptive, whereas others simply found them unrelated.

> I felt we were being manipulated . . . by showing these rising waters and floods. . . . I felt manipulated.

> They made the story seem faked because clearly we're not at the point where all these, you know, natural disasters are happening. I didn't think that the point of the story was that natural disasters have begun occurring because the polar ice caps are melting and whatever and yet they showed whatever and so that really undermined their story.

Uncertainties inherent in the science of both AIDS and global warming appeared to be made more confusing rather than less by the visuals used in the TV reports. With AIDS, for example, one of the problems with the new therapies is the side effects that can sometimes be intolerable. However, the pictures used made that appear to be an insignificant problem. With global warming, one of the uncertainties involves the extent and location of the effects of a warmer climate. Yet, the visuals used—of hurricanes and other natural disasters—suggested to viewers that those effects were well-understood and had already begun to occur.

Story Framing

The way a story is framed can have an effect on how people understand the issue presented. For example, in news stories, AIDS is framed as a disease whose origins and means of transmission are well-understood. On the other hand, news stories about global warming typically frame the topic as one about which there is considerable uncertainty among scientists as to whether global warming is actually occurring and, if it is, whether it is primarily due to natural or human causes. Reporters covering global warming seem to feel compelled to adhere to the journalistic tradition of balance, providing differing points of view within a story.

Even when the focus groups were presented with media stories reporting that a United Nations panel had reached consensus that human activity has a "discernible influence" on global warming, many study participants remained unconvinced. They wanted to see the evidence presented. They specifically mentioned that they were aware of the disagreement about global warming in the scientific community.

> I was actually surprised to hear this. Because I've always thought that there was a definite conflict between the theory that there was global warming going on because of human activity . . . or if it was just natural events.

> But I guess I still am not convinced. I'm certainly not convinced by this. . . . There have been changes that have naturally occurred and I'm not real convinced that this isn't just a, one of those issues that there's a lot of noise about.

> Throughout the whole interview, it was "possibility" and "might" and "we think." There is no consensus in the community as to what's happening, whether it might be man but it could be old Mother Nature blowing another Mt. St. Helen's, which affects the Earth's temperature for three years as much as three degrees.

When it comes to an issue such as global warming, in which the uncertainties are many but the consensus is quite robust, these focus group participants seemed to be saying that those he said/she said stories they encountered in the past led to more confusion than understanding.

CONCLUSION

Mass media accounts of uncertain science—like mass media accounts of any topic—are only one source of information people encounter in their daily lives. Yet, that does not relieve journalists of their obligation to do the best job they can to make their stories informative, understandable, and useful for their audiences. That task is especially challenging and important when journalists are dealing with new and controversial issues.

So, how can reporters bridge that gap between the interests and needs of audiences and the content of the stories they produce, taking into account such constraints as time, space, and resources? What can audiences—newspaper readers, radio listeners, and TV viewers—tell us about the type of information they need to make sense of the stories they read and hear?

First, in a very basic sense, journalists need to make a greater effort to understand the audiences for whom they report. They cannot simply assume that the audiences share their background, knowledge, or attention to the news.

A great deal of research has been conducted over the years on the dynamic ways in which people process information to make sense of their world and to manage the uncertainties that are regular parts of their lives. Only a small part of that work is touched on in this chapter. Yet, journalism training would do well to incorporate more of this knowledge into classroom instruction alongside the time devoted to teaching the craft of writing.

The movement toward public journalism offers some promise here as well. One of the characteristics of public journalism is the development of a better understanding of audiences and the presentation of news in ways that are meaningful to them.

Furthermore, the Internet and World Wide Web could provide new and meaningful ways for journalists to become better acquainted with audience needs and interests. Opportunities for audiences to send e-mail messages to journalists and news media outlets, asking questions and commenting on stories, are now a reality. A couple of caveats are in order here. At this point, even though such e-mail channels of communication now exist, it is not clear that journalists and media sites are actually paying attention to the messages they receive. Also, although people's access to the Internet and World Wide Web is increasing rapidly, as this chapter is being written, such access is still largely the province of a limited segment of society.

This study has also uncovered some features in news stories that make it difficult for audiences to make sense of them. First, reporters certainly need to go beyond the basic "who, what, when, where, why, and how" in writing about uncertain science, as well as about other complex topics. Somewhat surprisingly, however, these audiences told us that even some of that basic information—the fiveWs and H taught in introductory journalism classes—was missing.

Even when those basics were there, however, they were not enough. These individuals consistently reported having to make assumptions in order to make sense of the stories about both AIDS and global warming. As journalism professors McAdams and Elliott (1996) stressed, writers need to provide complete information and avoid making assumptions about the background and knowledge level of their audience.

Similarly, writer and teacher William Zinsser (1994) pointed out that one of the key tenets of journalism is "'the reader knows nothing.'. . . You just can't assume that your readers know what you assume everybody knows, or that they still remember what was once explained to them" (p. 157). Journalists need to regularly remind themselves to incorporate this perspective in their writing.

Part of the problem, of course, is that much news coverage is event-oriented, with stories focusing on what happened at one particular time. Additional details about the topic might have appeared earlier, such as the previous day or week. But as these focus group participants reminded us, we cannot assume that audiences encountered those earlier stories or, if they did, that they attended to them or can recall them.

The focus group participants in this study really had to work to make sense of the information they received. Journalists could have made their stories easier to understand if they had followed the advice of Levy and his colleagues in *The Main Source* (1986), which suggested that journalists make information explicit rather than implicit so that audiences do not have to work too hard to get the point. They also called for reporters to slow down the news and to build the story around one central point or theme. Several of the stories used in this study, especially the newspaper AIDS story, would have benefitted from this advice.

Writing instructors regularly stress the necessity of explaining technical or specialized terms. Ten years ago communication scholar Katherine Rowan (1988) outlined an explanatory strategy for writing that could make a major difference in this area. She suggested three types of explanations that could facilitate understanding: elucidating explanations, quasi-scientific explanations, and transformative explanations (see also chap. 12, this volume). As is all too common with news stories, these types of explanations were missing from the stories used in these focus groups.

Would such explanation have made a difference? One can only speculate. Yet, consider, for a moment, the stories about global warming and the confusion resulting from previous stories that featured "dueling scientists." Might audiences have better understood the stories if the reporters had begun with an explicit acknowledgment of beliefs audiences might already have had and then explained how this new information related to that?

Of course, in addition to information and explanation, these audiences wanted context. As the 1958 NASW report concluded, science writers should "present science in its context, whether the topic be abstract or concrete, and not . . . present bits and chunks of facts in isolation" (Survey Research Center, 1958, p. 178).

Levy and his colleagues (1986) made the same point when they stressed the need for journalists to emphasize why the story is important. Crane (1992) also pointed out that audiences need to be given a sense of why they should care about the story and should be given enough background so that they can understand it. She emphasized that stories need to answer the "so what" question. Almost to a person, these focus group participants asked for that kind of information.

Context is especially important in stories of uncertain science that involve health or environmental risks such as AIDS and global warming. In outlining what they termed an *ethical risk communication protocol*, communication scholars Valenti and Wilkins (1995) concluded that journalists covering such stories "would find themselves producing longer pieces that include context. ... Risk, in this framing, would be treated as an issue rather than a news event" (p. 192). The context that they and others have said was so important was one of the key things missing from these stories, according to the focus group participants.

Focus group participants also raised serious concerns about the video used in each of the stories. Not only did they find that the video often failed to support the narrative, but they also said that the video, in some cases, actually contradicted it. Crane (1992) stressed the importance of using compelling video that supports the narrative in television stories. Her advice would hold true for other media as well. Good visuals can enhance even a print story, often helping audiences to comprehend complex issues.

It would be easy to dismiss these individuals as unrepresentative and these stories as atypical. Indeed, it is important not to generalize from the focus group participants to all media users, but the higher educational backgrounds of these individuals should have given them an even greater ability than the average person to make sense of these media accounts. In addition, the media accounts themselves, although purposively chosen for the study, were standard fare produced, in most cases, by journalists who specialize in science topics.

Over the decades, journalists' work routines and the resulting stories have evolved largely to meet the needs and demands of their mass media organizations and of their sources. By listening to what their audiences tell them about the type of information stories need to have so they can make sense of them, journalists will more likely produce a product that will better meet the audience's needs as well.

ACKNOWLEDGMENTS

I'd like to thank my coeditors for their valuable suggestions on this chapter, and my husband, Steve Quigley, for his helpful comments and support. I'd also like to thank the focus group participants, who gave so generously of their time.

REFERENCES

Crane, V. (1992). Listening to the audience: Producer–Audience communication. In B. V. Lewenstein (Ed.), *When science meets the public* (pp. 21–32). Washington, DC: American Association for the Advancement of Science.

Cushman, J., Jr. (1997, November 28). Public backs tough steps for a treaty on warming. *The New York Times*, pp. A36.

Dawson, D. A., Cynamon, M., & Fitti, J. E. (1987). *AIDS knowledge and attitudes, provisional data from the national health interview survey: United States, August 1987* (No. 146, DHHS Pub. No. (PHS) 88–1250). Hyattsville, MD: National Center for Health Statistics.

Dunwoody, S., & Neuwirth, K. (1991). Coming to terms with the impact of communication on scientific and technological risk judgments. In L. Wilkins & P. Patterson (Eds.), *Risky business: Communicating issues of science, risk, and public policy* (pp. 11–30). New York: Greenwood.

Environmental Defense Fund. (1995). *Global warming: The history of an international scientific consensus* [Online]. Available: http://www.edf.org/pubs/FactSheets/d_GWFact.html.

The Henry J. Kaiser Family Foundation. (1996a). *Covering the epidemic: AIDS in the news media, 1985–1996.* Menlo Park, CA: Author.

The Henry J. Kaiser Family Foundation. (1996b). *The Kaiser Survey on Americans and AIDS/HIV.* Menlo Park, CA: Author.

The Henry J. Kaiser Family Foundation. (1996c). *The Kaiser Survey on Americans and AIDS: The role of the media.* Menlo Park, CA: Author.

Hornig, S. (1993). Reading risk: Public response to print media accounts of technological risk. *Public Understanding of Science, 2*(2), 95–109.

Intergovernmental Panel on Climate Change. (1995). *Climate Change 1995* [Online]. Available: http://www.unep.ch/ipcc/syntrep.html.

Kinsella, J. (1989). *Covering the plague: AIDS and the American media.* New Brunswick, NJ: Rutgers University Press.

Konick, S. (1993). *Network news coverage of AIDS: An analysis of verbal and visual texts.* Unpublished doctoral dissertation, University of Maryland, College Park, MD.

Levy, M. R., Robinson, J. P., & Davis, D. K. (1986). News comprehension and the working journalist. In J. P. Robinson & M. R. Levy (Eds.), *The main source: Learning from television news* (pp. 211–228). Beverly Hills, CA: Sage.

McAdams, K. C., & Elliott, J. J. (1996). *Reaching audiences: A guide to media writing.* Boston: Allyn & Bacon.

National Institute of Allergy and Infectious Diseases. (1997). *HIV/AIDS statistics fact sheet* (Fact Sheet). Bethesda, MD: National Institutes of Health.

National Science Board. (1998). *Science & engineering indicators 1998* (Government document no.NSB 98–1). Washington, DC: U.S. Government Printing Office.

Nelkin, D. (1995). *Selling science: How the press covers science and technology* (Rev. ed.). New York: Freeman.

Neuman, W. R., Just, M. R., & Crigler, A. N. (1992). *Common knowledge: News and the construction of political meaning.* Chicago: University of Chicago Press.

Pew Research Center for the People & the Press. (1997). *Americans support action on global warming* [Online]. Available: http://www.people–press.org/nov97rpt.htm.

Prewitt, K. (1982). The public and science policy. *Science, Technology, & Human Values, 7*(39), 5–14.

Roberts, L. (1990, August 10). Counting on science at EPA. *Science, 249,* 616–618.

Rogers, E. M., Dearing, J. W., & Chang, S. (1991). AIDS in the 1980s: The agenda–setting process for a public issue. *Journalism Monographs, 126.*

Rowan, K. E. (1988). A contemporary theory of explanatory writing. *Written Communication, 5*(1), 23–56.

Scientists' Institute for Public Information. (1993). Science news: What does the public want? *SIPIscope, 20*(2), 1–10.

Singer, E., & Endreny, P. M. (1993). *Reporting on risk.* New York: Russell Sage Foundation.

Survey Research Center. (1958). *The public impact of science in the mass media: A report on a nationwide survey for the National Association of Science Writers.* Ann Arbor, MI: Institute for Social Research, University of Michigan.

Trumbo, C. (1995). Longitudinal modeling of public issues: An application of the agenda–setting process to the issue of global warming. *Journalism & Mass Communication Monographs, 152.*

UNAIDS/WHO Working Group on Global HIV/AIDS and STD Surveillance. (1997). *Report on the global HIV/AIDS epidemic* [Online]. Available: http//www.unaids.org/highband/document/epidemio/report97.html.

Valenti, J., & Wilkins, L. (1995). An ethical risk communication protocol for science and mass communication. *Public Understanding of Science, 4,* 177–194.

Wilkins, L. (1993). Between facts and values: Print media coverage of the greenhouse effect, 1987–1990. *Public Understanding of Science, 2*(1), 71–84.

Wilkins, L., & Patterson, P. (1991). Science as symbol: The media chills the greenhouse effect. In L. Wilkins & P. Patterson (Eds.), *Risky business: Communicating issues of science, risk, and public policy* (pp. 159–176). New York: Greenwood.

Wynne, B. (1993). Public uptake of science: A case for institutional reflexivity. *Public Understanding of Science, 2*(4), 321–337.

Zinsser, W. (1994). *On writing well* (5th ed.). New York: Harper Perennial.

Zucker, H. G. (1978). The variable nature of news media influence. In B. D. Ruben (Ed.), *Communication yearbook, 2* (pp. 225–240). New Brunswick, NJ: Transaction.

Chapter 12

Effective Explanation of Uncertain and Complex Science

Katherine E. Rowan

*Katherine E. Rowan is a professor in the Department of Communication at Purdue University. Her research focuses on risk communication and mass media explanations of scientific information. It appears in journals such as **Communication Education, Risk Analysis, Written Communication,** and **Journalism Educator.***

Years ago, forest fires were always bad. Currently, prescribed burning is a standard practice in forestry.

Years ago, swamps were wastelands. Now, environmental scientists say these wetlands are "nature's kidneys" because they cleanse polluted water, allow floodwaters to recede peacefully, and provide habitat for important flora and fauna.

Several years ago, we were told that salt was bad for our health. A recent TV documentary said the health risk of high salt intake has been substantially overstated and that high salt intake is harmful only to those with specific health ailments (Neufeldt, 1997).

Audiences for mass media science routinely receive these conflicting reports. They learn to talk about wetlands, hormones, toxic chemicals, and ozone layers, although exactly what these concepts mean and what the conflicting reports about them are saying is often unclear. Uncertainty about the validity and meaning of scientific claims is pervasive in science news.

Journalists routinely manage uncertainties. They learn to frame conflicting claims as certain types of stories, and they identify ways of researching unfamiliar subjects quickly (see chap. 2, in this volume). As experts in the arts of uncertainty management, they do not need a review of communication fundamentals, but they can use "step back" opportunities. Just as professional athletes benefit from coaching, so too can those who report and write science news benefit from learning about text features that help audiences consider conflicting information and understand complex ideas.

This chapter provides that sort of "step back" opportunity. Organized as a discussion of myths, this chapter first debunks the myth that science is a collection of facts that scientists spot and journalists convey. To critique this myth, the chapter discusses ways in which scientific knowledge and everyday knowledge differ, and then explains the implications of these differences for reporting science news. A key implication is that audiences are poorly served when scientific findings are reported without some account of the reasoning that led to them. Frequently, the finding and the reasoning are intertwined.

The second myth concerns balance in science news. Sometimes science news is reported with an announcement of findings, a statement from someone who agrees with the findings, and another from someone who disagrees. This approach suggests that those agreeing and those disagreeing have equally valid perspectives. Because science works by consensual puzzle-solving, this is rarely the case. The chapter explains why and offers an alternative way to report science news objectively.

The third myth says that jargon and lengthy sentences are the principal obstacles to making science news clear. Instead, there are other, harder to detect, but more important barriers to comprehending science. Three are identified along with research-supported ways of overcoming them.

MYTH #1: SCIENCE IS A COLLECTION OF FACTS THAT SCIENTISTS SPOT. JOURNALISTS CONVEY THESE FACTS THROUGH NEWS STORIES SO NEWS AUDIENCES CAN APPLY THEM TO THEIR LIVES

Like all myths, this one has some appeal. Most people encounter science through textbooks, and textbook science is typically a presentation of established scientific knowledge (Trachtman, 1989). Because a good deal of textbook science has been tested for decades or even centuries, it has the status of fact. Yet, this myth suggests that news about the findings of recent studies also constitutes facts and that news stories reporting these facts must be correct. Furthermore, it says that reporters simply convey scientific findings and provide a range of comments about them.

One way of questioning this myth is to analyze its impact in different situations. First, consider a reporter covering a city council meeting. The meeting is an event that reporters, editors, and news audiences can verify. Many have some way of judging the council news to determine if it makes sense. In sharp contrast, imagine that a respected local scientist calls a TV station to report seeing a UFO above Main Street. Reporters receiving this call have many ways to check it out, just as they do the city council story. They can talk with passersby to see if they saw anything unusual downtown. They can contact the scientists' colleagues to see whether they can corroborate the UFO sighting. They can interview family and friends of the UFO-spotting scientist to inquire about his mental health, and so forth. However, if this story is aired or published, there is one aspect of it that will probably not be reported—an aspect that is difficult for journalists and news audiences to assess. The scientist who believes he has identified a UFO has likely used special reasoning processes to reach his conclusion, as startling as it might be. Although these out of the ordinary patterns of thought might be attributable to mental instability, they are also the stuff of scientific discovery. Even though these reasoning processes are hard to explain, they are part of the story. The news is not simply that something occurred. The news is the range of questions, uncertainties, and interpretations the reporter, scientists, and other rational observers would use to identify and frame this event.

In one sense, scientific claims are always like this hypothetical scientist's claim that a UFO is hovering over downtown. Scientific claims refer to events in the world that may be both real and creations of a particular kind of human reasoning. The specialized reasoning needed to make scientific discoveries is frequently not reported in news stories because it is unfamiliar and hard to understand. Yet, reporting a scientific discovery without at least some of the reasoning that led to it is like reporting a baseball game's final score without an account of the game. The score is meaningful only to fans. For science news to be meaningful, enjoyable, and accountable to wide audiences, journalists need to package stories in ways that help people realize that the fundamental rule in considering them is not "true, unless good reasons suggest otherwise." The rule for judging science news should be "important, if true" (Sandman, 1986, p. 1).

In the 19th century, astronomers discovered Uranus, the seventh planet from the sun. About the same time, they spotted some round, blurry images in interstellar space that looked like Uranus. Astronomers named these round images *planetary nebulae* because they looked like planets and they were nebulous, or hazy. In 1997, astronomers using the Hubble Space telescope were able to see these fuzzy images more clearly. Scientists now say that planetary nebulae are not planets, they are not nebulous, and they are not always round.

News reports in late 1997 told of a scientist nearly falling off his chair when he saw Hubble's pictures of planetary nebulae (Wilford, 1997). Hubble's photos revealed these blobs to be neither blobs nor planets, but the gaseous emissions of dying stars burning away in shapes ranging from pinwheels to butterflies (Edmonds, 1997).

The difference of a century shows the integral connection between scientific facts or discoveries and the reasoning that leads to them. As the misleadingly named planetary nebulae show, scientific findings are partly "out there" and partly a function of currently available scientific tools and reasoning. As noted earlier, to report only findings, facts, or discoveries is similar to reporting sport scores without describing the corresponding games. Ideally, good sports coverage helps people to enjoy, vicariously participate in, and even check the accuracy of a game story. Similarly, coverage of science news should help audiences be scientist-like in the ways in which they respond to science news. A good science news story should help audiences learn to test or question scientific claims. Ideally, it feeds an audience's appetite for increasingly better explanations by giving people some basis for questioning or considering scientific claims—rather than frustrating them with unsupported claims that warrant only blind faith or unreflective cynicism.

Scientific Knowledge and Everyday Knowledge

Journalists who understand the differences between scientific knowledge and everyday knowledge can help their audiences think scientifically. Social scientists Reif and Larkin (1991) summarized these differences well. According to these authors, scientific knowledge and everyday knowledge vary because the goals of science and everyday life differ. People's goals for living are, roughly, to lead satisfying lives. Explaining confusing phenomena and predicting future events are important only in so far as they contribute to the general goal of having a satisfying life. Consequently, the criteria for explanation and prediction in everyday life are not stringent. For example, if you routinely park a car on steep hills, it is useful to predict that applying the parking brake will reduce your risk of injury. Yet, for everyday life, few people need the laws of physics to understand what will happen if they fail to exercise this caution.

In contrast, for scientists, explanation of natural and social phenomena is the principal goal. Consequently, the definitions, claims, words, and inferences used to explain and predict must be exceptionally precise and careful. Furthermore, because more refined, more precise, better explanation is always possible, no phenomenon, no matter how thoroughly studied, is ever fully explained or understood. In this sense, all scientific knowledge is uncertain. In addition, and more surprising from the perspective of everyday life, discovery is not the principal goal of science. Galileo discovered the sparks near Jupiter with his telescope, but his capacity to hypothesize that these sparks of light were probably moons was an integral part of his finding. Instead of facts being "out there" for collection, science is the process of building increasingly better ways of explaining reality through the testing of claims (Burleson, 1979; Kinneavy, 1971; Kuhn, 1962; Toulmin, 1972; Whedbee, 1993). In support of this view, Reif and Larkin (1991) cited physicist William Bragg, who said, "The important thing in science is not so much to obtain new facts as to discover new ways of thinking about them" (p. 739).

REVISION OF MYTH #1: SCIENCE IS A PUZZLE-SOLVING PROCESS DESIGNED TO PRODUCE BETTER EXPLANATIONS OF REALITY. WHEN JOURNALISTS REPORT SCIENCE NEWS, THEY SHOULD HELP AUDIENCES PARTICIPATE IN THIS PUZZLE-SOLVING BY REPORTING SOME OF THE REASONING THAT SUPPORTS OR QUESTIONS THE FINDINGS

For audiences to gain the most from science writing, journalists need to assist them in learning to "play" the game of demanding increasingly better explanations and increasingly more evidence for any claim. As Reif and Larkin noted, audiences are capable of learning very precise rules for reasoning when they understand that these rules are needed. For example, people learn the precise rules needed to play board games or to balance their checkbooks. Just as journalists assist audiences in understanding and evaluating unfamiliar sporting events, so too do they need to assist audiences in understanding and evaluating scientific claims.

Unfortunately, reporting scientific findings with little evidence of their merit has become a frequent practice. Pellechia (1997) sampled 30 years of newspaper science stories. She found that stories often omitted information on how scientific studies were conducted. An Associated Press (1997) story seemed to illustrate Pellechia's finding:

> NEW YORK (AP)—A derivative of vitamin A reversed emphysema-like abnor-
> malities in the lungs of rats, suggesting a possible lead for a treatment. . . .

"This is the first time that anyone has identified a means of reversing emphysema," said Dr. Claude Lenfant, director of the National Heart, Lung, and Blood Institute.

But Lenfant, whose institute paid for part of the work, said in a statement that much more basic research is needed "before we can even begin to think about applying this to humans." (p. 4)

This story summarizes a study published in *Nature*, a scientific journal. The Associated Press reporter was careful to note the study's funding source and to include a caution about overgeneralizing the finding in rats to humans. Yet, another essential step may not have been taken. Readers need evidence if they are to make their own judgments, and they need writers to teach them how to evaluate the evidence. When they are not given evidence, audiences have no guidance on what to think if conflicting findings are reported 6 months from now. In its current version, this emphysema story is about as meaningless as the UFO-spotted-downtown story. A claim is made, but the reasoning behind the claim is missing. Audiences need that missing part of the story if they are to understand why that claim survived rigorous testing—or if it did.

Suggestions for Journalists

To help audiences think about science news, journalists should find out:

- What evidence, reasoning, or testing supports a finding.
- What "bugs," frustrates, or impresses scientists about their finding.
- What parts of the puzzle remain unsolved.
- What the best objections are from respected others.
- What has to happen before the finding is viewed as established knowledge.
- What people can do to learn more.

MYTH #2: CONFLICTING FINDINGS AND OPINIONS IN SCIENCE NEWS CAN BE REPORTED THE SAME WAY DISAGREEMENT IN ANY OTHER FORM OF NEWS IS REPORTED

In everyday life, we are often interested in public opinion on questions of value and policy. The range of opinion on immigration or taxation is important partly because decisions on these policies will be influenced by our votes. However, scientific knowledge or consensus is not built by elections or opinion polls. It is built through the testing of claims in scientific journals, conferences, and daily discussion. So, when journalists strive for balance in reporting, they cannot simply give audiences a report that "one scientist says it is and another says it is not." Instead, to achieve balance and accuracy in science news reporting, journalists need to let the public know whether an explanation is widely shared in the scientific community, the bases for its support or lack of support, and some of the better critiques of this position.

REVISION OF MYTH #2: BECAUSE SCIENTIFIC PUZZLE-SOLVING WORKS BY TESTING CLAIMS AND BUILDING CONSENSUAL SUPPORT FOR ONE EXPLANATION OVER OTHERS, NEWS AUDIENCES NEED TO KNOW HOW WIDELY A SCIENTIST'S OPINION IS SHARED BY OTHER SCIENTISTS

Global warming is an issue that illustrates the importance of reporting the extent of scientific support for claims. This climatic phenomenon refers to an average increase in global temperature caused by increasing amounts of greenhouse gases (Hammitt, 1995). Currently, there is widespread scientific agreement that amounts of atmospheric greenhouse gases have increased over the last several centuries. Evidence of these increases may be found in such phenomena as fossilized plants and tree ring records. These entities provide indicators of changing atmospheric gas content (Williams, 1992, p. 197). In contrast, however, there is considerable disagreement among scientists about the long-range physical, social, and economic impacts of these increases.

Ideally, a balanced story on global warming would let audiences know which claims in this complex puzzle are supported by scientific consensus and which are not. A story that cited one scientist who said greenhouse gases have increased since the 1600s and another scientist who said they had not would be balanced in the classic sense, but it also would be extremely inaccurate and misleading. Reporters are more likely to achieve balance, accuracy, and objectivity in covering science news if they let audiences know how widely key claims are supported by most scientists. The puzzle-solving orientation of science means that groups of scientists continually try to find consistent ways of viewing, testing, and solving core problems. That is, they work within paradigms. The trick in science reporting is to indicate broad support for claims that have survived rigorous testing but still help audiences see that currently accepted perspectives are the best working hypotheses.

Although mass media reports may tend to underestimate the amount of scientific consensus on certain claims, in some cases there may be, in fact, relatively little consensus. News audiences have become accustomed to conflicting answers on questions about the merit of fat and sugar. Unfortunately, research suggests that, rather than helping audiences cope with complex issues, stories that present conflicting information sometimes breed confusion or cynicism (Qian & Alvermann, 1995; Rukavina & Daneman, 1996; Schommer, 1990). Reflecting the public's frustration, Greenfield (1984) wrote, "By now the public suspects that what is banned today is likely to be given intravenously tomorrow" (p. 80).

Such cynicism is sometimes warranted. But, because science is an unending quest for better explanations and because the phenomena it attempts to explain are complex, a great deal of science news involves inconsistent information. Interestingly, a recent line of work suggests that the ways writers frame or package science news may assist audiences in interpreting conflicting findings (e.g., Qian & Alvermann, 1995; Rukavina & Daneman, 1996). In brief, this research shows that when writers cast scientific information as a puzzle or a dilemma, where there is no single answer, some individuals are better able to comprehend it. Specifically, Rukavina and Daneman (1996) found that labeling conflicting accounts as an unsolved puzzle with two possible answers and then discussing the strengths and weaknesses of each answer significantly improved comprehension of these ideas among many high school and college students. In contrast, students who received the same information in texts that presented the two theories successively were less likely to understand the theories or even note that they conflicted.

Journalists are not always able to frame scientific findings as a puzzle. Sometimes science news gives results from only one study. However, the puzzle frame is appropriate when several studies present mixed results. For example, a 1997 story begins, "The quandary faced by millions of American women of whether to enter menopause with or without hormone replacement therapy is likely to be exacerbated by a new set of studies published this week" (Bowman, 1997, p. A2). The story's next two paragraphs briefly summarize two research reports: a *New England Journal of Medicine* study that says hormone therapy may increase risk of breast cancer and a *Neurology* study that says this hormone therapy may reduce risk of Alzheimer's. The story then describes these studies and includes a recommendation that women consult their physicians to determine the best choices for them. If Rukavina and

Daneman (1996) are right, audiences' abilities to reason about science news such as this may be improved by the reporter's lead paragraph labeling the situation as a quandary to which there are few simple answers. Without this story frame, some readers may infer that a fatalistic or cynical view of post-menopausal options is the only possible perspective. The puzzle format may increase awareness of other choices.

Suggestions for Journalists

To provide balance, accuracy, and objectivity in science news, reporters should:

- Learn if a claim is widely supported by scientists.
- Find out if the scientists being interviewed endorse this consensus.
- Ask whether there are important variants on the consensus view.
- Frame conflicting findings as puzzles, noting the strengths and weaknesses of key puzzle-solving efforts.

MYTH #3: JARGON AND LONG SENTENCES ARE THE CHIEF OBSTACLES TO UNDER-STANDING SCIENCE NEWS

Intuitively, we know that unfamiliar words and long sentences are often hard to understand. Research supports these intuitions. For example, Hayes (1992) operationalized *lexical difficulty* as relative frequency of word usage. He demonstrated that scholarly articles in journals such as *Science*, *Nature*, and *Cell* are among the most lexically difficult forms of discourse, whereas mothers' talk to 3-year-olds and farmers' talk to cows are among the least lexically taxing. Numerous other readability studies, in which *readability* is defined in terms of word and sentence length, have come to similar conclusions (e.g., Klare, 1963).

However, there are important limitations to readability research. First, it offers a very narrow depiction of possible sources of confusion. Readability research assumes that the only sources of difficulty in comprehending complex ideas are the length and familiarity of words and sentences (Shuy & Larkin, 1978). Although this set of obstacles is important, audiences find many ideas difficult to comprehend, even when they are expressed in the simplest and most familiar words (e.g., the idea that the Earth is weightless is hard to understand).

Furthermore, studies show that if writers try to simply shorten sentences by excising transitional words and phrases, they may occasionally make their texts less—rather than more—understandable (Davison, 1984; Duffy, 1985). Transitional words and phrases may illuminate links between key points; these links, in turn, help audiences build mental models of complex phenomena. So, ironically, a text with multisyllabic words and long sentences may be more understandable than one with short sentences and a seventh-grade reading level—if the ideas it expresses seem intuitively plausible.

A third problem with readability research is that it is atheoretical. Grade levels for readability are simply correlations between indexes of word and sentence length in reading passages and the likelihood that students in various grade levels can answer questions on these passages correctly. It is unlikely that word and sentence length are the only factors affecting student comprehension.

REVISION OF MYTH #3: THERE ARE MANY OBSTACLES TO UNDERSTANDING SCIENCE NEWS

When it comes to excising jargon and making sentences clear, journalists have considerable support from textbooks, computerized aids, and editors. Yet, science writers and journalists have far less assistance in anticipating their audience's conceptual confusion. This may be one reason why Long (1995) found that science news stories devoted only 10% or less of their content to explaining complexities.

One way to think about likely sources of conceptual confusion is to review research on these phenomena. According to research, scientific ideas may be misunderstood in three principal ways. The first source of confusion occurs when familiar terms are used in unfamiliar ways. In everyday life, the word *force* may be associated with movement that requires effort, such as pushing or shoving; for scientists, however, this term typically refers to Newtonian force, which has nothing to do with effort. In everyday parlance, *hormones* are often considered artificial, excessive, or unnecessary substances; however, in scientific contexts, the term *hormones* may refer to essential substances found in all cells, both plant and animal.

The second source of conceptual confusion concerns structures or processes that must be envisioned or mentally modeled at new levels of precision or abstractness. Instead of simply referring to digestion, scientists might need to envision these processes in great detail to learn, for example, why stomachs do not digest their own linings. Similarly, a scientist considering a traffic accident might want to envision it abstractly in terms of an equation: Force equals mass times acceleration ($F = MA$). Journalists may have to help audiences to picture these entities in these new ways.

A third source of conceptual confusion lies with notions difficult to understand because they are counterintuitive. For instance, the ideas that the Earth is weightless, that forest fires can be good for forests (Patterson, 1992), or that plants naturally produce carcinogens and pesticides (Ames, Magaw, & Gold, 1987) are each supported by many scientists. Nevertheless, these ideas seem implausible to many people.

Scholars in a variety of fields have explored these obstacles to understanding science, identifying text features effective at overcoming each. I refer to people's efforts to minimize these difficulties as certain types of explanation (e.g., Rowan, 1988, 1992, 1995). These include elucidating explanations, which establish the meaning and use of terms; quasi-scientific explanations, which help audiences see the outlines of complex scientific phenomena; and transformative explanations, which help audiences understand counterintuitive scientific ideas.

Elucidating Explanations

Elucidating explanations are designed to help people understand the meaning and use of a term. The name *elucidating* is used because this sort of discourse clarifies meanings. Research in instructional design and linguistics shows that when people are struggling to understand the meaning of a term, they are in fact struggling to distinguish a concept's essential meaning from its associated meaning. So, good elucidating explanations focus attention on this distinction. Specifically, good elucidating explanations contain a typical instance of the concept, a definition that lists each of the concept's essential features, an array of varied examples and nonexamples (nonexamples are instances likely to be mistaken for examples), and opportunities to practice distinguishing examples from nonexamples (Merrill & Tennyson, 1977; Tennyson & Cocchiarella, 1986).

Because good elucidating explanations include sets of varying examples and nonexamples as well as definitions, they are more effective at emphasizing a concept's critical features than definitions alone. That is, concept mastery is more likely when people practice considering ways in which certain examples embody each critical feature of meaning and certain nonexamples do not.

Typically, elucidating explanations begin with definitions or examples. Yet, sometimes, they first help audiences recognize a concept's unessential meanings.

Journalists make this move when the name of a concept is misleading. For example, in a special section for *The Quill*, a journalism magazine, Hammitt (1995) noted that the term *global warming* is misleading. As he wrote, "Global warming is not likely to produce a uniform warming of the Earth's surface. . . . Some regions may even experience cooler than average temperatures" (p. 3). Similarly, writers discussing dietary fiber frequently say that not all dietary fiber is fibrous or stringy.

Second, good elucidating explanations list all of a concept's essential meanings. Wetlands are not simply any patches of moist soil. There are many legal definitions, but typically wetland is distinguished by permanent or periodic soil saturation, creating anaerobic conditions and distinctive vegetation that grows in water ("Federal manual," 1989). Because wetlands may be protected from farming or development by law, some people have become alarmed when *wetness* and *land* were viewed erroneously as the only defining criteria for wetlands.

A third feature of a good elucidating explanation is an array of varied examples. Intuition tells writers to give an example of a confusing concept, but research suggests that the best elucidating explanations offer many examples that illustrate the concept's essential meaning in differing ways (Merrill & Tennyson, 1977, p. xx). This effort to illustrate a concept's essential features in multiple guises minimizes the likelihood that a random feature of some single example will be interpreted as essential. *The Washington Post* writer Lawrence G. Prouix (1996) does a good job of offering a range of varied examples in a story on what counts as dietary fiber:

> Much of fiber is chemically similar to starch, but its atoms are so arranged that our stomach enzymes cannot break it down. It comes in two types, insoluble and soluble, and plant foods are the source of both. Insolubles, such as cellulose, fit the popular sawdust-like image of fiber (think of wheat bran). They absorb water and add bulk to the stool but pass out of the body unchanged. . . . Soluble fibers are softer things, including gums and pectin; apples and oats are good sources. (p. D2)

This passage is a good elucidating explanation because it offers varied examples of fiber (from the sawdust-like to the "softer things" like oats). The text might be even clearer if it explicitly defined *dietary fiber* and offered an even wider range of examples. One definition says dietary fiber is "plant cellular material resistant to digestion by human beings" (Slavin, 1987, p. 1164). Audiences are sometimes surprised to learn that french fries count as fiber and that "the fiber content of canned vegetables may be higher than that of fresh vegetables because browning reactions may occur with cooking" and "the browning products are [a kind of fiber called] . . . lignin" (p. 1167). Ideally, the wider the range of examples writers can offer, the clearer the essential features of a concept become. In this case, differing examples help readers understand the array of fiber sources.

A final important step of an elucidating explanation is discussion of nonexamples. Research shows that audiences can make important distinctions when they are offered apparent examples that nonetheless are erroneous illustrations of the concept (Merrill & Tennyson, 1977; Tennyson, Woolley, & Merrill, 1972). For example, Prouix (1996) could further help audiences recognize fiber by discussing a nonexample: tough meat. Tough meat is fibrous or string-like, but it is not an instance of dietary fiber because it is not plant material. Providing this nonexample would be one more way to clarify the essential versus the associated meanings of this concept.

Quasi-scientific Explanations

The second type of explanation is the quasi-scientific. This type helps audiences envision main points, key structures, or critical connections in complex phenomena. For instance, quasi-scientific explanations help audiences understand hard-to-picture phenomena, such as how the Pathfinder spacecraft relayed Mars images to Earth or why butterfly wings dissipate heat effectively. I use the term "quasi-scientific" for this type of explanation because it is similar to the sort of explanation scientists produce for one another. That is, scientists aim to represent some aspect of reality; journalists make these scientific accounts widely accessible partly through use of graphic aids, textual highlighting, and figurative language.

Picturing the Complex. Science news is often difficult to understand because it describes hard-to-picture structures or processes. Good quasi-scientific explanations overcome this obstacle by helping audiences to construct mental models of the intricate or abstract. Research shows that texts characterized by features suggesting the structure of to-be-learned material help audiences not only to understand such information, but also to use it. These text features include signaling devices, such as titles, previews, headings, bullet points, topic sentences, and transitions; and figurative language, such as organizing analogies (e.g., "Wetlands are nature's kidneys: They filter impurities") and graphic aids such as drawings, models, and animation. Overall, studies show that texts and videos enhanced by these features are better understood and applied than is the same information without them (Gentner, 1988; Gilbert &

Osborne, 1980; Loman & Mayer, 1983; Mayer, 1983; Mayer & Anderson, 1992; Mayer & Sims, 1994; McDaniel & Donnelly, 1996; Rukavina & Daneman, 1996).

For example, Mayer, Bove, Bryman, Mars, and Tapangco (1996) gave randomized groups of college students materials explaining how lightning strikes. One group of students received a text account accompanied by captioned cartoons that highlighted key steps in the process (e.g., particles in a cloud and on the Earth become oppositely charged; opposites attract; lightning strikes if a "leader"—an antenna, a tree—facilitates the particles' attraction. See Fig. 12.1). The other group of students read a text account without the captioned cartoons. The researchers found that those who had the captioned cartoons, plus the text, were better able to use their new knowledge to solve problems than were those who were given the text only. For instance, the text-plus-captions group was better able to describe conditions under which lightning would not strike than were their counterparts.

Good quasi-scientific explanations minimize distracting detail. That is, if the key challenge involved in understanding some intricate structure or process is its envisionment, then material that distracts people from building rough mental outlines is likely to hinder comprehension. In the lightning study, Mayer et al. (1996) found that those students who received an additional 550 words of text along with their captioned cartoons did not do as well on measures of comprehension and problem solving as the group that received the captioned cartoons plus text without the unnecessary words.

Good explainers often sense an audience's need for mental models. Effective teachers preview a lecture's main points. Similarly, scientists being interviewed may search for pencil and paper to draw, for example, the structure of some enzyme. They may also offer an analogy that captures the gist of the science they are trying to explain. In a news story on a new memory drug, for example, reporter Robert S. Boyd (1996) quoted a scientist who provided a particularly vivid comparison:

> "In summer, a forest is full and thick. In winter, you can see clear through the trees. Unfortunately, that's what your brain looks like with age," [Dr. Gary Lynch] said. "As the number of healthy brain cells shrinks, ampakines [the new drug] increase the ability of the remaining neurons to communicate with each other," Lynch explained. (p. A2)

An Associated Press version of this story appeared in a local paper without the seasonal analogy (Recer, 1996). Without it, the story seemed less effective at explaining this source of memory loss and its treatment.

The Process of Lightning

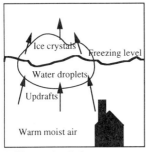

1. Warm moist air rises, water vapor condenses and forms cloud.

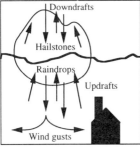

2. Raindrops and ice crystals drag air downward.

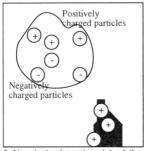

3. Negatively charged particles fall to bottom of cloud.

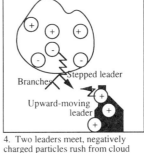

4. Two leaders meet, negatively charged particles rush from cloud to ground.

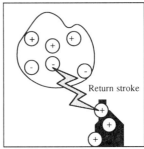

5. Positively charged particles from the ground rush upward along the same path.

FIG. 12.1. A captioned set of diagrams or cartoon used by Mayer et al. (1996) to explain how lightning works. Students who saw this illustration understood how lightning works better than those who read a text account but saw no illustration. Copyright 1996 by the American Psychological Association. Reprinted with permission.

Conflicting scientific findings may be considered a special kind of confusing, hard-to-picture structure. Rukavina and Daneman (1996) argued that this explains why readers are more likely to understand conflicting theories when those theories are introduced as differing approaches to an unsolved puzzle, for which there are two possible answers, than when conflicting research is presented without this frame. The puzzle label suggests a way to organize and consider what may otherwise be viewed as senseless information.

Transformative Explanations

Transformative explanations help audiences understand ideas that are difficult to comprehend because they are counterintuitive. That is, some scientific notions can be expressed with simple words and are easy to envision, but they are still profoundly difficult to understand. For instance, people struggle to understand how forest fires could possibly be good for forests, how the Earth could be weightless, or why going outdoors without a jacket is not the cause of head colds. In these cases, powerful nonscientific, or lay, theories are the principal source of confusion. Research in science education shows that transformative explanations help audiences recognize, test, and overcome lay theories. Transformative explanations are so named because they assist audiences not only in recognizing an implicit lay theory, but also in understanding its strengths and limitations, in fathoming the reasons scientists endorse the counterintuitive explanation, and in transforming the lay theory into science-based information that can be comprehended and accepted.

Scholars have explored lay theorizing in detail, for it particularly blocks people's mastery of Newtonian principles and scientific accounts of familiar phenomena such as weight, light, or disease (e.g., Alvermann, Smith, & Readance, 1985; Anderson & Smith, 1984; diSessa, 1982; Guzetti, Snyder, Glass, & Gamas, 1993; M. G. Hewson, & P. W. Hewson, 1983; P. W. Hewson, & M. G. Hewson, 1984). Fortunately, it is possible to predict the contexts in which lay theories are most likely to develop. People develop lay theories about very familiar aspects of life that have great import. Lay theories explain weather, accidents, gender relations, nutrition, and so forth. For example, powerful lay theories may tell people that bad air is the cause of a disease or a glider's crash. Lay notions erroneously assure people that everything natural is good or that infants riding in cars are just as safe in a parent's arms as they are in a car seat.

Lay theories are difficult to overcome for several reasons. First, they are often tacit or unspoken, although they still guide thought and action (e.g.,

Rowan, 1991). People who memorized force equals mass times acceleration may be surprised when they learn a train traveling only 10 miles an hour can cause a horrific accident. Their unspoken lay theory says that impact or force is a function of speed. Third, lay theories often exist side by side with their more orthodox scientific counterparts (Anderson & Smith, 1984). As in the train example, everyday experiences may seem to support the lay notion that slowness equals "lightness." To reconsider a lay notion, people must sometimes be surprised into awareness of the discrepancy between a lay theory and its more accepted scientific counterpart. Media coverage of an accident caused by a slow train may be the impetus creating this surprise. Good reporting can take advantage of such opportunities and help people rethink the connections among mass, acceleration, and force.

Researchers have identified message features that help audiences recognize and reflect on lay theories. In general, good transformative explanations treat audiences like scientists, and scientists do not give up their theories until they have compelling reasons to do so. Similarly, people do not give up lay notions simply because someone says they are wrong. Specifically, good transformative explanations help audiences overcome lay theories when they state the lay theory, acknowledge its apparent merit, create dissatisfaction with it, and show how a more orthodox notion better explains the phenomenon in question (Alvermann et al., 1985; Anderson & Smith, 1984; Guzzetti et al., 1993; Hashweh, 1988; Hewson, & Hewson, 1983; Hewson, & Hewson, 1984; Kuhn, 1989; Schommer, 1990; Shymansky & Kyle, 1988).

Transformative Explanations in the Mass Media. A good example of transformative explanation appeared when *The New York Times* covered the devastating Hamptons fire in 1995. In one story, reporter Andrew Revkin (1995) effectively explained the counterintuitive idea that a policy of controlled burning might have prevented these fires. In the story, he alluded to the lay theory that "forest fires must be bad for forests" and explained its inadequacy:

> For several years, environmental experts had been warning that the forests, which have evolved in a natural cycle that includes frequent fires, need to be burned in a planned pattern to avoid disastrous wild blazes.

> But, unlike Southern California where fire—both wild and managed—is almost an annual rite, Long Island has not seen a vast blaze in more than two generations, said Bruce Lund, director of preserves for the conservancy.

> Controlled burning has been successful for years in other areas with pine barrens, including a preserve in Albany, . . . foresters say.

The shrubs' waxy leaves, the resin-rich pine branches, and the dense mats of twigs and other litter typical of such barrens form one of the most combustible forest types in the country, said Dr. William Patterson, a professor of forestry at the University of Massachusetts.

"That's the unique thing about pine barrens," Dr. Patterson said. "So much can burn so fast that it's very hard to react. Once it starts, often the only thing to do is to get out of the way." (p. A25)

Revkin's story does a good job of explaining a practice that may seem absurd to New York residents unfamiliar with controlled burning. Furthermore, his story is well-researched, clear, and thought-provoking. The story acknowledges the understandability of the lay viewpoint, suggests its inadequacy, and then explains the greater range of situations accounted for by the expert view. It contains all of the attributes of a good transformative explanation, with one exception: The story does not explicitly state the lay theory to be critiqued or debunked. Presumably, the unstated lay theory is, "Forest fires are always bad for forests," or "If open flames are harmful to people and animals, they must be harmful to trees." By explicitly stating these lay views and then critiquing them directly, Revkin's story might be even more effective.

Transformative explanation can also be used in weather news. For example, a woman and two children recently sought shelter in an electrical storm underneath a tree. Lightning struck the tree, and all three were killed when the tree fell on them. During a TV news show, Indianapolis meteorologist Paul Poteet (WTHR-TV, 1997) commented on the story, noting that although trees seem to be safe havens in storms, they are anything but safe. In fact, although it seems unlikely, Poteet told viewers, if you are caught outside in an electrical storm, an open field is the better place to be. Poteet's explanation in this context was probably informative to many. He did an effective job of acknowledging the understandability of the lay theory and then presenting the expert view. Ideally, he also could have explained why standing under a tree is dangerous in a storm. (As Fig. 12.1 shows, trees can act as leaders, facilitating the attraction of negatively charged cloud particles to positively charged particles on the ground, and drawing a lightning strike.)

Because they work by surprising people into rethinking some of their most unquestioned notions, transformative explanations are often fascinating to audiences. In a sense, this chapter functions as a transformative explanation as it tries to reframe some fundamental notions in journalism. The challenge in transformative explanation is to explain scholarly or scientific notions compellingly, while acknowledging that they are nonetheless open to critique.

Suggestions for Journalists

Three major sources of conceptual confusion can mar audiences' comprehension of science news. To explain complex scientific information, journalists should determine the most likely sources of confusion presented by a story and then take steps to minimize these difficulties. Specifically, when reporting, interviewing, and writing, journalists should:

- Identify familiar terms being used in specialized ways and distinguish their essential from associated meanings.
- Use diagrams, analogies, or previews, and frame conflicting findings as puzzles to help audiences mentally model complicated subject matter.
- Explain counterintuitive scientific notions by identifying lay theories that make them seem implausible, acknowledging the understandability of lay views, demonstrating the lay views' limitations, and illustrating the greater adequacy of the orthodox scientific theories.

SUMMARY OF GUIDELINES

To help audiences think like scientists about science news, journalists should find out:

- What evidence, reasoning, or testing supports a finding.
- What bugs, frustrates, or impresses scientists about their finding.
- What parts of the puzzle remain unsolved.
- What are the best objections.
- What has to happen before the finding is viewed as established knowledge.
- What people can do to learn more.

To provide balance and accuracy in science news, reporters should:

- Learn whether a claim is widely supported by scientists.
- Find out if scientists being interviewed endorse this consensus.
- Ask whether there are important variants on the consensus view.
- Frame conflicting findings as puzzles, noting the strengths and weaknesses of key puzzle-solving efforts.

To understand and explain complex scientific information, journalists should:

- Identify familiar terms used in specialized ways and distinguish their essential from associated meanings.

- Use diagrams, analogies, and previews to help audiences mentally model complicated subject matter.
- Explain counterintuitive scientific notions by:
  — Identifying lay theories that make them seem implausible.
  — Acknowledging the understandability of lay views.
  — Demonstrating the lay views' limitations and the greater adequacy of the orthodox scientific theories.

CONCLUSION

This chapter began by promising a step back opportunity for writers. After reading it, a writer may wonder whether science news involves so much stepping back that one is likely to fall attempting it. Reporting information that can never be certain is intimidating. To make it less so, this chapter provided some coaching. Although this chapter emphasizes ways in which science news is distinct from other types, in many ways, reporting science is similar to covering any real, uncertain, and complex event. Research shows that most adults find science news fascinating and learn the bulk of what they know about contemporary science from the mass media (Atwater, 1988; Durant, Evans, & Thomas, 1989; Nunn, 1979). Journalists have the challenging job of helping audiences locate science news they can use, while still appreciating that today's best answer to an important puzzle may be overturned by tomorrow's better approach. In a sense, perhaps the best test of science reporting is the extent to which it helps audiences be like ethologist Konrad Lorenz: confident enough to enjoy learning from science news, but sophisticated enough to understand his point that "truth in science can be defined as the working hypothesis best suited to open the way to the next better one" (Reif & Larkin, 1991, p. 739).

ACKNOWLEDGMENTS

Several people helped me think about, find examples for, and improve this chapter. Thanks go to the editors of this volume—Sharon Friedman, Sharon Dunwoody, and Carol L. Rogers—as well as Brant Burleson, Kathy Campbell, Christopher Dowden, Michael Rowan, and Karen Whedbee. Any errors that remain are mine.

REFERENCES

Alvermann, D. E., Smith, L. C., & Readance, J. E. (1985). Prior knowledge activation and the comprehension of compatible and incompatible text. *Reading Research Quarterly, 20,* 420–436

Ames, B. N., Magaw, R., & Gold, L. S. (1987, April 17). Ranking possible carcinogenic hazard. *Science, 236,* 271–280.

Anderson, C. W., & Smith, E. L. (1984). Children's preconceptions and content-area textbooks. In G. Duffy, L. Roehler, & J. Mason (Eds.), *Comprehension instruction* (pp. 187–201). New York: Longman.

Associated Press (1997, May 28). Emphysema cured in rats. *The Purdue Exponent,* p. 4.

Atwater, T. (1988). Reader interest in environmental news. *Newspaper Research Journal, 10,* 31–38.

Bowman, L. (1997, June 19). Latest estrogen studies fail to resolve dilemma. *The Indianapolis Star,* pp. A1, A2.

Boyd, R. S. (1996, November 18). New drug improves memory. *The Indianapolis Star,* pp. A1–A2.

Burleson, B. R. (1979). On the foundations of rationality: Toulmin, Habermas, and the a priori of reason. *Journal of the American Forensic Association, 16,* 222–231.

Davison, A. (1984). Readability formulas and comprehension. In G. Duffy, L. Roehler, & J. Mason (Eds.), *Comprehension instruction* (pp. 128–143). New York: Longman.

diSessa, A. A. (1982). Unlearning Aristotelian physics: A study of knowledge based learning. *Cognitive Science, 6,* 37–75.

Duffy, T. M. (1985). Readability formulas: What's the use? In T. M. Duffy & R. Waller (Eds.), *Designing usable texts* (pp. 113–143). New York: Academic Press.

Durant, J., Evans, G., & Thomas, G. (1989, July 6). The public understanding of science. *Nature,* 340, 11–14.

Edmonds, P. (1997, December 12–14). This is the way the world will end. *USA Weekend,* pp. 16–17.

Federal manual for identifying and delineating jurisdictional wetlands. (1989, January). Washington, DC: Government Printing Office.

Gentner, D. (1988). Are scientific analogies metaphors? In D. S. Miall (Ed.), *Metaphor: Problems and perspectives* (pp. 106–132). Atlantic Highlands, NJ: Humanities Press.

Gilbert, J. K., & Osborne, R. J. (1980). The use of models in science teaching. *European Journal of Science Education, 2,* 3–13.

Greenfield, M. (1984, June 25). Give me that old-time cholesterol. *Newsweek,* p. 80.

Guzzetti, B. J., Snyder, T. E., Glass, G. V., & Gamas, W. S. (1993). Promoting conceptual change in science: A comparative meta-analysis of instructional interventions from reading education and science education. *Reading Research Quarterly, 28,* 117–155.

Hammitt, J. K. (1995, November/December). Global climate change: Are we overdriving our headlights? *The Quill,* pp. 35–38.

Hashweh, M. (1988). Descriptive studies of students' conceptions in science. *Journal of Research in Science Teaching, 25,* 121–134.

Hayes, D. P. (1992, April 30). The growing inaccessibility of science. *Nature, 356,* 739–740.

Hewson, M. G., & Hewson, P. W. (1983). Effect of instruction using students' prior knowledge and conceptual change strategies on science learning. *Journal of Research in Science Teaching, 20,* 731–743.

Hewson, P. W., & Hewson, M. G. (1984). The role of conceptual conflict in conceptual change and the design of science instruction. *Instructional Science, 13,* 1–13.

Kinneavy, J. L. (1971). *A theory of discourse.* New York: Norton.

Klare, G. R. (1963). *The meaning of readability.* Ames, IA: Iowa State University.

Kuhn, D. (1989). Children and adults as intuitive scientists. *Psychological Review, 96,* 674–689.

Kuhn, T. S. (1962). *The structure of scientific revolutions.* Chicago: University of Chicago Press.

Loman, N. L., & Mayer, R. E. (1983). Signaling techniques that increase the understandability of expository prose. *Journal of Educational Psychology, 75,* 402–412.

Long, M. (1995). Scientific explanation in U. S. newspaper science stories. *Public Understanding of Science, 4,* 119–130.

Mayer, R. E. (1983). What have we learned about increasing the meaningfulness of science prose? *Science Education, 67,* 223–237.

Mayer, R. E., & Anderson, R. B. (1992). The instructive animation: Helping students build connections between words and pictures in multimedia learning. *Journal of Educational Psychology, 84,* 444–452.

Mayer, R. E., Bove, W., Bryman, A., Mars, R., & Tapangco, L. (1996). When less is more: Meaningful learning from visual and verbal summaries of science textbook lessons. *Journal of Educational Psychology, 88,* 64–73.

Mayer, R. E., & Sims, V. K. (1994). For whom is a picture worth a thousand words? Extensions of a dual-coding theory of multimedia learning. *Journal of Educational Psychology, 86,* 389–401.

McDaniel, M. A., & Donnelly, C. M. (1996). Learning with analogy and elaborative interrogation. *Journal of Educational Psychology,* 88, 508–519.

Merrill, M. D., & Tennyson, R. D. (1977). *Teaching concepts: An instructional design guide.* Englewood Cliffs, NJ: Educational Technology Publication.

Neufeldt, V. (1997, January 9). *Junk science.* (ABC News Special). New York: American Broadcasting Corporation.

Nunn, C. Z. (1979). Readership and coverage of science and technology in newspapers. *Journalism Quarterly, 56,* 27–30.

Patterson, R. (1992, November/December). Fire in the oaks. *American Forests,* pp. 32–34, 58–59.

Pellechia, M. G. (1997). Trends in science coverage: A content analysis of three U. S. newspapers. *Public Understanding of Science, 6,* 49–68.

Prouix, L. G. (1996, March 21). It's no punch line: Fiber's good for you. *The [Lafayette, IN] Journal and Courier,* p. D2.

Qian, G., & Alvermann, D. (1995). Role of epistemological beliefs and iearned helplessness in secondary school students' learning science concepts from text. *Journal of Educational Psychology, 87,* 282–292.

Recer, P. (1996, November 18). Memory drug to be tried on Alzheimer's. *The (Lafayette, IN) Journal and Courier,* pp. A1–A2.

Reif, F., & Larkin, J. H. (1991). Cognition in scientific and everyday domains: Comparison and learning implications. *Journal of Research in Science Teaching, 28,* 733–760.

Revkin, A. C. (1995, August 26). Controlled burning adopted, but too late. *The New York Times,* p. 25.

Rowan, K. E. (1988). A contemporary theory of explanatory writing. *Written Communication, 5*, 23–56.

Rowan, K. E. (1991). When simple language fails: Presenting difficult science to the public. *Journal of Technical Writing and Communication, 21*, 369–382.

Rowan, K. E. (1992). Strategies for enhancing comprehension of science. In B. Lewenstein (Ed.), *When science meets the public* (pp. 131–143). Washington, DC: American Association for the Advancement of Science.

Rowan, K. E. (1995). A new pedagogy for explanatory public speaking: Why arrangement should not substitute for invention. *Communication Education, 44*, 236–250.

Rukavina, I., & Daneman, M. (1996). Integration and its effect on acquiring knowledge about competing scientific theories from text. *Journal of Educational Psychology, 88*, 272–287.

Sandman, P. (1986, November). *Explaining environmental risk*. Washington, DC: Office of Toxic Substances, U. S. Environmental Protection Agency.

Schommer, M. (1990). Effects of beliefs about the nature of knowledge on comprehension. *Journal of Educational Psychology, 82*, 498–504.

Shuy, R. W., & Larkin, D. L. (1978). Linguistic considerations in the simplification/clarification of insurance policy language. *Discourse Processes, 1*, 305–321.

Shymansky, J. A., & Kyle, W. C. (1988). A summary of research in science education—1986 [Special issue]. *Science Education, 72*, (3).

Slavin, J. L. (1987). Dietary fiber: Classification, chemical analyses, and food sources. *Journal of the American Dietetic Association, 87*, 1164–1171.

Tennyson, R. D., & Cocchiarella, M. J. (1986). An empirically based instructional design theory for teaching concepts. *Review of Educational Psychology, 56*, 40–71.

Tennyson, R. D., Woolley, F. R., & Merrill, M. D. (1972). Exemplar and nonexemplar variables which produce correct concept classification of behavior and specified classification errors. *Journal of Educational Psychology, 63*, 144–152.

Toulmin, S. (1972). *Human understanding*. Princeton, NJ: Princeton University Press.

Trachtman, L. E. (1989). What does public understanding of science really mean? *Bulletin of Science, Technology, and Society, 9*, 369–373.

Whedbee, K. E. (1993). *John Stuart Mill's theory of practical argument and political advocacy.* Doctoral dissertation, University of Wisconsin, Madison, WI.

Wilford, J. N. (1997, December 18). Hubble takes gaudy photos of dying stars. *The New York Times*, p. A17.

Williams, J. (1992). *The weather book*. New York: Vintage.

WTHR–TV (1997, August 17). *Morning news*. Indianapolis, IN.

Chapter 13

Using Systematic Thinking to Choose and Evaluate Evidence

Robert J. Griffin

Robert J. Griffin is the director of the Center for Mass Media Research at Marquette University, where he is a professor of journalism in the College of Communication and winner of the university's premier award for sustained teaching excellence. He has authored or coauthored articles and chapters on reporting about science, environment, and energy; he is lead editor of the book **Interpreting Public Issues.** *His recent research focuses on risk communication and methods of teaching statistical reasoning to journalism students.*

> *"God does not play dice with the universe."*
>
> —Albert Einstein, c. 20th century

> *"How can I be sure, in a world that's constantly changing?"*
>
> —The Rascals, c. 20th century

> *"Be sure of it; give me the ocular proof. . . . No hinge nor loop to hang a doubt on."*
>
> —William Shakespeare (Othello III, 3), c. 16th century

Uncertainty will always plague us. You can bet on that. For a journalist, dealing with uncertainty is part of the job. Sometimes we feel uncertain because we sense that we lack enough knowledge of something we could know more about. Sometimes we feel uncertain because we cannot predict the seeming vagaries of real causal forces in the world as they influence card games, football games, volcanic eruptions, elections, human health, and other aspects of our surroundings ranging from the microscopic to the cosmic (Kahneman & Tversky, 1982). In either case, a journalist's audience usually wants at least enough certainty in the information they are given so that they can deal with their world with some confidence (Eagly & Chaiken, 1993).

Of course, if the audience's world is in fact uncertain, a good journalist accurately points that out. For example, the results of preelection political polls and other sample surveys of the public are couched in sampling error. A journalist who reports such a survey accurately and responsibly will always take into account the survey's margin of error when interpreting the poll for the audience. Similarly, health risk estimates are often posed as a range of probabilities that indicate a person's chance of being victimized by a given injury or illness. For example, the local health department might proclaim that a person who is not vaccinated might have a 1 in 100 to 1 in 500 chance of catching the latest strain of flu.

Due to the nature of scientific inquiry, there is always some degree of uncertainty in scientific findings. In fact, the scientist lives in a world in which absolute proof is virtually impossible. Yet, based on the fruits of scientific inquiry, government officials often have to make decisions affecting public policies, including controversial actions such as limiting the emissions of greenhouse gases or requiring that additives be put into gasoline in certain cities to reduce urban air pollution. Judges and juries often have to determine, based on scientific evidence, whether plaintiffs have been harmed by hazards such as workplace carcinogens, defective products, or medical malpractice. At best, these decisions are made only after carefully weighing the bulk and quality of scientific findings that bear, pro and con, on the policy or judgment.

CONFIDENCE GAMES

Even careful decisions can be corrupted by those who have a stake in misrepresenting scientific certainty. Basically, there are at least two kinds of practitioners of these scientific "confidence games": those who present scientific results as being more certain than the findings warrant and those who want to dismiss even strong scientific findings because the results are less than absolutely certain.

The former can include some scientists who have a professional stake in presenting findings that are noteworthy and some of the people who allege that they have been victimized by technology, products, or malpractice. The latter can include some industry representatives whose job is to cast doubt on scientific revelations about deleterious effects of products, medical practices, or manufacturing processes. These two sides often collide in the courts, where judges have been given more and more discretion to act as what the U.S. Supreme Court terms gatekeepers of scientific evidence. For example, judges in product liability cases can exclude expert testimony if "there is simply too great an analytical gap between the data and the opinion offered," according to Chief Justice William Rehnquist (Biskupic, 1997, p. A2). As members of the fourth estate, journalists will continue to have a responsibility to help ensure that governmental and judicial decisions are balanced and based on valid scientific evidence and principles.

Of course, everyday people also have to make decisions based in part on scientific findings. These decisions can include which products to purchase, which scientific, technical, or environmental policies to support as citizens, and which changes in lifestyles or habits might affect their personal health and safety. Confidence hucksters can muddy those choices as well. So, it is also part of a reporter's job to help audiences sort empirical fact from junk science when people consider various consumer, political, and health-related options. In fact, people tend to rely a lot on the mass media as sources of information about health risks in particular (Freimuth, Edgar, & Hammond, 1987; Singer & Endreny, 1987).

One of the best ways for a journalist to discover whether scientific-sounding claims are valid is to subject them to the rigors of systematic thinking, that is, to the rules of evidence and reasoning scientists routinely apply to their investigations. Systematic thinking does not require journalists to be experts in research methodology and mathematics, although some basic knowledge of scientific procedures and statistics is certainly helpful (see, e.g., Cohn, 1989; Meyer, 1991). In fact, contrary to what many may believe, journalists are not inherently math dummies. Freshman college students going into journalism are just as adept at math as the average college freshman (Becker & Graf, 1994). "It is time to let the secret out," as Paulos (1995) wrote in his book, *A Mathematician Reads the Newspaper*. "Mathematics is not primarily a matter of plugging numbers into formulas and performing rote computations. It is a way of thinking and questioning that may be unfamiliar to many of us, but is available to almost all of us" (p. 3).

So, most journalists should be able to handle the kinds of reasoning processes required to think systematically about the news and, because science and statistics underlie many news stories, they have an increasing responsibility to their audiences to do so. However, one of the most common practices of the journalistic craft—relying on anecdotal information in gathering and presenting the news—can markedly interfere with a reporter's attempts to apply systematic thinking.

THE STORYTELLERS

Basically, the journalist's job is to tell a story. So it is quite natural for a journalist to think in terms of anecdotes to present the news. If there is a new treatment for diabetes, interview a few diabetics and find out how that will make life easier for them. If the state health department warns people about health dangers from eating fish that might contain mercury or PCBs, tap some anglers on the shoulder and ask them if they are worried. If a new study shows that TV viewing influences the academic performance of preteens, ask some local grade school teachers what they have noticed. If a federal report shows that urbanization is seriously encroaching on land used to grow food, write a story that follows a farm family through years of economic struggles.

The common wisdom among journalists is that anecdotes draw audience interest, humanize a news story and, because anecdotes tend to be vivid, make the news memorable. Unfortunately, relatively little is known about the actual effects these techniques have on audiences. What is known suggests that journalists should exercise some caution when employing anecdotal information in stories so as not to mislead audiences or themselves.

Certain Examples, Uncertain Evidence

Anecdotes can be fine examples, but they are usually poor evidence, especially in the news. It is easy for a reporter to assume that the grassroots quotes she just gleaned from a dozen motorists at the local filling station were not just great copy for her story about gasoline taxes but typify a cross section of public opinion as well. To a social scientist, those same interviews are a convenience survey of an unrepresentative sample of 12. In other situations, a reporter might find an example of a prominent local athlete who is struggling to overcome drug dependence to illustrate his story on addiction in the city. To a social scientist, the athlete is strikingly atypical of the problems everyday people face.

Problems multiply when journalists present anecdotal information directly as evidence. For example, *Newsweek* ran an article headlined, "Conspiracy mania feeds our growing national paranoia" (Marin & Gegax, 1996–1997, p.

64). Claiming that "conspiracy paranoia is surrounding us," the article takes a brief yet critical tour of some popular conspiracy theories. The news peg, as reflected in the headline, is that popular belief in conspiracies is growing. "This great nation has always had its share of conspiracy freaks. . . . But the ranks of the darkly deluded may be growing," the authors stated (p. 66). "Clearly, something is heating up in the more tropical climes of the American psyche," Marin and Gegax concluded, based primarily on the following evidence cited in the article:

- Three quarters of Americans believed that the government is somehow involved in conspiracy, according to a survey reported in *George* magazine.
- America Online had begun a channel for fans of the paranormal and the paranoid.
- Mel Gibson starred in a movie called *Conspiracy Theory.*
- The editor of *The Skeptical Inquirer*, a publication that debunks the farout, said that there certainly seems to be a resurgence in sympathy toward conspiracy theory and an increase in paranoia.

Most of the evidence is anecdotal and none of it would support the conclusion that, nationally, paranoia and belief in conspiracies are growing. That conclusion requires evidence that compares representative surveys of Americans at two points in time and asks about their beliefs in a variety of conspiracies. Such evidence might balance the anecdotal information presented in the story and relegate it to what it is: example instead of evidence.

Reliance on anecdotes might affect audiences in other ways as well. With our minds and our worlds filled with uncertainties and our days filled with only 24 hours, we often fall back on judgmental shortcuts, called *heuristics*, to make sense of things (Tversky & Kahneman, 1982). Heuristics are intuitive and can often bias our judgments. For example, people might overestimate the risks of cancer in the population if someone they know has the disease. Reading about a cancer case in the news will probably not have quite the effect on a person's judgment as would firsthand knowledge. Nonetheless, vivid anecdotes, which are a news staple, could influence a person's judgments of risks and should be employed carefully by journalists.

SYSTEMATIC THINKING AND UNCERTAINTY

The use of anecdotes by journalists is certainly not going to disappear, but it is important to gather and present anecdotal information as examples rather than evidence, to find typical examples instead of extreme cases to illustrate a story, and to couch description within a context that shows how representative or unrepresentative the cases may be. In most situations, this requires the systematic gathering of representative data of some type. However, just because information is in numerical form does not mean that it is necessarily any more representative than a typical verbal anecdote. In fact, undigested statistical information is often nothing more than a quantitative anecdote.

Although we will probably never overcome all of our uncertainty about the world, the techniques of systematic thinking employed by scientists serve to reduce the uncertainty that is brought about by faulty reasoning and improper evidence. The next sections illustrate three steps to systematic thinking that journalists can employ in their daily work.

As Compared to What?

Journalists often encounter raw statistics, such as the number of people afflicted by heart disease or involved in automobile crashes annually. Some of these raw numbers can be quite astounding and equally misleading. For example, in 1992, *The New York Times* reported that four of America's largest cities—Los Angeles, San Diego, Dallas, and Phoenix—each tallied a record number of killings the previous year. As Arnold Barnett (1994) observed in *Technology Review:*

> The implication was that even one all-time high among such cities was unusual, let alone four. The report failed to point out, however, that all four of these cities also reached new highs in population in 1991; thus, even if their per capita murder rates had not changed since Cain slew Abel, their absolute 1991 murder tolls would have set new records. (p. 44)

First Step: Find the Baseline

Indeed, the first step in systematic thinking is to establish an appropriate baseline. A common means of establishing a baseline is to turn a raw statistic into a rate (e.g., 1 out of every 1,000) or percentage (e.g., .1%) by using an appropriate denominator. If *The New York Times* had used one of these techniques to establish a baseline, a different picture of urban murders might indeed have emerged. Thus, baselines provide essential interpretive context for any raw statistic.

Baselines also give context to an anecdote, especially by helping audiences see how representative the case is. For example, in a feature on the growing proportion of senior citizens who resort to suicide, *Milwaukee Journal Sentinel* reporter Fran Bauer (1996) started the story with this brief account:

> Recently, an elderly man parked his car, walked to the top of the High Rise Bridge, stepped over the guard rails and jumped to his death.
>
> Divers tried frantically to rescue the man from the icy waters of the Milwaukee River below. But he died within minutes, a suicide.
>
> For most, the case was quickly forgotten.
>
> Yet statistics tell a far grimmer story. (p. G1)

Bauer then gave readers context for the anecdote by including national data on the disproportionate upturn of suicides among older citizens, especially males, from 1980 to 1992 and showing that, although persons aged 65 and older accounted for only 13% of the population, they made up nearly 20% of all suicides. In doing so, the reporter made it clear that the proportion of suicides in the older age group is not just a simple reflection of their numbers in the population. The rest of the article discussed the factors such as isolation, depression, changing cultural attitudes, and even longevity itself that might contribute to suicides among the aging.

To help bring this message home, the paper accompanied the story with a graphic titled "1994 Suicides by Age Group in Milwaukee County" (Fig. 13.1). Unfortunately, however, that graphic confused the picture the reporter had so carefully presented in text. At first glance, the pie chart seems to show that suicides are decimating the young but are rare among the old. What caused this pie chart to go sour? Instead of depicting suicides in each age group on a per capita basis, as would be appropriate for the story, the chart shows the portion of the total number of suicides that occurred in each age group. In short, the graphic confuses the meaning of the story because it ignores the baseline, specifically, the size of each age group in the local population. To better illustrate Bauer's trend story, the newspaper might have used a couple of charts—one portraying per capita suicides in each age group in 1994 and another showing the same breakdown for 1980. That way, two essential baselines are used: the population base and the prevalence of suicides at a comparative time in the past.

Second Step: Make a Dynamic Comparison

Despite its flawed graphic, the suicide article showed how comparing rates across groups and across time can reveal dynamic patterns that are otherwise

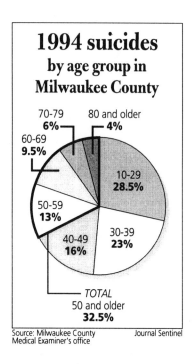

FIG. 13.1. 1994 Suicides by age group in Milwaukee County.

obscured when reporters employ only simple descriptions in the form of anecdotes, raw statistics, or even raw rates and percentages (e.g., reporting only the overall suicide rate for the population in general). A phenomenon such as illness or suicide now becomes a variable to be compared with another variable, such as age or sex differences, giving clues to sometimes subtle forces at work in society and in human lives. Of course, as Cohn (1989) noted, these comparisons can take many forms and must be rigorous and fair. However, looking for these dynamic comparisons is the second step in systematic thinking. By habitually asking "as compared to what?" and searching carefully for solid evidence of the answer, journalists can get new insights into the news and avoid some flimsy or misleading conclusions.

For example, *Discover* magazine once reported that 90% of the people who survived airplane crashes had formed in their minds a plan of escape before the accident happened (Nolan, 1986). Their recommendation? Look for the emergency exits and plan how to get off before you take off. This advice seems sensible enough, but it is not as factually based as it would seem. Note that *Discover*'s advice is based on a comparison that is implied but for which there is no evidence.

As Gilovich (1997) observed, it is impossible to find out what percentage of the nonsurvivors had also formulated escape plans. In short, there is no way of knowing whether those who planned their way out actually fared any better.

In another case, an Associated Press (1995) article about the success of cardiopulmonary resuscitation (CPR) appeared under the headline: "Bystanders' CPR Efforts Often Backfire, Study Says." The lead paragraph read: "Chicago—Bystanders who attempted CPR on cardiac arrest victims got it wrong more than half the time, reducing patients' already slim chances of survival, a study found" (p. 6A).

Notice that the clear implication of the newspaper headline and of the first paragraph is that people who try to do CPR on a heart attack victim, but who do it improperly, are doing more harm to the victim than if they had done nothing at all. That is pretty important advice, advice with ethical and legal implications, as well as with implications for the life of the poor victim.

The news item was based on an article by Gallagher, Lombardi, and Gennis (1995) that appeared in the *Journal of the American Medical Association* (*JAMA*). The brief Associated Press news story quotes one of the article's authors, John Gallagher of the Albert Einstein College of Medicine in New York, as stating that improperly administered CPR "does not seem to be any better than no CPR." He did not say that improperly administered CPR is worse than no CPR, which should have tipped off the reporter that something was amiss in the lead paragraph.

An abstract of the *JAMA* article, then readily available to journalists with Internet access, briefly explained the research method and basic findings of the study. Emergency hospital personnel, who arrived at the scene of a cardiac arrest, recorded whether any bystanders had attempted CPR on the victim and, if so, whether the technique they used was *effective*, that is, whether it was performed according to medical guidelines. The patient *survived* if he or she was able to return home from the hospital. The researchers also controlled for some other factors that might affect the outcome of the study. The abstract explained that:

> the survival statistic for those receiving CPR was 19 out of 662 compared to 11 out of 1405 who did not receive CPR.... Of those patients who received effective bystander CPR, 14 out of 305 survived (4.6%) compared with 5 out of 357 (1.4%) who received CPR judged to be ineffective.

A careful reading of the numbers shows that only 0.8% (11/1,405) of the victims who received no CPR had survived. In situations like this, a simple but systematic jotting down of the numbers on a notepad, such as a reporter might have done in Fig. 13.2, can help journalists—and their audiences—understand

No CPR	Ineffective CPR	Effective CPR
0.8% survived	1.4% survived	4.6% survived

FIG. 13.2. *JAMA* number comparisons.

what comparisons are being made. Although giving ineffective CPR might not really improve the victim's odds of survival as compared to administering no CPR at all, it certainly does not "backfire" by "reducing patients' already slim chances of survival," as the story headline and lead had erroneously reported.

Perhaps the statistics most in need of dynamic comparisons and reportorial finesse are vital statistics data representing health and disease, life and death. "They are much applied, misused, and misunderstood," stated Cohn (1989, p. 74). "Yet these statistics can yield fascinating stories if we learn something of their power and limits and the rather special vocabulary of human lives." Cautioning that disease data are often applied too broadly to the population, Crossen (1996) observed:

> One in five American men will get prostate cancer. One in eight American women will get breast cancer. At least two million Americans are manic-depressive, and more than two million are schizophrenic. At least 60 million Americans have high blood pressure, 12 million have asthma and four million have Alzheimer's disease. One in three Americans is obese.
>
> With numbers like these, it is amazing there is anyone still here—let alone people living happy, healthy lives. Projections of the incidence of disease are rampant these days, as a growing number of health advocacy groups compete for people's limited attention and money. Most of the numbers are extrapolations or estimates—at best. Yet as the media report them, often uncritically and without context, these conjectures assume the mantle of quantifiable fact. (p. B1)

Crossen suggested that a better way to present information to people about risks of a disease is to project, for example, how risks vary by gender and age. Figure 13.3 illustrates data her story provided on the probability of developing cancer in 10, 20, and 30 years, and eventually for men and women of various ages who are currently free of cancer. The chart shows some very interesting patterns. For women, for example, the overall risk of getting cancer sometime in life actually decreases as they get older. The same is not true for men. Of course, heart and circulatory problems claim more human lives than does

Probability of Developing Cancer

In 10, 20, 30 years and eventually

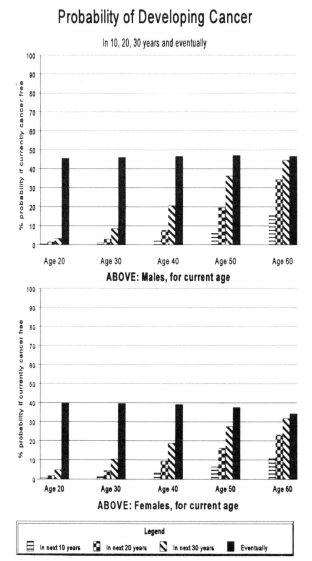

ABOVE: Males, for current age

ABOVE: Females, for current age

Legend			
⊟ In next 10 years	▨ In next 20 years	◹ In next 30 years	■ Eventually

FIG. 13.3. Based on data from *The Wall Street Journal.*

cancer, Crossen said, and people should remember that, despite increasing longevity, no one lives forever.

Figure 13.3 is an example of what statisticians call a *multivariate analysis.* Tables such as these are very useful because they illustrate the ways different factors (here, age and sex) might combine in different ways to produce different outcomes (here, the risk of cancer). Notice that this is a much more dynamic and realistic picture of the way life really is than one gets from the more crude descriptions provided by simple anecdotes and undigested statistics. However, because data such as these can become quite complicated for people to understand, journalists will need to become more adept at reasoning from data and interpreting data for audiences. Innovative and clear graphic displays of statistical information (e.g., Tufte, 1983, 1997; Utts, 1996; Wainer, 1997) are essential to that task. In particular, computers and other new technologies offer exciting opportunities to use hypertext (Fredin, 1997), animation, and interactive environments to help people understand data dynamics.

Error and Uncertainty

Journalists also should remember that even the most carefully gathered statistical information contains some uncertainty in the form of error. Some of the error rests in the techniques and measures used to gather the information, such as relying on the completeness of health department records, the precision of a medical test, or a person's ability or willingness to report illnesses, socially undesirable activities, or highly personal information to a survey interviewer. Some of the error rests in extrapolating or generalizing from, for example, animal tests to humans or from a sample to the population. So, in making dynamic comparisons, it is important to take into account what the range of error might be. As a general rule, we should be cautious about small differences between groups, especially if the differences are only a few percentage points. They might simply be the result of error and, therefore, have no real meaning. If the data are from a well-designed probability sample survey (of people in a city, for example) or laboratory experiment in which subjects were randomly assigned to conditions (a placebo versus a new drug, for example), then a reporter can more readily get a handle on how much room to allow for error by relying on the reported statistical significance of the results or by applying the standard formula to determine the margin of error in surveys. Of course, even these statistical tests will not compensate for errors in the measures and techniques themselves, so it is still wise to exercise some caution.

So, a good revision of the question posed at the beginning of this section is this: "As compared to what, given error?"

SIDEBAR:
EXAMPLES AND SAMPLES, OR
HOW A LITTLE HOMEWORK CAN GO A LONG WAY

Parents from the Milwaukee suburb of Shorewood had complained that their seventh-grade offspring were being given an unusual amount of homework, so much so that their backpacks were becoming laden with books and too heavy for a kid to carry.

So, to check out these parental allegations, reporters decided to compare the heaviness of the backpacks of Shorewood Intermediate School students to the weight of backpacks carried by their peers at two schools in neighboring communities. In a large, color graphic that accompanied the front-page article ("Full Load," 1997), the paper listed the weight of each of the 14 backpacks sampled at each of the three schools along with the average backpack weight at each school: 20.43 pounds at Shorewood, 16.93 pounds at University School, and 11.93 pounds at Morse Middle School. The data are reproduced in Figure 13.4. The reporters concluded that "for the most part, the [Shorewood] parents were right." To further illustrate the point, the newspaper used an example as part of the graphic: a photo of a student from the Shorewood school whose backpack was heavier (at 31 pounds) than any of the other backpacks from any of the schools. "What's it like carrying around 31 pounds?" asked a tag line above the student's photo. The answer, also illustrated, is that 31 pounds is equal to the weight of nearly two bowling balls or 191 toy "beanie babies" and is greater than the weight of a Trek 750 bicycle. The story itself is peppered with quotes from students at the three schools about what it is like to lug their burdens.

All in all, the reporters endeavored to conduct a dynamic comparison across three schools and tried to use comparative data on the average weight of backpacks at each institution to provide a moderating context for the quotations from students. Without the weigh-ins, the entire story might have had to rely on the use of anecdotes as evidence instead of as examples. The interesting graphic tried to translate the weight of backpacks into terms many readers might understand.

Unfortunately, two enduring journalistic problems—using unrepresentative examples and unrepresentative samples—seemed to mar this otherwise laudable effort:

1. The illustration used the decidedly atypical backpack—the one that weighed more than any of the others and half again as much as the average for Shorewood Intermediate School—rather than a typical backpack (the mean,

(continued)

Sidebar *(continued)*

It's tough being a backer packer

It all began when some Shorewood parents complained how heavy their kids'
backpacks have become because of the amount of homework brought home.
Do their concerns carry weight? We found out, by weighing backpacks from 14
students from each of the schools below. The results? Well, for the most part, the
parents were right. And how do the kids feel about carrying all that weight?
Some shrugged it off, but others said it feels like the weight of the world.

Shorewood Intermediate School		University School		Morse Middle School	
Sampled backpack weights	TOTAL WEIGHT: 286 LBS.	Sampled backpack weights	TOTAL WEIGHT: 237 LBS.	Sampled backpack weights	TOTAL WEIGHT: 167 LBS.
11 20 25	AVERAGE WEIGHT: **20.43** pounds	**6** 17 19	AVERAGE WEIGHT: **16.93** pounds	**8** 11 13	AVERAGE WEIGHT: **11.93** pounds
15 20 25		11 18 20		9 12 14	
15 20 30		13 18 21		11 12 14	
15 20 **31**		16 19 **24**		11 13 **15**	
18 21		16 19		11 13	

What's it like carrying around 31 lbs.?

FIG. 13.4.   LOUIS K. SALDIVAR/Journal Sentinel

median and mode are 20 pounds) to represent that school. Journalists too often
use the atypical as an example, and in this case the reader can too easily be
confused about the average weight of backpacks at that school.

2. The reporters used what they described in the text of the story as a "very
unscientific survey" (p. 1A) to choose which backpacks to weigh. Although
they did not describe how they selected backpacks, "unscientific" usually
means "nonrandom sample" and opens the possibility that expectations about
finding heavier backpacks at the Shorewood school might have unconsciously
affected reporters' choices. A random sample of some type would probably not
have been too hard to conduct, especially given the effort reporters had already
devoted to the story. And it would have given the reporters a big advantage:
they would have had a means to control for sampling error. As it is, there is no
way to reduce the large amount of uncertainty in their results. In short, it is not
clear what they actually found. In fact, had the same data been the result of a
random sample, the results would show that the average backpack weight at
Shorewood Intermediate School is not different, beyond sampling error, from
the average backpack weights at University School, according to a statistical

(continued)

Sidebar *(continued)*
test called the "analysis of variance" commonly available on desktop computer statistical packages. The real finding would be that Morse Middle School backpacks are the lightest and that, for the most part, the Shorewood parents were wrong.

WHY AND SO WHAT?

Interpretation is an essential component of good reporting and usually requires answering the questions "why?" and "so what?" The answer to the question "why?"—for example, "Why does urban sprawl affect water quality?" or "Why would eating fatty foods increase a person's risk of heart attack?"—calls on the reporter to address cause-and-effect relations. Similarly, the answer to the question "so, what?"—for example, "So, what policy solutions can mitigate the effects of sprawl on water quality?" or "So, what personal actions can one take to lower the risk of a heart attack?"—also requires analysis of causality.

Because people tend to base their preferences for solutions to a problem on their perceptions of what caused the problem (Didier, 1987), it is important for reporters to present causal information carefully to audiences. Doing so means being especially alert to some of the common mistakes we all make in everyday causal reasoning. Many of these miscues stem from the need to quickly overcome uncertainties in our world in order to go about everyday life pressures that certainly affect reporters at least as much as everyone else. For a reporter, however, taking a more careful and responsible approach to interpreting causality requires taking a more systematic look at what causes what, adopting in less formal ways the standards of proof scientists require.

Third Step: Use Causal Caution

Dynamic comparisons reveal what are commonly known as *correlations* between variables. In the sciences, establishing a correlation between two variables is an essential step in determining whether one may be a cause of the other. Suppose there were no correlation between being a cigarette smoker and having a higher risk of lung cancer. Under those conditions, smoking could not be a cause of lung cancer. However, the opposite is not true: Simply showing an association between smoking and cancer did not prove that smoking contributed to the risk of lung cancer. Additional rigorous evidence was needed, as is true with any area of scientific inquiry into causality. Along with showing correlation, evidence of causality requires evidence that the alleged causal agent occurs prior to the condition it causes (e.g., that smoking precedes the development of cancers) and—the most difficult task—that other explanations are discounted or accounted for.

"One of the first things they teach in introductory statistics is that correlation is not causation," quipped Sowell (1996, p. 11) in *The Country Chronicle*. "It is also one of the first things forgotten." Remembering these rigorous standards of causal proof and adopting the caution they impart constitute the third step in systematic thinking.

Correlation and Causal Conclusions.   In everyday life we often jump to conclusions about causality. Sometimes those judgments are based on what is, at best, incomplete or flimsy evidence of correlation, much of it anecdotal and based on what we happen to have noticed or experienced. Unlike the scientist, who relies on systematic sampling and statistical techniques, the layperson "must rely upon intuitions and subjective impressions based on limited access to relevant data," explained Ross and Anderson (1982, p. 140). The result is often a biased base on which to build causal conclusions.

Some of those premature causal conclusions find their way, unexamined, into the media, as illustrated by the story about the effects on survival if passengers mentally map their emergency routes out of an aircraft. Some are even embarrassing for the media. Take, for example, the media's response to information proffered by various advocates for battered women including, ironically, the group Fairness and Accuracy in Reporting (FAIR) that reports of domestic violence rise 40% on Super Bowl Sunday. In short, the causal implication is that watching the Super Bowl makes men more likely to batter their female partners. As Hohler (1993) of *The Boston Globe* related:

> The image was alarming. Men across America, incited by booze, gambling losses and the body-slamming exploits of their football heroes, could make Super Bowl Sunday the worst day of the year for domestic violence.
>
> Activists trumpeted the warning, saying national studies supported their claim. Much of the nation's media echoed the alarm.
>
> And NBC, heeding the prediction, aired as its only public service announcement in the countdown to the Super Bowl a 20-second television spot that dramatized for 40 million viewers the horror of domestic violence.
>
> But in an embarrassing setback for the campaign against domestic violence—and for the news media—some of the groups that pressured NBC to air the free spot,

including Fairness and Accuracy in Reporting, acknowledged yesterday that they had based their predictions in part on incomplete, inaccurate or anecdotal information. (p. 1)

According to Hohler, the media watchdog group FAIR had extrapolated the 40% figure, which FAIR described as anecdotal, from a book of photo essays on domestic violence. There were other errors in advocates' claims as well, but there did not seem to be any significant, systematic evidence of an increase in domestic violence after the Super Bowl game.

"People are extraordinarily good at ad hoc explanation," Gilovich (1991, pp. 21-22) observed. "To live, it seems, is to explain, to justify, and to find coherence among diverse outcomes, characteristics, and causes." Gilovich noted that people can find patterns even in random phenomena—randomness being the ultimate in uncertainty and lack of correlation—and quickly explain the patterns in terms of their own preexisting theories and beliefs about causality.

People can have a number of intuitive, preexisting theories about causality (see, e.g., Hilton, 1988; Kahneman, Slovic, & Tversky, 1982). Many concern human behavior—the stuff that much reporting is made of. These intuitive beliefs can bias our perceptions of causality, especially when causes and effects are otherwise uncertain. For example, people tend to overestimate the role of forces inside the individual, such as personality, ability, disposition, and motivation, as causes of human behavior and to underestimate the role of environmental or situational factors, such as the varied opportunities and obstacles that exist for people in different social classes. Heider (1958) called this bias the *fundamental attribution error*, and it affects us more when we interpret the behavior of others, as reporters tend to do, rather than our own. When applied to whole classes of people, the attribution of behavior to shared internal states can form the basis for social stereotypes (Hamilton, 1979), such as we might have of others of a different race or sex when we believe that whole groups of people are inherently lazy, ignorant, insensitive, and so forth. Media portrayals might be associated with the ways audiences attribute to internal or external causes the way members of certain groups in society behave (Griffin & Sen, 1995). Attributional biases, of course, could have a lot of ramifications if they influence media content, audience perceptions, and social policy.

Although it would be nearly impossible for reporters to effectively counteract all sources of error when making statements about "why" and "so what," adopting a more rigorous set of standards for causal proof will reduce the likelihood of inaccurate causal conclusions. To that end, here is a brief overview of the other steps scientists take in finding evidence of causality.

The Right Time Slot.   People develop causal beliefs because they repeatedly witness the association between an event and something that follows
it (Hilton, 1988). Scientists use the same approach, although more rigorously.
In essence, a purported cause must be shown to precede its effect in real time,
whether it be epochs or nanoseconds. Many scientific procedures, such as most
controlled laboratory experiments or panel design surveys, directly observe
before-and-after changes as they happen. In many other cases, such as in
geology or deep space astronomy, the evidence of before-and-after is often
gathered indirectly. Sometimes, attempts are made to discern causal sequences
from only one point in time, such as in a cross-sectional epidemiological or
public opinion survey. In all cases, however, it is wise to be cautious about the
evidence of time sequence. It is often helpful for a reporter to determine whether
the proposed order of the cause and effect variables could just as realistically
be reversed.

The Network.   Most of the things that happen are the result of a variety
of factors, many interwoven with one another. One of the most difficult tasks
in systematic thinking and investigation is to separate the influence of an
apparent causal agent from other variables, often called *confounds*, which also
might affect the outcome attributed to the causal agent.

Cohn (1989), for example, related the story of a scientist who proposed the
possibility that left-handed batters were overrepresented among the best hitters
in baseball because of hemispheric lateralization of the brain. A more baseball-
savvy critic had a simpler explanation: Left-handed batters happen to enjoy a
natural physical advantage in the game, specifically, most pitchers are right-
handed, which gives left-handed batters an edge, and left-handed batters are
already moving toward first base after they swing, making it easier for them to
reach the base.

Usually the simpler, more parsimonious explanation is preferred as long as
it predicts the phenomenon—in this case, the better hitting performance of
lefties in baseball—at least as well as the more complicated one. Of course, it
is also quite possible that both the scientist and the baseball-wise observer were
right, because a phenomenon can (and usually does) have multiple causes.
Thus, it is wise for a reporter to ask what other causal agents might be on the
scene and how they have been accounted for.

Here are some of the other common patterns of relationships among causal
agents that a reporter might encounter. For convenience, the suspected causal
agent will be referred to by its common nickname, X, the variable it apparently
influences as Y, and the other dynamic variable in the mix as Z. X is also often

referred to as an *independent variable*, Y as a *dependent variable*, and Z as a *third* variable (no matter how many there are).

Contingency. Sometimes a variable (Z) can work like a switch or catalyst for the relationship between X and Y. Only if Z takes on certain characteristics, for example, does X affect Y. In Fig. 13.3, sex might be considered to be Z, age as X, and lifetime cancer risk as Y. If Z (sex) is female, then advancing age (X) decreases overall cancer risk (Y). If Z (sex) is male, then age and overall cancer risk are unrelated.

Intervening Variable. For a variable to effect change in another variable, the two must be functionally related. That is, the link between the variables should be clear and the processes by which X affects Y well defined. Sometimes X can affect Y only through an intervening variable Z that is the more proximate cause of changes in Y. Thus, intervention is like a chain of relationships. For example, researchers often look for, and find, differences in all sorts of social, psychological, and even health-related variables based on demographic differences in the population. Flynn, Slovic, and Mertz (1994) found that white men perceive risks differently than white women and minority men and women. Yet, to explain why this difference occurs, the authors suggested that white males may simply feel more in control of their environment than everyone else, and that sense of control affects their perceptions of being at risk. Thus, a sense of control is posed as an intervening variable (Z). In general, demographic variables often need such assistance. The alert reporter, trying to assess whether the services of an intervening variable are needed, might ask whether it is crystal clear *why* X might affect Y. Take another look at Fig. 13.3 in that light.

Lurking Variable. This one's a real con artist. In what is sometimes called a *spurious relationship*, the lurking variable Z deceives you into thinking that X and Y are related when they really are not. In reality, the lurking variable itself affects both X and Y, making them correlate with one another without any real connection between them. For example, suppose a study were to show that Internet users who browse on-line news services know more about international current events than other Internet users. It might indeed be tempting to say that their greater use of net news (X) is making these folks more savvy about what is happening in the world (Y). Might a Z be lurking about? Perhaps these folks are better educated than those who do not use the on-line news services. They might visit the on-line news sites as part of a pattern of greater attention to a lot of news channels, including television, newspapers, and news magazines. Their superior knowledge of international current events might be a byproduct of their educational preparation coupled with their use of these more traditional news media. A good study will control for alternative possibilities such as this.

In general, the authors of most scientific studies are very cautious about claiming causal relationships, preferring instead to claim not much more than association. Nonetheless, systematic thinking on the part of a journalist can serve as a check on unwarranted causal claims.

SUMMARY: PREPARING FOR THE 21ST CENTURY

"So certain are you."

—Yoda, *Star Wars*, Century uncertain

Computers, the Internet, and the other new communication technologies are changing the information landscape. For journalists and the public alike, landmarks that used to identify trustworthy sources and valid information are disappearing. For example, rumors can attain about the same status as news on the Internet, to the point that even veteran journalists have been befuddled. Whether new landmarks appear in this world of uncertain information is anyone's guess. If these trends continue, the new millennium will require people to have cognitive tools, or at least considerable guidance, to verify what is valid and what is not. More than ever, journalists will need to apply the tools of systematic thinking, tools that, by their grounding in the sciences, are effective in sorting out facts from fantasy, puffery, politics, and even the preening of scientists.

Fortunately, there are many fine sources that journalists can use to prepare themselves. Philip Meyer's now classic works, *Precision Journalism* (1979) and *The New Precision Journalism* (1991), continue to offer reporters superb guidance in the use of surveys, sampling, statistics, and related tools of the social sciences, and—just as valuable—guidance in the thinking that goes along with using them. Victor Cohn (1989) similarly provided an excellent guide to reporting a wide range of scientific controversies, methods, and thinking in *News & Numbers*, a book that includes a fine chapter on scientific uncertainty. Even though audiences might not generally be familiar with the role of uncertainty in science, clear reporting of uncertainty may indeed help people understand it better (see Johnson & Slovic, 1995).

Unfortunately, the mass media have provided critical observers with a wealth of examples of how not to report and display scientific and statistical information. Journalists can learn a lot about how to do things better—and learn a lot about systematic thinking in the bargain—by reading books such as Paulos' *A Mathematician Reads the Newspaper* (1995), his best-seller *Innumeracy: Mathematical Illiteracy and its Consequences* (1988), and Gilovich's *How We Know What Isn't So* (1991). Journalists also should take advantage of the movement within the teaching of statistics and mathematics that urges universities to ensure that college graduates are quantitatively literate, that is, that they can apply mathematical thinking, beyond mere formulas, to everyday problems (Subcommittee on Quantitative Literacy Requirements, 1995). Various universities are responding to this need by offering courses incorporating or devoted to quantitative reasoning. The Chance Project at Dartmouth College in Hanover, New Hampshire, has a wealth of examples of correct and incorrect quantitative reasoning in the news and also has a storehouse of related teaching materials, all available on-line (www.dartmouth.edu/~chance). One superb how-to book that employs the systematic thinking approach to statistics and that definitely belongs on the journalist's bookshelf is Jessica Utts' very readable *Seeing Through Statistics* (1996).

The growth of computer-assisted reporting will require journalists to think adeptly and systematically about the numbers they encounter. In fact, journalists without the requisite computer and quantitative skills will probably find themselves at a real disadvantage in the journalism job market (Feola, 1995). The growth of new media, which overwhelmingly use visual displays to present information, will demand that reporters and illustrators become masterful at presenting quantitative information graphically and accurately. Computerized animation and interactive formats could help audiences understand dynamic comparisons and even the influence of third variables. For example, one's chances of contracting heart disease at a given age might be illustrated by a curve on an attractive graph that changes as the viewer provides the computer program with different information about his or her own unique background and habits. The curve might be animated to show change based on lifestyle alterations, such as stopping smoking or adopting a low-fat diet, that the viewer might be considering—and a range of uncertainty could be illustrated around the curve. Of course, to date, media have sometimes distorted quantitative information when presenting it graphically. Some fine books that show how to prepare valid, attractive, still-life graphic displays of data include Utt's *Seeing Through Statistics* (1996), Tufte's *Visual Explanations* (1997), and especially Tankard's "Visual Crosstabs" (1994) and Wainer's *Visual Revelations* (1997).

Journalists in the 21st century must be able to reason from verbal and quantitative information, know how to assess what information is missing, be able to gather and validate the required information, be adept at understanding and explaining the uncertainty that scientific information inevitably contains, and be able to interpret information to nonexpert audiences verbally, quantitatively, graphically and, most of all, accurately. These cognitive and communication skills are absolutely essential if journalists are to meet their responsibilities to society and their audiences in the new millennium.

ACKNOWLEDGMENTS

Special thanks to Dr. Laurie Snell, professor of mathematics and Director of the Chance Project at Dartmouth College in Hanover, New Hampshire, for helping to provide many of the examples used in this chapter, and to Ruth Boulet, master of arts graduate in journalism from Marquette University, for her superb help with the research.

REFERENCES

Associated Press (1995, December 27). Bystanders' CPR efforts often backfire, study says. *Milwaukee Journal Sentinel*, p. 6A.

Barnett, A. (1994, October). How numbers can trick you. *Technology Review*, 39–45.

Bauer, F. (1996, April 1). Senior suicides on rise. *Milwaukee Journal Sentinel*, pp. G1, G3.

Becker, L. B., & Graf, J. D. (1994). *Myths & trends: What the real numbers say about journalism education*. Arlington, VA: The Freedom Forum.

Biskupic, J. (1997, December 16). Trial judges have wide discretion on scientific testimony, Court says. *The Washington Post*, p. A2.

Cohn, V. (1989). *News and numbers*. Ames, IA: Iowa State University Press.

Crossen, C. (1996, April 11). Fright by the numbers: Alarming disease data are frequently flawed. *The Wall Street Journal*, p. B1, B4.

Didier, M. (1987). Attributions in the evaluation of alternative solutions to social problems. *Journal of Social Psychology, 127,* 357–365.

Eagly, A. H., & Chaiken, S. (1993). *The psychology of attitudes.* Fort Worth, TX: Harcourt Brace.

Feola, C. J. (1995, March). Making the cut: Enhance your job opportunities by developing your computer skills. *The Quill*, 24–26.

Flynn, J., Slovic, P., & Mertz, C. K. (1994). Gender, race, and perception of environmental health risks. *Risk Analysis, 14,* 1101–1108.

Fredin, E. S. (1997, September). Rethinking the news story for the Internet: Hyperstory prototypes and a model of the user. *Journalism and Mass Communication Monographs, 163.*

Freimuth, V. S., Edgar, T., & Hammond, S. L. (1987). College students' awareness and interpretation of the AIDS risk. *Science, Technology, & Human Values, 12*, 37–40.

Full Load. (1997, November 11). *Milwaukee Journal Sentinel*, p. 1A.

Gallagher, E. J., Lombardi, G., & Gennis, P. (1995). Effectiveness of bystander cardiopulmonary resuscitation and survival following out–of–hospital cardiac arrest. *Journal of the American Medical Association, 274*, 1922–1925.

Gilovich, T. (1991). *How we know what isn't so*. New York: The Free Press.

Gilovich, T. (1997, March/April). Some systematic biases of everyday judgment. *Skeptical Inquirer, 21*(2), 31–35.

Griffin, R. J., & Sen, S. (1995). Causal communication: Movie portrayals and audience attributions for Vietnam veterans' problems. *Journalism and Mass Communication Quarterly, 72*, 511–524.

Hamilton, D. L. (1979). A cognitive–attributional analysis of stereotyping. In L. Berkowitz (Ed.), *Advances in experimental social psychology* (Vol. 12, pp. 53–84). New York: Academic Press.

Heider, F. (1958). *The psychology of interpersonal relations*. New York: Wiley.

Hilton, D. F. (1988). Introduction: Images of science and commonsense explanation. In D. F. Hilton (Ed.), *Contemporary science and natural explanation: Commonsense conceptions of causality* (pp. 1–8). Brighton, Great Britain: Harvester.

Hohler, B. (1993, February 2). Super Bowl gaffe: Groups back off on violence claims. *The Boston Globe*, p. 1.

Johnson, B. B., & Slovic, P. (1995). Presenting uncertainty in health risk assessment: Initial studies of its effects on risk perception and trust. *Risk Analysis, 15*, 485–494.

Kahneman, D., Slovic, P., & Tversky, A. (Eds.). (1982). *Judgment under uncertainty: Heuristics and biases*. Cambridge, England: Cambridge University Press.

Kahneman, D., & Tversky, A. (1982). Variants of uncertainty. In D. Kahneman, P. Slovic, & A. Tversky (Eds.), *Judgment under uncertainty: Heuristics and biases* (pp. 509–520). Cambridge, England: Cambridge University Press.

Marin, R., & Gegax, T. T. (1996–1997, December 30–January 6). Conspiracy mania feeds our growing national paranoia. *Newsweek*, 64–71.

Meyer, P. (1979). *Precision journalism* (2nd ed.). Bloomington: Indiana University Press.

Meyer, P. (1991). *The new precision journalism*. Bloomington: Indiana University Press.

Nolan, D. (1986, October). Airline safety: The shocking truth. *Discover*, 30–31, 52–53.

Paulos, J. A. (1988). *Innumeracy: Mathematical illiteracy and its consequences*. New York: Vintage.

Paulos, J. A. (1995). *A mathematician reads the newspaper*. New York: Basic Books.

Ross, L., & Anderson, C. A. (1982). Shortcomings in the attribution process: On the origins and maintenance of erroneous social assessments. In D. Kahneman, P. Slovic, & A. Tversky (Eds.), *Judgment under uncertainty: Heuristics and biases* (pp. 129–152). Cambridge, England: Cambridge University Press.

Singer, E., & Endreny, P. (1987). Reporting hazards: Their benefits and costs. *Journal of Communication, 37*, 10–26.

Sowell, T. (1996, June 26). By the numbers. *The (Grafton, NH) Country Chronicle*, p. 11.

Subcommittee on Quantitative Literacy Requirements. (1995). Quantitative reasoning for college graduates: A complement to the standards [report]. Mathematical Association of America. [Online]. Available: http://www.maa.org.

Tankard, J. (1994). Visual crosstabs: A technique for enriching information graphics. *Mass Comm Review, 21,* 49–66.

Tufte, E. (1983). *The visual display of quantitative information.* Cheshire, CT: Graphics Press.

Tufte, E. (1997). *Visual explanations.* Cheshire, CT: Graphics Press.

Tversky, A., & Kahneman, D. (1982). Judgment under uncertainty. In D. Kahneman, P. Slovic, & A. Tversky (Eds.), *Judgment under uncertainty: Heuristics and biases* (pp. 3–20). Cambridge, England: Cambridge University Press.

Utts, J. M. (1996). *Seeing through statistics.* Belmont, CA: Duxbury/Wadsworth.

Wainer, H. (1997). *Visual revelations.* New York: Copernicus.

Chapter 14

Beyond the Basics: A Roundtable Discussion

Rita R. Colwell

Peggy Girshman

Cora B. Marrett

Paul Raeburn

F. Sherwood Rowland

Tom Siegfried

Rita R. Colwell is director of the National Science Foundation. She is the founding director and former president of the University of Maryland Biotechnology Institute. She also is a former president of the American Association for the Advancement of Science, the American Society for Microbiology, and the International Union of Microbiological Societies. She is the author or co-author of 16 books and more than 450 scientific publications.

Peggy Girshman is a science and medical producer for Dateline NBC. Previously she served as the deputy senior national editor of National Public Radio News and a senior producer of a 26-part series on statistics for the Public Broadcasting Service. She is co-recipient of the American Association for the Advancement of Science-Westinghouse Science Journalism Award for a series about the brain and of an Emmy for a documentary about viruses.

Cora B. Marrett is the provost/vice chancellor for academic affairs at the University of Massachusetts, Amherst. She is a former assistant director for Social, Behavioral and Economic Sciences at the National Science Foundation and was a professor of sociology and Afro-American studies at the University of Wisconsin-Madison. She was a member of the President's Commission on the Accident at Three Mile Island.

Paul Raeburn is senior editor for science and technology at *Business Week*, where he directs coverage of science and technology, medicine and the environment. An award-winning science writer, he is the author of *Mars: Uncovering the Secrets of the Red Planet* and *The Last Harvest: The Genetic Gamble That Threatens To Destroy American Agriculture*. Raeburn is an officer of the National Association of Science Writers and the Council for the Advancement of Science Writing.

F. Sherwood (Sherry) Rowland is the Bren Research Professor of Chemistry at the University of California-Irvine and the foreign secretary of the National Academy of Sciences. A 1995 Nobel Prize Laureate in Chemistry, he has served as president of the American Association for the Advancement of Science, and has also been elected to the American Academy of Arts and Sciences and the American Philosophical Society. His other awards include the Tyler World Prize in Environment and Energy and the Charles Dana Award for Pioneering Achievements in Health.

Tom Siegfried is a columnist and science editor at *The Dallas Morning News*. He is a past winner of the American Chemical Society's James T. Grady-James H. Stack Award for Interpreting Chemistry for the Public and of the American Association for the Advancement of Science-Westinghouse Science Journalism Award. He also is a former member of the board of the National Association of Science Writers and of the Science Journalism Center at the University of Missouri.

Question: What does the phrase scientific uncertainty mean to you?

Tom Siegfried: In writing about science, scientific uncertainty involves whether what you are writing about is right or wrong. That is a stark way of putting it, but you have to consider that question on two levels. At one level, everything in science is uncertain, which scientists know, as do experienced science journalists. All or nearly all scientists may agree that we know how the sun shines, yet they realize there is some small chance that today's best theories may someday be replaced by something different. At the second level, there is real disagreement among scientists about whether something is right or wrong, such as whether electromagnetic fields are dangerous to living organisms. So there is the distinction between unavoidable ultimate uncertainty on the one hand, and more serious, practical uncertainty on the other. And then some claims or reports are almost surely wrong so you do not report on them, while some things are probably wrong, but are so important that you have to report on them. In that case, a good reporter provides information to try to convey that these things probably are wrong.

Rita Colwell: Scientists deal with uncertainty every time we write a paper. We have assembled facts and data, analyzed them, and determined that we feel sufficiently comfortable or certain that what we have discovered and presented will be able to pass the test of our peers. So, *certainty* for us is that whatever is being reported is reproducible and quantifiable, and, therefore, is a relatively certain finding or discovery that we can share openly and publicly. In doing so, we put our reputations at risk. Such decisions are made regularly by scientists who decide whether what they have found merits the scrutiny of their peers.

Sherry Rowland: There are two different meanings to *scientific uncertainty* and one has to do with measures such as standard deviation, which is a quantitative estimate of uncertainty. However, in terms of dealing with the media, the meaning that is most involved is right versus wrong. Scientists might propose something that is fundamentally right even though it might be hard to evaluate quantitatively. Atmospheric carbon dioxide undoubtedly absorbs outgoing terrestrial infrared radiation, and this, in turn, tends to warm up the Earth. But other things are happening in the atmosphere at the same time, and the amount of warming will depend on the total change, and not just the carbon dioxide increase. Scientists are aware of the vagueness, but their reputations depend on their findings being right most of the time. Sometimes, however, there are people who are wrong almost all the time and they are still quoted in the media 20 years later very consistently.

Cora Marrett: As Sherry noted, some people define uncertainty from a statistical approach, saying that uncertainty is a condition in which the event, process, or outcome is known but the probabilities that it will occur are not known. But I think that is only one side of the issue. In some instances, admitting or accepting the fact that scientists or government leaders are uncertain about what is happening is risky politically and even monetarily. This was clearly the case in 1979 with the partial meltdown of the Three Mile Island [TMI] nuclear plant near Harrisburg, Pennsylvania.

Peggy Girshman: When I first think about uncertainty, what I think of is purely statistical: What are the odds of certain things happening? Evaluating that in any subject I cover would be an important element in reporting on an event or scientific study. The second thing is factoring in a more squishy element, which is how people feel about the topic on which I am writing. So, it is almost like the nonscientific definition of uncertainty is factored into the scientific definition. The nonscientific definition is how will the public feel about an issue? They are often uncertain about what reporters and scientists are saying. They do not know how to evaluate findings, even if we write that this is what a discovery might mean.

Paul Raeburn: When we write about uncertainty, we deal with a spectrum in the stories we produce. There are stories for which there is a fair amount of certainty. For example, you could write a story about the latest reports on the amount of carbon dioxide in the atmosphere and there is a fair degree of certainty about what is going on there. However, you also could write a story about how much expected warming would result from the increased carbon dioxide and there is a fair amount of uncertainty here. In many stories we do, there is a lot of uncertainty because there is disagreement in the scientific community. To us, that is another kind of uncertainty. That is something that we on the outside find hard to assess.

Tom Siegfried: This brings up an interesting point related to disagreement among scientists and what is meant by uncertainty. Often, journalistic coverage of scientific disagreement is what is translated as scientific uncertainty in stories. In many cases, this means quoting person A and then quoting person B on different sides of the issue. However, a better way to do it is to look beyond the scientists' disagreement to the pieces of evidence involved. Reporters do not often examine the evidence that supports what scientists say. Daily deadlines certainly make this more difficult to do. However, using only quote-based reporting impairs the media's ability to do a good job of elucidating uncertain issues.

Question: How has scientific uncertainty played a role in an issue with which you were involved?

Paul Raeburn: A story that I wrote in 1995 for The Associated Press was on *calcium channel blockers*, which are very widely used drugs for treating heart disease. The particular issue in this story was using them to treat high blood pressure. The drugs had been approved by the U.S. Food and Drug Administration and were believed to be safe and effective. However, several recent studies suggested increased risk of death and heart attacks in people taking these drugs. So while it was relatively certain that the drugs lowered blood pressure, it suddenly became very uncertain whether they in fact saved people's lives over a longer period of time.

I happened to be the only representative of a major news organization who wrote the story, and I found myself besieged with calls from doctors and industry representatives who said my story had needlessly alarmed patients taking the drugs. It was a difficult experience because it was an area where scientists clearly disagreed. It was one in which most scientists thought the drugs were safe, and a few thought they were dangerous. But I encountered scientists who thought that using the drugs was problematic, and I had to try to deal with that.

Peggy Girshman: The accident at the TMI nuclear plant is an example for me. I reported on the story for Channel 9, which is the CBS affiliate for Washington, DC. Two factors stand out in dealing with uncertainty in this story. The first was deadline pressure and how it affected the story. As one of the science writers at the station, I was expected to know immediately what was going on and understand it. However, with a daily deadline, all of us are generalists and none of us know enough about any topic. So I started calling around to information sources and who I reached on the telephone determined how I was going to report the story in an hour. For example, if I got one guy who said this is horrible, then he was going to color my whole view of the story and there was nothing I could do about it that night.

The second factor dealt with public fears. Just telling people that they have nothing to worry about does not work. People are not stupid; they know the company operator or government officials want to avoid a panic by providing such reassurances. Conversely, the public readily accepts sources who tell them to worry, and although these sources may be scientists too, they often are dismissed by some experts and officials as "kooks." Even though experts may disagree with those concerns, reporters have to deal with them because they are a part of the story.

Rita Colwell: An example of public fear occurred near where I live during the TMI accident. One evening, the siren at the local fire station short circuited. Although this was only a fire alarm, not a nuclear alert, the neighborhood went berserk. People streamed out of houses; kids were frightened and crying. When we tried to phone the fire station, the lines were jammed. This specific fear of a radiation release coming our way fed on the general fear that had developed during the accident. For a brief time, uncertainty translated into a certainty for at least this population.

Cora Marrett: The uncertainty at TMI began with the plant operators; initially no one in the nuclear plant was certain about what had happened. They did not know that there had been radiation releases. But, at the same time, both government officials and reporters were asking the operators what was happening. Since no one inside the reactor building was going to say "We don't have the foggiest idea," they said some things when knowledge was not there during the first few hours of the accident. Later, when it became clear that there had been radiation releases, questions arose about the potential health effects of those releases. These questions were not easily answered and could only be dealt with using probabilities, rather than facts.

Sherry Rowland: The TMI accident is one kind of science event that requires an immediate response. My example is something that I have dealt with—stratospheric ozone depletion—where there have been 20 years of media coverage. Everyone has had plenty of time to look into the issue, the question of uncertainty, how it is handled, and the action of scientists. The uncertainties included the absence of any measurements of the key chemicals over Antarctica when the hole in the polar ozone was recognized in 1985—solved by sending scientific expeditions to get the data. Unfortunately, the length of time this issue has been covered has not necessarily clarified it in the public mind because the public gets much of its information about science from nonscientific sources.

Tom Siegfried: The ozone issue is a good one to bring up. It relates to the point I made earlier about quoting people versus examining the evidence. The appearance of uncertainty was created about the atmospheric chemistry of ozone depletion by what appeared to me to be a well-orchestrated campaign by special interest groups. There is very little uncertainty in the scientific evidence, which is well-researched and well-documented. However, the public became uncertain about the issue because of media interviews with selected scientists from the interest groups. In this instance, the coverage of the issue was dictated by a small group of scientists as opposed to the actual evidence. I think this example points to a real deficiency on the part of the media in dealing with scientific uncertainty and their inability to really go beyond the rhetoric and get to the evidence. It is a weakness the media have and they should attempt to correct it.

Paul Raeburn: I certainly think that the ozone case is one example of where apparent uncertainty has been created. Another example is the tobacco story, where some people probably are still uncertain whether nicotine is addictive. Yet, this is a matter where there is very little uncertainty. Few scientists outside of the tobacco industry will dispute that nicotine is addictive. But in April 1994, people saw the spectacle of the heads of major tobacco companies swearing before Congress that they did not believe nicotine was addictive.

Question: What role do scientists play in communicating uncertainty to the public? Let's look at global warming as an example.

Peggy Girshman: Clearly, James Hansen, director of the National Aeronautics and Space Administration's Goddard Institute for Space Studies, was a major factor in getting the public and the media to pay attention to global warming when he testified in 1988 before a Congressional hearing that global warming had begun. The Congressional hearing was being held because it was a very hot summer, but that was irrelevant.

Sherry Rowland: What Hansen actually had done was run his own computer model of warming and cooling trends to see what the statistics were for natural variations, and the statistics in his model did not fit what was happening to the weather outside. He did not just look at that hot summer of 1988, but looked at trends over the decade of the 1980s up to that point. His conclusion was that he was seeing more than just natural variation in weather patterns. Natural fluctuations were not large enough to account for what he had seen. Of course, the media story was much better because the temperature soared to 105 degrees in Washington and it was one of the hottest years in the last 10 or 15. Hansen might have been earlier than most in his conclusion that global warming was occurring, but he did not draw that conclusion on the basis of that summer alone.

Peggy Girshman: Since the public does not always comprehend short- and long-term probability, does a scientist such as Hansen, who had both a political and research agenda, take advantage of his position to get his point of view accepted?

Sherry Rowland: I think he had a research agenda, but I am not sure that he had a political agenda unless appearing before a Congressional committee is by definition a political agenda.

Paul Raeburn: I believe that Hansen did not exploit that opportunity to promote his view and that his actions were not motivated by anything other than disinterested scientific pursuit. However, that brings up an interesting point. As journalists, we cannot be sure what people's motivations are. Yet, most of us have a feeling about the people we talk to and whether they are being straight with us and obviously there is uncertainty in that.

Cora Marrett: How does that enter into your stories then—your sense of whether sources are being straight?

Paul Raeburn: My judgments about the source and my feelings about whether I am getting a straight story influence how I play that story. I trust my perceptions as a journalist. When you have talked to a lot of people over the years and later learned whether they were being straight, you hone that sense. So I trust those feelings and go with them.

Tom Siegfried: I agree with that and I think that is an essential part of doing good science journalism. I just want to add one point: Part of making those judgments goes beyond just your gut feelings to look at the person's record. This means looking at the literature, the evidence. You also look at how sources use and present the evidence and then you make a judgment about who you believe is a reliable source. Especially when dealing with issues of uncertainty, you should not try to equally represent all sides of an issue. You should seek what you think is the best information to convey, and an essential part of that is judging which people are reliable sources. So if I am going to write a story about the addictive nature of nicotine, I am not going to talk to anyone from the tobacco industry even though the standard journalistic practice of balancing views in a story suggests that I ought to. I regard that form of balance as a disservice to the readers since I believe the tobacco industry's information is not reliable. Of course, if a particular company is accused of something specifically, you are journalistically obligated to give it the opportunity to reply. But that is a different issue.

Question: Do scientists suffer consequences when they discuss uncertain science with journalists?

Rita Colwell: When you talk with journalists about uncertain science, you have to be very careful about what you say. In fact, you probably will not talk to a reporter until you have a confidence level that allows you to state that if someone else did the experiment again he or she would get the same results no matter what. In particular, when you have a theory that runs counter to what other scientists think, it is very tough to go out there, talk to a reporter, lay your reputation on the line, and then be maligned by so-called authorities in a very unpleasant way. This leaves you vulnerable and unable to strike back except by publishing more data and more papers, which takes a long time.

This is particularly true for women scientists. During my career, some of my work has run counter to prevailing views and I have literally taken slander and public ridicule from a few individuals with clout and that has been very unpleasant. The major example is my hypothesis that the causative agent of cholera is a naturally occurring aquatic bacterium. This is now accepted, but it was not 20 years ago when I first proposed it. You have to have a sense of confidence in the data you have gathered and how you have interpreted them. Doing all of this is not easy and it can be painful, and it takes time to accumulate the irrefutable evidence, which I did.

Peggy Girshman: You cannot win in a way, because if you are not willing to talk to a reporter, then we will look for someone who is willing and may be less cautious about expressing a point of view.

Rita Colwell: That is correct, and then if you do talk, you are at the mercy of your opponents, who do not accept your theory, who may be the authorities on the issue, and who then make statements disparaging your work. Your peers and even your allies have problems with whom to believe because they are not doing the experiments. For you to succeed, a whole lot of trust needs to be developed.

Sherry Rowland: During the first couple of years of the research Mario Molina [professor of chemistry at the Massachusetts Institute of Technology and cowinner of 1995 Nobel Prize for Chemistry] and I did on stratospheric ozone depletion, the aerosol industry, which then accounted for two thirds of the U.S. chlorofluorocarbon [CFC] usage, bore the brunt of calls for controlling CFCs. So those people criticized us heavily. Molina and I read *Aerosol Age* avidly because we wore the "black hats" in every issue. The magazine even went so far as to run an article calling us agents of the Soviet Union's KGB, who were trying to destroy American industry.

While such criticism was discouraging, what was more disconcerting was when scientists on the industry side were quoted by the media, claiming our calculations of how many CFCs were in the stratosphere were off by a factor of 1,000. Because they had chosen the upper stratosphere where essentially no CFCs were left, the question of one part per thousand or one part per million of CFCs remaining in the mix of atmospheric chemicals made no difference in the overall calculations. Still, if someone says you have made an error of a factor of 1,000, it sounds like it is a very serious error.

Even after we won the Nobel Prize for this research, our politically conservative local newspaper, *The Orange County Register,* damned the award with very faint praise saying that our theory had been demonstrated in the laboratory, but that scientists with more expertise in atmospheric science had shown that the evidence in the real atmosphere was quite mixed. This ignored the consensus views of the world's atmospheric scientists that the results had been spectacularly confirmed in the real atmosphere.

Tom Siegfried: When someone brings up something that is contrary to the major theories in a scientific field, journalists must decide how to deal with the issue. This presents a very difficult problem, even for good science journalists. It requires that journalists view an uncertain issue in a more sophisticated way, asking such questions as how certain the theories are and what are the theories based on. If you do not have journalists who are able to deal with the different levels of uncertainty and respond to new ideas more appropriately, you get really bad reporting.

The constraints of traditional newspaper reporting, such as the daily deadline and the need for hard news, make reporting on scientific uncertainty—and particularly studies that go against dogma—a difficult thing to do well. Because of the way newspapers operate, you have to write something today no matter whether you know something new or not. You have to write a lead that makes a point. This distorts the reporting of scientific evidence in a way that collapses uncertainty.

Cora Marrett: Let us assume for the moment we are talking about only the good science journalists and that we recognize the obvious problems of deadlines and other constraints. How does uncertainty affect stories in other ways?

Tom Siegfried: If something is important and should go on page one, you often have to deal with other editors who do not understand uncertainty. Trying to explain it to them is very difficult. They may want to put a story in the newspaper that is too one-sided or not very important, but they do not know this because they do not understand the uncertainty in the issue. Claims that a new drug can reverse the aging process are highly uncertain, yet many editors would consider a report like that to be big news without appreciating the uncertainties involved. Another problem that affects coverage involves scientists who are inarticulate when they try to explain their work or some, mostly in the biomedical area, who do not want to talk to reporters at all.

Rita Colwell: For the scientist who gets a request to be interviewed there are problems as well. First, there is the uncertainty of whether he or she is going to be quoted accurately. Second, there is the question of whether the reporter doing the interviewing really understands what the scientist is saying. Scientists have to worry about their reputations, which poorly written articles can affect, particularly if the scientists are dealing with uncertain issues or studies that disagree with the accepted theories in their field.

Peggy Girshman: I want to bring up a specific example that created problems for me as an editor for National Public Radio: bovine growth hormone, BGH—the genetically engineered compound that is given to cows to increase their milk production. It is rare to cover something where there is such solid agreement among the U.S. scientific community. The scientific consensus is that BGH is not harmful to humans. Yet, we were forced to cover the charges of an economist and biotechnology critic, Jeremy Rifkin, because he filed a lawsuit against its use, claiming that it was unsafe. Despite the fact that he was not a scientist, I had tremendous internal and public pressure to cover Rifkin in some way. I do not want to deal with people like Rifkin because of their lack of scientific training. However, when he files a lawsuit against BGH, you have no choice; it is part of the story. So, he gets a 30-second sound bite as do some scientists. To the public, Rifkin and the scientists appear to be of equal merit in the broadcast.

You also have no control over what other reporters or editors from your organization want to do. On this same issue, there was the problem of doing a story on Wolfgang Puck, the chef at Spago, a fancy Los Angeles restaurant. At Rifkin's suggestion, Puck decided not to serve any bioengineered foods on his menu. Even though existing scientific evidence did not support such behavior, Puck was an interesting character with this interesting idea, so NPR staff people wanted to interview him about it.

Paul Raeburn: One important point to include in such stories would be that most scientists believe that the hormone is safe but that there are some people like Rifkin, who is a longtime critic of the biotechnology industry. I have spent a lot of time with Rifkin to try to figure out why he does what he does, but I have not written about him much. However, I did a different type of story a few years ago about BGH. The story did not deal with the safety issue. Rather, it focused on how the introduction of BGH would affect the businesses of family farmers. It would be a great advantage to the large dairy farmers in California and a major disadvantage to the small dairy farmers in Wisconsin. That aspect was a more interesting story with much more importance.

Rita Colwell: Fear of genetically engineered products also was raised with the Flavr Savr tomato. In this case, the only genetic alteration of the tomato has been to change a natural enzyme so that it acts a little more slowly to retard ripening. The genetic engineering did not produce a different product, and in no way did it make any changes other than slower ripening. So, people get a tomato that has not been sprayed with chemicals to make it ripen and it does not have to be harvested when it is golf-ball size in order to transport it to market. Yet, some people who follow Rifkin created an aura of fear about this tomato, saying that because it was genetically engineered, it was unsafe. The tomato is probably less of a health hazard than tomatoes genetically selected by traditional methods, grown, harvested before fully ripening, and sprayed with chemicals so they will ripen at the time they get to market.

Paul Raeburn: What is interesting to me is how critics like Rifkin create such changes in popular perceptions. Clearly, they are throwing seeds on fertile ground. People do not want industry adulterating their food, which is a very legitimate, rational reaction when they hear about something like the Flavr Savr tomato.

Cora Marrett: I am curious about why people develop different impressions of issues. It could be because there are heated debates about risky or uncertain issues, but I do not think that is all of it. Perhaps there are other less tangible factors operating. For example, with BGH, there are some issues that have nothing to do with the hormone itself, such as what this development will do to farmers. Similarly, some people's concerns about uncertain issues might be associated with promises made by scientists about the certainty of their work, which turned out to be less than certain. Promises made and not kept reduce the level of trust the public has in science.

Tom Siegfried: That is a good point. Examples arise of scientific evidence being overturned and people seize on that. I think there is always residual uncertainty in any science. This is where Rifkin and other critics promote their own agenda by capitalizing on the uncertainty that exists, making it appear much greater than it is. They magnify and use this uncertainty as a tool. The media often further this behavior by quoting them. This is how such people manipulate the media and get their points across. That is one of the problems with science coverage.

Author Index*

*n = indicates reference found in footnote.

Subject Index*

A

Absence of knowledge, 36
Accountability, 98, 138, 140
Accuracy, 76, 132, 207, 209, 219
Acid rain, 15–17, 38
Advertisers & advertisements, 34
African-Americans, sickle-cell anemia and, 48
Agendas
    hidden, 84
    media and, 53
    scientists and, 64, 255
Agent Orange, 114, 115, 116
AIDS
    agenda setting, 53
    media coverage, 185–186
        context lacking, 191–193
        information lacking, 188–191
        story framing, 195
        story structure, 193
        visuals, 188, 194, 198
    public understanding of, 181, 183–184
    scientific literacy and, 52
    11th International AIDS Conference, 187
Alar, *119*
American Association for the Advancement of Science, 157
American Medical Association (AMA), 116
American Paper Institute, 117
Analogy, 214, 219, 220
Anecdotes, 228–230, 231
Animal research, 160
Asserting negative evidence, 7
Assumptions, 167–170, 173, *see also* Biases; Interpretation
    of audience, 188–191, 196–197
Audience, 34, 38, 179, 226
    assumptions of, 188–191, 196–197

    conceptual confusion, 210–212, 216, 219
    evidence for, 205–206
    interpretation, 86
    pleasing, 53, 197–198
    poorly served, 202
    understanding of uncertainty, 86–87
    writing for, 205–220
Authoritativeness, 140, 145–146

B

Balance, 71–72, 89, 207–209, 219
    in dioxin coverage, 127
    disservice to readers, 256
    in the media, 33
    in science news, 202
Banbury conference, 118
Bangor Daily News, dioxin coverage, 130
Baselines, 230–231
Beat reporters, 83
Behavioral biology, 157–165
Beliefs
    causal, 241–242
    genetic engineering, 107–109
    popular, 101–102
Biases, 83, 89, *see also* Assumptions; Interpretation
    in environmental reporting, 168–169
    fundamental attribution error, 241
    heuristics, 229
Big Crunch, 138
Biotechnology, 64, 96, 97, *see also* Genetic engineering
    media's presentation of, 54
    sources, 104
Boundaries, 63
Bovine growth hormone (BGH), 259–260
Bovine somatotropin (bST), 102–104, 109

---

*n = indicates reference found in footnote.

269